PASSAGE TO PORO[S]

"On the beguiling island of Poros, Ed Tick combines his love for the people and culture of modern Greece with the wisdom, mythology, and healing practices of the ancients. On Poseidon's island, we encounter mythical heroes, renowned artists, local personalities, refugees, an array of expats, and American veterans, all of whom have come to appreciate the value of *philoxenia* (hospitality) found in this magical place. As I read this book, I was transported to Poros, with its *kali aura* (beautiful air), serene waters, and magnificent sleeping goddess. This is a book that feeds the soul."

PETER MEINECK, PH.D., ASSOCIATE PROFESSOR OF
CLASSICS IN THE MODERN WORLD, NEW YORK UNIVERSITY

"Ed Tick rebirths an ancient fountain of healing and life in this book. Having spent every summer on this island since 1974, it is wholesome to experience Poros through his eyes. He brings healing not only to the reader but also to the land itself."

LINDY MCMULLIN, PH.D., DIRECTOR OF PSYCHOLOGY PROGRAMS
AT THE HELLENIC AMERICAN UNIVERSITY

"This book is like the psychological tales of the travels of the winds from classical mythology as they surf over the tiny island of Poros, sift through particular pines, strike the ancient rocks of time, and finally gather at the mouth of the cave of Poseidon, who continues to speak— in this case, personally to Tick, and through him, to all of us. We should listen."

STEVEN B. KATZ, PH.D., PEARCE PROFESSOR EMERITUS OF PROFESSIONAL
COMMUNICATION AND ENGLISH AT CLEMSON UNIVERSITY

"Healers and storytellers, Homer assures us, are always welcome. There is no better or more urgent time to welcome Ed Tick, compassionate healer and inspired storyteller, into your life. In *Passage to Poros*, Tick takes us on a transformative journey, offering us asylum from a crazed world and entry into inner healing and peace. Part travel guide, part memoir, part poetic commentary, and part spiritual meditation—every chapter is a pilgrimage, a journey of soul. This book is a paean to sanctuary."

ROBERT EMMET MEAGHER, AUTHOR OF *HERAKLES GONE MAD*,
KILLING FROM THE INSIDE OUT, AND *WAR AND MORAL INJURY*

"This is the story of love for the island of Poros, love for the people, and love for the past, present, and future. Ed Tick invites us into the world of myths and archetypes that bring new light to our modern hardships, giving them roots and the wisdom of the eternal. With modesty and generosity, the author shares his insights and feelings with the reader, opening a door to a new dimension of the invisible world of symbols and imagination that heals our souls."

NATALIA PAVLIKOVA, JUNGIAN ANALYST AND PREVIOUS PRESIDENT OF
THE RUSSIAN SOCIETY FOR ANALYTICAL PSYCHOLOGY

"In Poros, Ed Tick found a home, and in Greece, he summoned Psykhe from her ancient Olympian home into our modern lives through Western medicine, psychiatry, and psychology."

IKHLAS GRACE AKRA, M.D., HOLISTIC NATUROPATHIC PSYCHIATRIST
IN THE ANCIENT HIPPOCRATIC TRADITION AND
FOUNDER OF ABATON BELIZE

"Ed Tick writes with a breadth of scholarship, depth of soul, and love. Reading *Passage to Poros* is like reading a love poem to Poros and to the archetypal ground of our human imagination."

ROGER BROOKE, PH.D., ABPP, PROFESSOR EMERITUS OF
PSYCHOLOGY AT DUQUESNE UNIVERSITY

"A spiritual book that revives myth in the heart of the present, reminding us that we need a safe place to seek refuge and reconnect with the universal soul."

GIANLUCA CINELLI, EDITOR OF *CLOSE ENCOUNTERS IN WAR JOURNAL*

"Edward Tick constructs a sublime, colorful mosaic. A precious reminder of the authentic wisdom of the ancients: how we can draw it into the present, restore it in our own lives, and preserve and protect it."

SUSAN RABY-DUNNE, MILITARY HISTORIAN,
VETERANS' ADVOCATE, AND AUTHOR

PASSAGE TO POROS

IN THE SANCTUARY OF THE SEA GOD

EDWARD TICK, PhD

Park Street Press
Rochester, Vermont

Park Street Press
One Park Street
Rochester, Vermont 05767
www.ParkStPress.com

Park Street Press is a division of Inner Traditions International

Copyright © 2025 by Edward Tick
Foreword © 2025 by Phil Cousineau

All rights reserved. No part of this book may be reproduced or utilized in any form or by any means, electronic or mechanical, including photocopying, recording, or any information storage and retrieval system, without permission in writing from the publisher. No part of this book may be used or reproduced to train artificial intelligence technologies or systems.

Cataloging-in-Publication Data for this title is available from the Library of Congress

ISBN 978-1-64411-379-0 (print)
ISBN 978-1-64411-380-6 (ebook)

Printed and bound in the United States by Lake Book Manufacturing, LLC

10 9 8 7 6 5 4 3 2 1

Text design by Priscilla Baker and layout by Kenleigh Manseau
This book was typeset in Garamond Premier Pro with Griffon and Mrs Eaves OT used as display typefaces.

To send correspondence to the author of this book, mail a first-class letter to the author c/o Inner Traditions, One Park Street, Rochester, VT 05767, and we will forward the communication, or contact the author directly at **EdwardTick.com**.

Scan the QR code and save 25% at InnerTraditions.com. Browse over 2,000 titles on spirituality, the occult, ancient mysteries, new science, holistic health, and natural medicine.

*dedicated to the spirituality and
people of the island of Poros—
from ancient times to the present—
and the memory of Giorgos Dimitriadis,
holy man and friend to all*

Glad is the soul that sees the mysteries of the gods.

EURIPIDES, *BAKKHAI*

CONTENTS

FOREWORD	RHAPSODY ON A THEME OF PILGRIMAGE by Phil Cousineau	IX
	ACKNOWLEDGMENTS	XV
INTRODUCTION	PASSAGE TO THE PAST	1
1	PORTRAIT OF POROS Immersion in the Greek World	14
2	COUNSEL WITH THE DEAD Poet George Seferis on Poros	36
3	THE GIFT OF THE SEA TURTLE A Meeting in Poseidon's Sanctuary	51
4	POSEIDON The Powerful, Unpredictable Protector of the Sea	57
5	GREEK MYTHOLOGY ON POROS The Naming of an Island	80
6	A HISTORY OF ASYLIA (SANCTUARY) Stories from Refugees through the Ages	89

7 *THE SUN OF POROS*   117
Writers and Artists on Poros

8 IN THE AGORA   136
Meandering the Streets

9 THE SHADOW OF PARADISE   154
Struggles Facing a Rural Community

10 A HEALING ISLAND   174
Physical, Emotional, and
Spiritual Transformations

11 ASKLEPIOS ON POROS   193
Dream Incubation and Therapeutics

12 RESTORING POSEIDON'S SANCTUARY   213
Living in Agape

NOTES   223

BIBLIOGRAPHY   229

INDEX   233

FOREWORD

RHAPSODY ON A THEME OF PILGRIMAGE

Phil Cousineau

Seek the depths—or else.
SAUL BELLOW, *HENDERSON THE RAIN KING*

If an island had the power to write its own autobiography, it would render a story similar to the one that Ed Tick has conjured up in his marvelous new book, *Passage to Poros*. His innovative work is based on thirty-eight years of visits to the Greek island, a revered pilgrimage site due to its healing powers and capacity to induce a kind of creative reverie in the artists, writers, and photographers who have sailed there.

Tick's writing is rhapsodic in every sense of the lapidary word, which has loamy roots that reach down and back to the Greek *rhapsode*. Originally, the ecstatic word referred to a wandering oral storyteller, one who ventured from town to town, palace to palace, performing by heart the verses of epic poets such as Homer and Hesiod. Our word *rhapsody* reflects the sense of being transported by euphoric expressions in all the arts, from epic poetry to art, music, and sculpture. These qualities also describe the emotional effect and celebratory nature of the author's narrative.

Celebration certainly conveys the overall mood of *Passage to Poros*, but the work reaches for more than the kind of cultural flattery found in so much travel writing. Instead, I found that Ed Tick's ambition is closer to one of his literary lions, George Seferis, the Greek winner of the Nobel Prize in Literature, in 1963, who invented the enormously useful term *mythistorema* in the belief that we all live in a *mythic history*. The poet's clever neologism links the two commonly opposed worlds of myth and history, and in its unique way resolves the tension between them.

The seeming paradox of *mythic history* may be heresy to the literal-minded reader but does bring us close to the ancient Greek sensibility that the world is surrounded by what the art critic Alexander Eliot colorfully called the "mythosphere." By this Eliot meant that the air we breathe is made up of sacred stories that are as real to the soul as the so-called facts of history are to the mind. During my reading of *Passage*, I was reminded of Mary Shelley's observation that her literary invention of *Frankenstein* was more real than truth. For J. R. R. Tolkien, "myth equals a truth that cannot be explained by fact . . . the sacramental nature of life."

In turn, Seferis's insight about the inextricably connected sources of wisdom is a reminder that the mythic imagination is worthy of our reverence, a conviction that Tick builds on in a marvel-filled memoir because he, too, is in search of both and truth about the human adventure. He finds that they are as intertwined as the serpent on Hermes's caduceus.

To tell his tale, Tick honors the original meaning of Poros itself, *passage* or *resource*, by deftly weaving together the island's recorded history with his own ruminations about its ancient folk traditions, mythologies, and healing rituals. Lest the narrative become too romantic, these scintillating passages are balanced by the inclusion of elegiac observations about the rapidly disappearing customs on Poros caused by the threat of the tenacles of tourism and climate change that are strangling so many of the Old-World sites we claim to love. His musings serve as a powerful buildup for the last section of the book that focuses on the therapeutic techniques he has developed to help heal veteran and non-veteran travelers who sometimes accompany him to the island because they are suffering from an ongoing "war in the soul."

The cumulative effect makes *Passage to Poros* a feat of literary pilgrimage. As I wrote in *The Art of Pilgrimage*, the ancient act of traveling to sacred sites can be spirituality transformative—if performed with genuine intention and attention. Traditionally, tourism simply refers to the basic act of visiting a famous place, then going home. But there is no promise or expectation of returning *changed*. In dramatic contrast, pilgrimage is the trip you can't *not* take because it offers the possibility of transformation. The double negative is necessary to describe the profound need to respond to the call of the soul at one of life's crossroads.

Passage to Poros is proof of the healing forces at work in a bona fide pilgrimage for people in a midlife crisis, suffering from post-traumatic stress disorder, or in spiritual hunger. His account is tripartite: part travelogue, in the spirit of the first century geographer Pausanias, often regarded as the world's first travel writer; part memoir, in the style of Henry Miller and Nikos Kazantzakis; and part *nekyia*, a descent into the dark night of the soul, reminiscent of Mark and Kurt Vonnegut's haunting account, *The Eden Express*.

With a touching vulnerability, Tick reveals how he embarked on the American version of the Grand Tour in the mid-1980s, on an early-midlife journey to the ancient world in search of its timeless wisdom, or at least for an exciting adventure. But when he arrived in the Aegean, he didn't step off the ferry as an earnest and callow backpacker. Instead, Tick admits he was "in a solemn and pensive mood, facing midlife storms and challenges, seeking direction."

This is what I think of as the pilgrim mood.

At first, Tick was struck by the rich vein of local culture but was eventually moved by his encounters with the modern version of what Homer described as *filoxenia*, the "love of strangers," in effect, the art of Greek hospitality. While reading about his many colorful examples of local friendliness and generosity, I was struck by the irony that we have inherited half of the venerable custom, a twisted version, as evidenced in *xenophobia*, the hatred or fear of strangers.

In such curious ways do we learn life lessons from the ancients. This helps restore gifts of humanism that we moderns have nearly lost.

What I find most unique about Ed Tick's book is the way he smoothly incorporates his practice of transformational travel to augment his work as a "transformational psychotherapist" with the seekers who join him on the island. What made this possible was that he had unwittingly landed on an island that was drenched in beauty and romance, but also steeped in the ancient rite of *asylia*, or sanctuary, that had offered "inviolable safety" for the last three thousand years. And like so many pilgrims before him, Tick found sanctuary for his own passage, his own rebirth.

Passage to Poros is exactly that, a book of transitions, a kind of portal to another time, Kairos not Chronos, another place, not utopia (literally "no-place"), nor a paradise, but a refugee's sanctuary. The mythosphere around the island has made it an ideal writer's retreat, a healing zone, and a place to pause and reconsider your life . . . if the visitor learns to see with the eyes of the heart.

I find Tick's own description of the purpose of the book to be trustworthy. He describes it as "a testament and guidebook for the generous pilgrim who is feeling hunger for a soul-stirring adventure." This is not a humblebrag but an honest self-assessment. His *Passage* is an effective plunge into the origins of one humble but vital corner of Greek civilization, what he calls "enduring Greece," as well as a tumble into his own troubled soul. This qualifies him as the quintessential "wounded healer," which makes the last section of the book that much more compelling. The *presence* of the island itself, he reveals, has its own wily wisdom, and has helped heal him and many of the seekers he takes there on pilgrimage.

Beyond the extraordinary, I was moved by Tick's vivid vignette of one of his ordinary days on the island. Gradually, as in an engaging play or movie, we see him transform over the course of his three-plus decades on Poros through simple meetings in the local *kafenia*, or coffeehouses, talking, joking, philosophizing with the colorful locals. Reading the book, I thought of the veteran travel writer Tim Cahill's insight that the finest thing we meet in our travels is the friends we

RHAPSODY ON A THEME OF PILGRIMAGE ❧ xiii

make: "A journey is best measured in friends, rather than miles." Watching Tick make time to make friends reveals Poros's power to offer a "passage" through space but in time, from the mundane to the numinous.

As often happens with big-hearted travelers, Ed Tick reveals how he went to Greece to learn about its esoteric side, its mythology and ancient rites, but ended up finding more than he asked for, notably many of the healing tools the modern world has forgotten about. And in the venerable tradition of mythic heroes everywhere he has not hoarded those tools but passed them on to us for what they are: gifts, boons, treasures.

For the probing reader, this book is an *opportunity*, in the mythic sense, a word rooted in Portunus, the Roman god of harbors, whom sailors importuned to receive the blessing of soft breezes, calm seas, and safe landings.

In a world where travel has transmogrified into greedy, narcissistic, disrespectful tourism, *Passage to Poros* reveals that we have a chance to move around the world in the pilgrim mood. Soulful, curious, reverential, and beaming with gratitude. And like pilgrims everywhere, we can leave gifts behind us when we leave and bring back boons when we return home.

Transformed into our better selves.

PHIL COUSINEAU is a freelance writer, filmmaker, independent scholar, and writing consultant, who lectures around the world on a wide range of topics from mythology, film, and writing to beauty, travel, sports, and creativity. He has more than thirty documentary film credits, including *The Hero's Journey: The Life and Work of Joseph Campbell* and *Forever Activists: Stories from the Abraham Lincoln Brigade.* His forty published books include *The Art of Pilgrimage, Once and Future Myths, The Blue Museum, The Lost Notebooks of Sisyphus, Who Stole the Arms of the Venus de Milo?* His latest work is *Moonlight Over the Parthenon: Poems In and Out of Greece.* Cousineau has been leading art and myth tours and writing retreats to Greece since 1993. He lives with his family on Telegraph Hill in San Francisco.

Author's Note to the Reader

All stories and full names reported herein are real and used with permission. Single first names are used to protect the person's anonymity. Where possible and not awkward, spellings and close approximations of Greek names, places, and concepts are used to facilitate readers' immersion.

ACKNOWLEDGMENTS

I especially honor and thank my Poriotes friends and associates who have embraced me and helped make this work possible:

George Seferis, the great and passed poet whose work first brought me here

Yannis Maniatis, library director and the living encyclopedia of Poros

Babis Kanatsidis, regional historian and journalist

Pamela Jane Rogers, American artist in residence and bridge between our worlds

Giorgos Dimitriadis, Christos Drougas, and the staff of Taverna Sti Rota—masters of filoxenia

Nikki Protopapa and Giorgos Kaikas of 7 Brothers Hotel

Tasos Rodis, teacher and guardian of culture

I thank and honor my agent Joe Kulin, Jon Graham, and the able and supportive editorial staff of Inner Traditions; my friends, colleagues, and supporters in Athens and around Greece; and the many American and international pilgrims who have journeyed with me since 1995 and shared their stories.

And as always to my beloved life and work partner, Kate Dahlstedt.

INVOCATION

Homeric Hymn to Poseidon
Anon., ca. 800 BCE
A New Translation

I call you Poseidon, great god, invisible,
Earth embracing and ever moving,
Founder and Protector,
Lord of the deep and true.
Your task is double, Earthshaker honored by the gods,
To be tamer of horses and savior of ships.
Hail, Poseidon, Earth-cupping, dark-maned.
O blessed One, be kindhearted to all of us who sail your
  wide waters.

INTRODUCTION

Passage to the Past

Pilgrimage—travel on long, distant, and demanding adventures to sacred sites that deepen the soul, bring wisdom, and heal wounds—has been a spiritual practice for millennia. Asylum—seeking a place of holiness and inviolable safety—has likewise been an ancient and sacred practice afforded those in distress. For three thousand years, to this day and for transformations achieved by modern pilgrims, including me, the small Greek island of Poros has been a site of pilgrimage and asylum.

Passage to Poros: In the Sanctuary of the Sea God guides you on a pilgrimage of discovery, healing, wisdom, living community, myth, and divine presence. We track a journey that stretches over millennia from mythic and ancient times to the present. This journey is to discover and restore asylia, the original meaning and practice of sanctuary that provides safety, inspiration, and belonging, and facilitates transformational healing and connections to the divine, on a small and humble island.

Poros is an island of only twelve square miles merely a one-and-a-quarter-hour hydrofoil ride from Athens's port of Piraeus. It has a rich and ancient mythology and history largely unknown by visitors and even many residents alike. It is full of marvels, mystery, and stories historical, modern, and inclusive of this author's thirty-eight years of visits and healing work there. Its small permanent population of less than four thousand contains some of the warmest, kindest, and most upright inhabitants of our planet. As Giorgos Dimitriadis, owner of Taverna

Fig. I.1. The view of Poros town along the waterfront where fishing boats and yachts dock.

PHOTOGRAPH BY TASOS RODIS

Sti Rota on Poros's waterfront, said, "We are still a small village maintaining real community even though surrounded by modernity and drenched in tourism." Fay Sokaris, a Greek American woman from Boston whose family was originally from Ikaria, has traveled all over Greece for decades. She declares, "Poros people are the warmest, kindest, most welcoming I have met anywhere. Many places practice *filoxenia*, guest-friendship. But on Poros their hearts are big, and it is real."

Today Poros serves primarily as a short stop on a rapid daylong cruise in the Saronic Gulf, a weekend getaway for Athenians, or a second home or vacation destination for the sun-hungry and affluent. Its true character remains largely unknown. Aside from its common mention in travel guides, only a few books in English—most out of print—mention or have been written about this little-known gem of the Saronic Gulf.

I have been traveling to Poros since 1987 and leading pilgrimage there since 1995. *Passage to Poros* explores the history, people, culture, mythology, literature, and sacred sites of Poros. It documents my decades of healing work guiding pilgrimage there, and my own life-transforming and soul-awakening relationship with this island over almost four decades. We immerse on Poros by exploring its three-millennia-old history and its contemporary village life and characters. We hear its impact on Nobel Prize–winning poet George Seferis whose hermitage island it was, as well as Marc Chagall, Lucien Freud, and other artists and writers who retreated here. We demonstrate cultural and mythological immersion as spiritual pilgrimage, learning how visitors are changed in body and soul, identities, values and faith, on this island. And we witness three decades of dream healing in the ancient Asklepian tradition that I have led on and near this island.

As Phil Cousineau has written, pilgrimage is "a transformative journey to a sacred center . . . a journey to a holy site . . . or a natural setting . . . or to a revered temple. . . . To people the world over, pilgrimage is a spiritual exercise, an act of devotion, . . . always a journey of risk and renewal."[1] Through this immersion in everything Poros, the reader may experience spiritual pilgrimage. This is a testament and guidebook for those who hunger for soul-stirring adventure, travel as pilgrimage, and deep immersion into the roots of our civilization and souls.

There are countless books published about ancient and modern Greece and a plethora of Greek travel guides with hotel, restaurant, shopping, and site guidance. Many guides include Poros in the cluster of Saronic Gulf islands; it is a popular stop for tourist-laden sightseeing ships and vacationers for a few hours. But there have only been a few books in English that explore the character, spirit, and offerings of this island.

The play and movie *Shirley Valentine* has become a modern myth. Through one woman's story it reveals and replicates the life stories of countless modern women. Too often, marriage, family, and workplace become confinements where the authentic self, with its passions and creative gifts, becomes trapped and the love relationship meant to awaken, support, and bless us becomes a prison cell. Joan, one of my many travelers here, adopted the name Shirley to remind her of her inner longings and help her emerge from unhappy confinement.

4 ∽ PASSAGE TO THE PAST

These patterns are not new or contemporary, but archetypal. What patterns and role models are portrayed in the unhappy, conflictual marriage of Zeus and Hera or the endless philandering of gods and punishing rages of goddesses? Disloyal, dysfunctional relationships are paraded and dramatized throughout Greek mythology and the Bible, the foundational texts of Western civilization. And likewise, we are told of transformational journeys of all kinds and pilgrimages and relocations to sacred and safe sites. During these journeys, we identify our personal life stories with the myths. This is one psycho-spiritual practice in which we recognize the archetypal, eternal dynamics in the story we are living. When we identify the archetypes, the god-powers that are active in us, we can give them new positive shape and direction. We take more charge of the myth that is living through us.

Anne Ibbotson, from the United Kingdom, published *Coming Slowly: A Kaleidoscope of Life on, and Around, the Greek Island of Poros* in 2006. Her book is a Shirley Valentine–type memoir of encounters with Poros's people and places when, as a young woman, she found refuge from the stresses of modern life and identity crises of adulthood. Spending most of her adult life on Poros, she concludes, "I hope you will . . . see the charm and understand something of the magic of this tiny island. . . . I came, fell in love with it and made a life here, and it has been, and still is, one of the best decisions of my life."[2]

Peter S. Gray was an American journalist, novelist, and philosopher. He lived on Poros from 1930 to 1932, and 1937 to 1939. In 1942, he published *People of Poros: A Portrait of a Greek Island Village*, a memoir of his encounters and relationships with the residents of the island, and its customs, culture, and way of life during the 1930s. He presented everyday people, their daily lives, working to eat and survive from one challenge to the next, the fears, stresses, and drastic changes visiting them with the approach of World War II, and the philosophy and humanity of simple islanders.

It is well-recorded in World War II history that early in the conflict Greece repulsed the nearly overpowering Italian invasion. This miraculous success helped delay the German advances elsewhere so the Allied powers could regroup and prepare their defenses and strategies. It was instrumental in contributing to the eventual Allied victory.

Yannis Maniatis is a retired high-ranking naval officer and now the devoted director of Poros's Hatzopouleios Public Library. Yannis explains that because Gray's book was published in English in 1942 during the war, though about a humble island, "it helped people the world over to understand the importance of Greece and its soul. It helped maintain a positive world image of Greece during these darkest of times." Yannis found the book when he was stationed as an officer at the United State naval base at Quantico Bay, Virginia, in 1984 for advanced training. The book was so rare that the Library of Congress let him examine but not photocopy it. His base librarian located and borrowed a copy, and he photocopied the entire book. He translated it into Greek as *Oi Poriotes Sto Nisi Tous* (The Poriotes of our island).[3] It was published in 2002 and Yannis went to great lengths to identify the actual people presented in the text.

The poet George Seferis won the Nobel Prize for Literature in 1963. He used Poros as his writing refuge and retreat immediately after World War II. Many of his poems originate from or comment on this island where he found "a fisherman's chat" to be more authentic than the modern chatter of urban or intellectual environments. The American writer Henry Miller was a friend of Seferis and spent time on this and other regional islands. He mentioned his impressions of Poros in *The Colossus of Maroussi*, an account of his long pilgrimage through Greece with Seferis, Lawrence Durrell, the writer, editor, and intellectual George Katsambalis who was Miller's "Colossus," and other writers of the era. Seferis and Miller both affirmed, and I attest to the same in chats with fisherfolk, the laundryman, a retired postman, artists and refugees, and countless others who find asylum here. There is a serene belonging and presence on Poros like no other. We will hear of *galini*.

Our Western concept of the soul first awakened in Greece over 2,400 years ago with Sokrates and the so-called Greek miracle. But millennia earlier, the region was inhabited and suffused with spiritual beliefs and practices. For thousands of years here and throughout the ancient world, people sought oracles, visions, dreams, and had experiences that put them in touch with primal and cosmic powers that over time became their gods and goddesses, the personifications, carriers, and embodied imagery

6 ∽ PASSAGE TO THE PAST

of these powers. As a result, since ancient times small Greece has been a magnet for the soul and has given birth to countless famous and little-known books of immersion, pilgrimage, and spiritual encounter. From Homer's *Odyssey* and Pausanias's first travel guide written around the second century, through Lawrence Durrell's *Prospero's Cell* written about the island of Corfu and Henry Miller's *Colossus*, retreat for cultural and spiritual restoration has been a practice as old as civilization and Greece itself.

It continues to this day. I first wrote about Poros three decades ago.[4] Pamela Jane Rogers is an American expatriate artist who has lived and worked on Poros for thirty years, painting more than a thousand canvases in several mediums, studying the penetrating light, colors, and textures here.[5] She too is replicating an ancient tradition of the traveling artist finding and rendering her soul space in glorious colors while adding her name and work to the island's legacy. The Greek American translator and poet Kimon Friar and American poet James Merrill resided here. Marc Chagall, Lucien Freud, John Craxton, and other artists over the last three centuries retreated here, and their art was transformed. Travelers seeking such immersive experience can find Poros to be a welcoming portal through which we cross from the mundane to the divine, the temporal to the eternal. As Pamela said, Poros is "an entrance into the real, ancient, and enduring Greece."

Passage to Poros is a spiritual, mythological, literary, cultural, historical, and psychological pilgrimage, an immersion in the sacred dimensions of the island, and a guidebook for modern travelers and those seeking to penetrate the spiritual dimensions of travel, here and everywhere.

Crossing the Strait

> *Let us feel that where the heart is,*
> *There the muses, there the gods sojourn . . .*
> RALPH WALDO EMERSON, "INTELLECT"

Always seeking spiritual guidance and growth and more comprehensive dimensions of healing, always hungry to penetrate the invisible and discover the marvelous in the everyday, I have been studying the Greek tradition as a living entity almost my entire life. I have studied its literature and mythology since childhood, embracing its wisdom for life guidance, devouring its myths for identification, emulation, warning. I have had countless dreams with mythic figures, images, themes that challenge and guide my own growth. For four decades I have traveled all over Greece and had life-changing experiences. Since 1995 and to this day I lead pilgrimage and practice radical ritual modeled on Asklepian and other ancient Greek practices for healing, psycho-spiritual growth, and wisdom that are rare in our modern world but accessible and can be achieved in both well-known and remote sites all over the country. For decades I have used Poros as my base.

I guide people as pilgrims seeking and experiencing life-transforming dreams, visions, and synchronistic events that are beyond rational explanation. Yet they are comprehensible and useable as they reveal in our times and lives ancient and eternal, archetypal, and mythic dimensions of existence—the place the soul lives. The natural and cosmic powers that were once personified as gods and goddesses and known in myths and oracles are still alive and accessible. They are the forces of the universe; they are *what is*. The American writer Henry Miller experienced, during his pilgrimage here, that "the curtain had been lifted on a world which had never really perished but which had rolled away like a cloud and was preserving itself intact, inviolate, until the day when . . . [we] would summon it back to life again."[6]

As I have written elsewhere, I call the ancient personifications known as gods and goddesses the god-powers. They are embodiments, images, and versions of the archetypes that are eternal in the personal, cultural, and collective unconscious. We can invoke them to achieve "experiences akin to the ancients."[7] As Plato and Carl Jung both indicated, the "forms" or archetypes are living forces. They have been buried and dried out in our postmodern, materialistic, hyperrational, and violent world. "Archetypes are like riverbeds," Jung wrote, "which dry up when the water deserts them." We must water them again and well to restore our psyches, and the longer they flowed in a place the more readily they can return.[8] Immersion in living mythology, especially in its homeland, can provide this.

8   PASSAGE TO THE PAST

When we immerse in the "spirit of place," meet its long-time residents, drench in its mythology, pay attention to our dreams and synchronistic events, we awaken not only ourselves. As Prof. Roger Brooke explains, we are no longer in physical but "in psychological space.... The space around is not merely geometric space; it is indeed a place that carries history, imagination, and psyche." We enter "the soul of the place."[9]

Numerous numinous events unfolded for me around Greece and on Poros, an island in ancient times whose god was Poseidon and under whose protection asylia, inviolable sanctuary, was practiced. These events on Poros and other sites impelled me to explore, develop, and use mystery and healing practices modeled on the ancients, and apply them in my own life and those of my patients and students for contacting the Self within, the core soul that wants rediscovery, exposure, expression, and healing. The soul wants us to live its life. Or, as George Seferis wrote, there is a soul that fights to become yours.

In our modern times and society, I am identified as an archetypal or transformational psychotherapist. However, my identification has passed beyond these modern iterations to embrace the archaic Greek roles of *therapeut, moirarchos, Asklepiad,* and *didaskalos.*[10] A therapeut is a servant of the god-power who channels its energies to those in need of healing. A moirarchos is one who guides us toward our destinies. An Asklepiad is a doctor or practitioner who has been initiated in the ancient tradition of the healing god Asklepios and the use of dream incubation for channeling transpersonal messages and energies. A didaskalos is a wandering, itinerant teacher who does not have a "job"—a permanent position—but meets, guides, explores in the agora, the open public spaces. Sokrates is our prime model.

Immersion in the ancient Greek world allows these depths of experience and awareness. It is as Plato and Hippocrates taught—we grow from the core soul upward to the heart and mind and outward to the body; and Sokrates—we must not neglect the wants of our souls; and Hippocrates—"All illnesses begin in the soul and end in the body." In our spiritually starving and stress-filled modern world, people have lost these vital connections and often try to restore or induce them using alcohol ("spirits"), drugs, and medications. But we can naturally achieve intuitive, imaginal, and altered states or transpersonal experiences that lead us back to our authentic selves and destinies. This is a core quality of living well that is neglected by our modern world. Without it we suffer in emptiness and despair and descend into soul sickness, wounding, and loss.

Poseidon, Asklepios, Athena; the hero Theseus and his tragic son Hippolytos; the Persian invasions and defeats; the Mycenean warrior culture and its powers; spiritual practices at least three thousand years old; nymphs and mountain spirits; Dionysos and Persephone exploding in the land and people; the nearby citadel of Agamemnon, commander of the Greeks at Troy; the Muses and stories bursting as if just experienced; the marketplace of today replicating the ancient agora; the Taverna in the Wake and others where philosophers and refugees gather as they did at Simon the Sandal Maker's shop in ancient Athens; the wise beggar Diogenes; the angry rebel Demosthenes and other personages of the past; the presence of St. George and his determination; Panagia, Mother Mary and her compassion—all these are alive. They are revealed in dreams and uncanny experiences and encounters, and they live in the people of the region. These are of the soul, the deeper invisible ecology of Poros.

This reawakening of the ancient is not only happening on Poros and through my small work. The religion of the Twelve Olympians has been surreptitiously practiced in northern Greece for generations. Some people believe in literal gods and sacred fires burn at the base of Mt. Olympus today. After a sixteen-hundred-year silence, the religion of the Olympians was legalized in 2017. Elsewhere around Greece modern therapists and artists are reviving mystery practices of Dionysos, Orpheus, Eleusis, and others. One colleague is a nurse by day and priest of Poseidon by night. Others revive Dionysian ecstatic dancing. Still others use ancient tragedy as modern mythic psychodrama. Professors and geophysicists scientifically research the natural healing energies of some of the ancient sites. A therapist is teaching Asklepian self-healing. A leading medical doctor and professor uses Pythagorean principles for healing modern stress. A pioneering orthomolecular physician affirms that the soma takes its directions from the soul and is researching how this happens on the cellular level. Taken together we are mining the ancient ways to make them accessible, marry them to modern science, and provide missing

10 ∽ PASSAGE TO THE PAST

ingredients for soul healing and spiritual growth for individuals and our suffering modern world.

In indisputable and nearly unbelievable ways, in that which Freud called "the uncanny" but did not understand or experience, Poros became retreat, sanctuary, asylum, temple, incubation, and healing chamber where I could help others achieve, and myself have, "experiences akin to the ancients." Poros became the thin mouth of the great funnel through which the ancient Greek world pours through.

From the Ancient to the Modern World

Poros. A dead poet first brought me here. A giant sea turtle met me here. Pilgrims and refugees find sanctuary here. Forgotten god-powers gift dreams and visions here that have guided healing for many and for me. These meetings and numinous experiences led me to new directions for soul growth and healing. I felt sent home to seek and develop them, then bade to return again and again.

Poros is small. It is a limestone island emerging from the Saronic Gulf, thirty-six miles southwest of Athens. It lies just two hundred meters off the eastern Peloponnese coast. To get there, travelers must arrive by sea from the port of Piraeus or the other Saronic islands, or on their own boats or yachts. Or they must travel by land along the eastern Peloponnesos and cross the strait of glistening azure waters from the gleaming village of Galatas on the mainland opposite.

The island wears as its quiet glory two humble jewels. One is the Monastery of Zoodogos Pigi, the Virgin of the Life-giving Spring. It is snuggled into a pine- and cypress-treed bayside, thriving after three centuries, and a long-time center of asylum. The second is the once grand but long-abandoned Sanctuary of Poseidon, god of the sea, lying in its own mountaintop ruins and carpeted with wildflowers, gnarled old olive trees, and wind-twisted pines. Black-and-white images run through the text to connect you with this island, and a color insert is included to help you immerse yourself in this place.

Poros means both "passage" and "resource" in ancient Greek. On the concrete level, the island's name refers to the deep and narrow strait of

Fig. I.2. The view of Poros town from the Galatas side.
Photograph by Tasos Rodis

water separating it from the mainland. It provides safe passage and harbor for the crowded tour ships and private yachts that regularly put in today and feed its contemporary economy now dependent on tourism. Its small harbor town, also called Poros, provides a refuge from modern life as a restful and scenic recreational escape for international travelers and weary Greeks who fill its tavernas and hotels on weekends and holidays.

Yet for those who seek it Poros can be a spiritual sanctuary and place of refuge from our speed-drunk, stress-filled, materialistic, competitive, alienating, and threatening modern world. The small island can provide passage into a living village and between our visible everyday world and the psycho-spiritual and mythic dimensions, the invisible realms of which we are all a part but hardly aware. It can help reveal our small but significant places in the chain of history and tapestry of the cosmos. Poros offers itself, in Athenian poet Giorgos Kanabos's words, as *o kipo tis Theas*, "a garden of God,"[11] in which the

12 ∽ PASSAGE TO THE PAST

world-weary wanderer is drenched in beauty, serenity, and revitalizing energies of generous hospitality and unseen presence. From ancient times to our day, Poros has been a font of hidden resources that can be rediscovered by modern pilgrims from any tradition.

My first visit to Poros in 1987 gifted me an experience that changed my life and work permanently and for the better in ways I could never have imagined. I have returned to Poros numerous times since, seeking asylia, the rite of asylum, the origin of the English word. In ancient times it meant inviolable protection from violence and life's many dangers. The homeless, shipwrecked, and politically oppressed fled here— so too throughout history into modern times. Like so many, my psyche too was drenched in, and I sought refuge from, much that has fled Pandora's box and stampedes among us—war; famine; plague; debt; cruelty; abuse; alienation; hypocrisy; greed; and the assaults of technological and unregulated capitalistic cultures and global climate change, and of the mundane. In addition to helping heal personal suffering in ways that work, I sought to better understand the grand drama that shapes our lives and in which we are all players great or small. And I wanted to partake of magic and mystery. The ancients testified to it. I believed it must still be available somehow, somewhere, in our suffering world, and especially where it had existed for millennia. Greek mythology and ancient traditions have given me healing tools that the modern world does not have, and I wish to help bring them to us.[12]

Indeed, I have been renewed and enriched during every visit to Poros, by every sweet breeze and glorious vista, by depths of intimate and philosophical conversation with residents or others who find refuge there, by its human and natural history and wonders, by what seem to be touches from the ancient deities who dwelled here, and a few blessed times by events that seem miraculous and impossible to explain but are more real than real and lift us above "the mediocrities of the world."

Though Greece is now Orthodox Christian, we can experience and embrace the ancient gods' archetypal natures in a living mythic psychology. Poseidon, best known as the god of the sea, was for several thousand years the ruling deity on Poros. He was god of earthquakes and thunderstorms and sent many of our most daunting troubles. He is popularly known for his power, unpredictability, and the troubles and challenges he sent. But less well known, as his Homeric Hymn, almost three thousand years old, declares, he founded and protected cities. He tamed tempests. He rescued sailors caught in his storms, and tamed and gifted horses. His sanctuary on Poros, in undeveloped ruins today, was his most important and one of the most revered in the ancient world. Especially on Poros, he protected the oppressed who sought his succor. We meet him here.

From numerous visits and my own immersion in the spirit of this small and unassuming island, journeys to Poros and its ancient and modern sanctuary become a source of refuge, resource, passage, and teachings that can provide wisdom, safety, and transformational healing when life is most storm ridden. We gain passage and connection to powers and resources that provide sanctuary in hidden, rich, and secret, yet accessible, restorative, and life-transforming ways.

1

PORTRAIT OF POROS
Immersion in the Greek World

Since we cannot change reality, let us change the eyes which see reality.

NIKOS KAZANTZAKIS, *REPORT TO GRECO*

We are all on passage from life to death, the visible to the invisible, and the imperative to grow our souls. Poros, "passage," is an apt name for the small Saronic Gulf island and a blessed place for soul growth. Technically, *O Poros* and *O Skorpios* are the only two Greek islands with male names, all others being female. Poros is separated from the mainland by about seven hundred feet of sapphire or steel-blue, calm, quietly roiling or roughly wave-chopped waters and surrounded by undulating mountains carpeted with pine trees. Poros was born when the nearby Methana volcano erupted about forty-five thousand years ago and hurled its great boulders through the air to fall as a volcanic rock protrusion resting on the sea bottom. Methana is the Hephaestion, a volcano that in mythic times was ruled by Hephaistos, lame god of artisans and the forge, on the peninsula a short distance to the north.[1]

As the visitor approaches by ferry, hydrofoil, or cruise ship, the island is at first indistinguishable from the Peloponnesian coast. Novelist Henry Miller visited both his friend the poet George Seferis and the island in 1939. He described his first sighting, which presages rebirth we can experience upon visiting: "Coming into Poros gives the illusion of the deep dream. Suddenly the land converges on all sides and the boat is squeezed into a narrow strait from which there seems to be no egress. . . . To sail slowly through the streets of Poros is to recapture the joy of passing through the neck of the womb."[2]

Soon the narrow strait yawns and Poros seems to separate. Its harbor and only town, also named Poros, opens like a boat-lined amphitheater, thick with fishing caïques, yachts, dinghies, and water taxis that carry people across the passage to the village of Galatas on the opposite shore.

Sixty years ago, people hired rowboats to make the crossing; there were no cars or roads on the western side. A lone Volkswagen was the taxi service for the region. To cross the strait, two boats lined up, side by side, wooden planks were laid between them, and the car was carefully steered across the makeshift bridge. When small boats arrived in the 1960s, the fee for crossing was three drachmas, about nine cents. Today, for one euro thirty cents, wooden water taxis ferry people for the few-minute ride between the island and Galatas perched across the dancing waters on the eastern shore of the Peloponnese.

Small hotels, restaurants, shops, and lime-washed white houses with red tile roofs spread along the water's edge on both shores. On Poros they climb the hill, crowned with a white clock tower, the town's symbol. Across the strait in Galatas, the small buildings stretching along the opposite eastern shore seem to smile by day and their lights glitter at night like seeds of light scattered by the hands of a god.

Poros is actually a double island, large and small, attached by a thin causeway. Its larger island is named Kalaureia and derives from the Greek, *kali aura*, literally meaning "good wind." The name connotes the gentle, sweet, and pleasant breezes for which the island has always been known. Nikos Kazantzakis wrote of "the influence on the soul of pure air, easy breathing, and a vast horizon. Anyone would think that the soul, too, is an animal with lungs."[3] In the sweet

16 ～ PORTRAIT OF POROS

Fig. 1.1. An early photo of crossing the strait, when small boats were the only transportation, 1925.
PHOTOGRAPH FROM THE HATZOPOULEIOS PUBLIC LIBRARY ARCHIVES

breezes sweeping the pine mountain and sea vistas of Poros, we feel that animal soul peacefully reawakening. About this Poros air, Peter Gray wrote, "because of the singular quality of the air you feel that you have gained new vision, that your eyes for the first time are open to reality."[4] And poet Kate Dahlstedt, who has traveled here many times, affirms these qualities in our times. She writes:

> *It's not the handshakes*
> *Or the early morning smiles*
> *Not the mountains or the sea*
> *Hillside shanties or olive trees*
> *Not the ferry all day long*
> *The bouzouki player's song—*
> *Bigger than all of these*
> *A simple place to breathe*
> *Where my weary soul belongs*[5]

The smaller of Poros's connected islands is called Sfairia. It is a triangular volcanic stone island with little vegetation, upholding the town with its busy, popular, attractive harbor village, the island's only modern settlement. Sfairia is named for Sfairos, the charioteer of Pelops, an ancient king of Pisa, near Olympia, for which the great Peloponnesos—"Pelop's Island"—is named.

"Passage" does not only refer to the waterway separating the island from the mainland. For millennia, because of the island's proximity to Athens, Greek writers, artists, government officials, and businesspeople, as well as international visitors have used the island as a respite from the hectic pace of cosmopolitan life or the demands and threats of history and politics. They boat down this watery passage to another, more ancient and serene world.

Poros has been inhabited since at least about 1100 BCE. Its earliest settlement, discovered only a few decades ago on a tiny neighboring island, dates to 2300 BCE. It was part of the Cycladic culture of the central Aegean, "the area of the Argo-Saronic Gulf [that] was densely populated since early antiquity, apparently because of its position facing the Aegean and open to the communication routes,"[6] and suffused "with a net of communication in the region."[7] These predate by many centuries the powerful Mycenean era dominant in the central Peloponnesos whose capital of Mycenae was fifty-six miles west and inland from Galatas.

In classical times Poros was the center of the Kalaureian League, an alliance between seven important cities: Athens, Epidauros, Nauplion, and others, that together founded the League.[8] It dates to before 600 BCE. The League is known to have been religious rather than political, economic, or military. The island and its Sanctuary of Poseidon were its center of spiritual practice. In fact, it was the principal site for the worship of Poseidon in the ancient Greek world. Its purposes and rituals remain largely a mystery. Here the god was the sanctuary's protector, and he was known as *Poseidonos Kalavros,* the god of good winds.[9]

In the twentieth century Poros was a favored retreat of the poet George Seferis, who sometimes fled Athens to the rugged, sparsely

Fig. 1.2. Still waters in the bay perfectly mirror Poros town with its iconic clocktower. See also plate 1.
PHOTOGRAPH FROM HATZOPOULEIOS PUBLIC LIBRARY ARCHIVES

populated island during the challenging times following World War II and was in residence there from 1946 to 1949. He stayed in the reddish-stone villa called Galini, meaning "serenity" or "tranquility," fronting the bay across from the main town. In ancient times the word connoted safe harbor out of the storm winds. Seferis's famous and complex poem series *Tsichla*, "The Thrush" was written there, inspired by a naval vessel of that name sunken in the harbor during World War I. He wrote his famous poem "Arnisi" ("Denial") at Neorio Beach, a short walk down the bayside from the villa, a place where his literary friend Henry Miller liked to swim.

By the sea, mysterious
and white as a pigeon,
we were thirsty at noon
but the water was brackish.

On the blond sand, alighting
we inscribed her name. Beauty

PORTRAIT OF POROS 19

blew the breeze from the sea
and erased the writing.

With what heart, with what strife,
what breath and what ache
we received our life. A mistake!
And we changed life.[10]

Seferis wrote in *A Poet's Journal: Days of 1945–1951* that Poros was a place where "a boatman's chat, a fisherman's gesture . . . belong, even today, to a ceremonial world."[11]

In 1952, Poros was an artistic retreat for the Russian modernist painter Marc Chagall, who also stayed in Galini. Poros flooded Chagall with so much light and color that it changed his canvases as it illuminated his inner life and united his somber Russian tones with explosions of life-affirming sensuality.

Though somewhat marred and transforming today due to dependence on a tourist economy, development for the affluent that is sweeping the world, and the impact of climate change, for those who seek it Poros remains that source of archaic authenticity, ceremonialism, serenity, and beauty.

Poros town is home to 90 percent of the island's permanent population, today less than four thousand. It also has a small number of approximately two hundred permanent international residents: Albanian, Cypriot, Dutch, British, French, Bangladeshi, Armenian, Israeli, American. Notably, due to contemporary socioeconomic conditions, especially the little availability of employment, growth of tourism, and influx of the affluent, the Greek population is slowly and annually shrinking while the international population is increasing.

Small farms with orange and lemon trees and vineyards are scattered on the northeast side of the island. In town, several travel agencies offering accommodations and travel services front the busy harbor. Taxis, motorcycles, motorbikes, and small delivery trucks rumble back and forth. In previous years, and during my early visits, residents crowded the ferry slip at arrival times, greeting guests or offering visitors a room

Fig. 1.3. The century-old clock tower on the town's highest point has become the island's celebrated symbol. See also plate 4.
PHOTOGRAPH BY BABIS KANATSIDIS

in their hotel, home, or for the young, hardy, or thrifty, a cot on their roof if the weather was good.

Numerous stairways lead from the harbor street up into a labyrinth of *sokaki*, narrow, winding alleyways lined with old houses lush with bougainvillea and gardenias, orange and lemon trees, clinging grapevines. Occasional signs offer a room to rent. Small buildings here and there house gift or local goods shops, a few barber and butcher shops, late-opening tavernas.

These bright, meandering alleyways, lined with flowers, hung with gourds, lead upward from the water to the town's clock tower, built in 1927 with an innovative timing mechanism from America still in service after repairs in 2000. The clock tower has become the beloved symbol of the island. Before it flaps a tattered Greek flag. The flag is Greek blue and white—sky and sea. In the corner on a blue field is the white Cross of St. George, displaying the symbol of the warrior saint, leader, and protector of the army. The flag has nine alternating blue and white stripes. To this day the number of stripes is connected in

PORTRAIT OF POROS 21

popular thought to the nine syllables of the Greek phrase, *eleftherios i thanatos*, "freedom or death." This modern design was adopted at the First National Assembly in 1822. Said Makis Kordomenidis, a veteran of the Greek Special Forces, "The Spartans danced in fire before the Persian onslaught at Thermopylae. From ancient times to today Greek warriors march into battle calling this slogan and singing." Manolios, an elderly Poriotis* World War II veteran, lost an arm in combat. He waved his empty sleeve at me and said, "It is nothing to give my arm for Greece."

The view from the clock tower, especially at sunset with the flag above gently flapping or quietly drooping, shows the wide harbor gleaming and broad passage showered in golden droplets as small boats cut their wakes through the azure waters.

Across the channel the mainland village of Galatas receives travelers ferrying to or from other destinations. Galatas is less developed with less English spoken, its tavernas more local, hotels fewer and simpler, grocery stores and other local residential services more common. We feel the beating lives of ordinary people less impacted by tourism there.

Behind and to the north of Galatas, the tall, broad range of mountains is known in Greek as Koimomeni—or the Sleeping Woman Mountain, often called Sleeping Beauty. The names are telling of the shape and character of the mountain. I recorded my early 1997 encounter with her in my journal.

The blazing sun chariot is still an hour above the horizon. Its light glares off the waters of the strait that separates this beflowered island from the world, turning the blue waters into a blinding silvery sheet of glass. Below the sun, awaiting its fiery kiss on her belly, Koimomeni stretches her hazy gray silhouette across the horizon. Her brow, nose, and chin point upward, slightly taut. Her lips part as if to whisper a secret into the ear of the sky. Her long neck stretches. Her firm breasts rise, so full, then her chest tapers to a slender belly before her

---

*On the island, a man is known as *Poriotis* (plural *Poriotes*) and a woman is *Poriotissa* (plural *Poriotisses*).

Fig. 1.4. Sleeping Lady Mountain displaying her goddess form.
See also plate 6.
PHOTOGRAPH FROM HATZOPOULEIOS PUBLIC LIBRARY ARCHIVES

thighs slope upward to her raised knees. She is so perfectly a woman that looking at her I expect to see her breathe. I await the heave of her breasts, the pulsing of her throat, the quiver of her chin. Eternally, she lies there while we who pass watch and wait in wonder. To see her would alone be reason enough to visit this isle.

In archaic times, as Aeschylos described in the opening of Agamemnon, perhaps fires flared on her summit, announcing that after the decade-long war, Troy had finally fallen.[12] Now spires rise from her slopes like giant acupuncture needles. Windmills. Even this ancient woman in the mountain is touched, redressed, and put to new service in our needy modern world.

Plato perceived the forms, Jung the archetypes. The spiritual pulsates through the real. These ideal essences are behind every physical manifestation. Koimomeni evokes a goddess. There are things that so partake of eternity that, no matter what we humans do, their beauty cannot be marred.

Fig. 1.5. The blazing sun chariot eternally settles at dusk over the goddess form in the mountain. See also plate 11.

PHOTOGRAPH BY THE AUTHOR

Along Poros's harbor front are fruit and vegetable stands, tiny groceries, a few quality jewelry stores, several hotels, and numerous tavernas and both traditional and modern coffee shops and bars as well as the ubiquitous trinket shops. During the pandemic, some older small businesses were forced to close. In their place, modernistic boutique shops have opened selling upscale clothing and jewelry that cater to tourists and the wealthy yachting and second-home crowd now slowly but steadily changing the town's ecology while sustaining its economy. In afternoon heat and calm, or in cool and cloudy weather, fewer chairs are occupied among the neat dining and café areas along the street facing the waters. With sunset, warm weather, and on weekends and holidays, they fill to a noisy bursting.

East along the waterway is the town's modest archeological museum on Plateia Alexander Koryzis, in which stands his mounted marble bust. Koryzis was born in 1885 on Poros, where his father had been mayor. He briefly became prime minister of Greece during

24   ∞   PORTRAIT OF POROS

World War II. He refused to comply with Nazi demands that he expel British forces from Greece. In 1941 the Germans invaded, and he shot himself in the heart.

The museum building was originally his residence. It stands in one of several small squares along the waters that open on old, low, and quaint public or private buildings, a few with historical statues. The wharf is wider now than in previous decades. A hundred years ago in front of the museum, floating markets—small boats loaded with produce and dry goods—lined the waterway for island shoppers.

In the Square of Heroes, a plaque and monument memorialize regional victims of the Nazis and other local war dead going back to World War I. One carries the names of five island residents executed by the Nazis in 1943. Yannis Maniatis explains that this wartime action, and others like it around the world, "de-liberate" the invaded free countries and therefore should be called "possession" rather than the commonly used "occupation," since the invader intended to keep and retain rule over the captured territories. The monument also names Giorgos Kontos, Poros's most recent casualty, a vice colonel in charge of communications killed in the Korean War in January 1953. These names stand as sad reminders of the cost of world alliance and eternal war. On national holidays it seems as if the entire village gathers in ceremony before the monument to honor their memories and "the cost of freedom."

The small museum, which only charges a two-euro entry fee, houses relics and finds from Troizen, a remote but important ruin site across the water just six miles north of Galatas, as well as from Poseidon's sanctuary. The bull was his totem. One glass case holds dozens of small clay bull effigies offered as sacrifice and thanksgiving.

Troizen was the birthplace of the mythic hero Theseus, famous for entering the Cretan labyrinth, slaying the Minotaur, and returning to become king of Athens. Troizen's locale beneath rough mountains with rare rushing creeks gives a taste of the rugged childhood Theseus must have enjoyed in these wilds where he hunted boar and heard Poseidon's voice in the thunder.

In historical times Troizen was a place of sanctuary and refuge. Its unrestored foundations remain half-covered in poppies and sweet wild grasses. Troizen had an Asklepieion, a sanctuary of the healing god Asklepios, where holistic medicine and dream healing were practiced for centuries.[13] It had a temple to Hippolytos, tragic son of Theseus, who was mistakenly killed by a curse from his father enacted by Poseidon. At his temple, marriage and mystery rites were practiced. During the Persian invasions in 480 BCE, when Athens was sacked and the Akropolis burned, the women, children, and elderly of Athens, all who could not fight, fled to Troizen for safety.

The archeological museum has a copy of Themistokles's Resolution of 480 BCE. It originally declared the evacuation of Athens during the Persian invasion and before the Battle of Salamis. "Most Athenians sent their children and women to Trizina, where they were received with great honor, and taken care of with the greatest of hospitality." The original was found by an American professor in Trizina in 1959, where it had been made into a step on the school stairs.[14] Also from fourth-century BCE Troizen, a marble frieze shows a woman removing her veil, recording a traditional wedding ceremony ritual. A third-century funeral stele from Kalaureia shows the orator Xenokrates holding a scroll. He died in battle defending his home island. The museum is also refuge to a humble collection of pottery urns, shards, and column bases and both Doric and Ionic capitals from Poros's mountaintop Sanctuary of Poseidon as well as from Troizen and Methana, the nearby volcano and site of scattered villages a short drive up the Peloponnese coast. These date from the seventh through the fourth centuries BCE.

Humble and fractured statues and relics of Poseidon, Hygeia, Dionysos, and other deities as well as a collection of steles and votive offerings to the gods and shell-encrusted shipwreck finds adorn this simple two-story museum. Its prize may be a half–life-size statue of Asklepios from his temple at Troizen. Standing before statuary in quiet rooms, we may gain encounters. Some visits have provoked dreams. Once I watched a giant black spider drape and hug the smooth white marble shoulder of a statue of Dionysos as if it were the god's brooch. I was transfixed.

Small and moderate-sized Orthodox churches are scattered throughout the town, a few on or near the waterfront, others in the high labyrinth of streets. The dominant church is the St. George Cathedral. Famous icons decorate the lavish interior smelling sweetly of oft-burning incense. Villagers are especially proud of the numerous icons decorating the interior, painted in 1907 by Kostas Parthenis in what is known as Advanced Byzantine style. The cathedral is new and on the site that originally held five small chapels, including sites of St. George, St. Kiriaki, and St. Evangelista, patroness of the Annunciation. Only three chapels remain. Two were taken down for building materials. An old and small stone capital stands where an altar once was.

The cathedral is built atop an ancient temple to Athena, and some of her archaic stonework is built into the edifice. Greek Orthodox churches always face east and are built in a crucifix shape. But this cathedral faces north, is rectangular, and is in perfect triangular alignment with Athena's Parthenon in Athens and Poseidon's temple at Sounion, creating a great triangle of energy across the miles and seaways.

Behind my favorite hotel, 7 Brothers, a few steps down a picturesque alley, is the Church of the Ipapanti. A large stone fountain stands in front, its obelisk supporting a spigot. For centuries villagers drew their daily waters from this source, as did I during earlier visits here. With modern pollution, now villagers politely but firmly warn us to no longer drink this water.

Ipapanti is Greek for Candlemas, the holy feast day that celebrates the presentation of Jesus and purification of the family in the temple when the babe reached forty days old. It is celebrated in February about two weeks after Catholic Candlemas. The church is modest in size but inviting and serene in atmosphere. Along with many locals, I start my days lighting candles and sitting in contemplation and prayer before its icons. I especially love an icon of the Virgin and child. Her wide, watery eyes stare out at us in utmost compassion and gentleness. I have sat before her during difficult times, seeking help and support and feeling soothed and upheld.

The harbor road north leads past more boat moorage as the cluster of scattered tavernas thins out. Toward the farther end a modern bronze statue called *H Gorgoni*, or the *Mermaid*, stares out toward the sea and distant mountains for as long as bronze keeps its form. Sculpted by Giorgos Xenoulis in 1999 and dedicated at the changing of the millennium, her bronze is mottled and aging. Her breasts tilt upward. Her fountain base sprays water toward her graceful fins and hand upraised to mountains and sky. But they only flow in high season when enough travelers justify the trouble. Yet in air she curves like the sea, graceful and free.

Beyond the mermaid is an old arsenal, now a Naval Academy for petty officer recruits. The building was originally built in 1844 as a summer residence for King Otto. As modern history unfolded it served as a naval base for Venetians, Russians, English, and French forces. It finally became the first naval base of modern Greece. The *Averof,* fondly called a battleship, (actually an armored cruiser) was for a long time anchored offshore and part of the school. The *Averof* served prominently in the 1912 victory over the Turkish fleet in the battle of the Dardanelles and was for many years the flagship of the Greek navy. Though old and outdated, it continued to serve in World War I, in transport during the Turkish expulsion of its Greek population, and in convoy and transport operations in World War II. It was decommissioned in 1952. During its Academy residency, until it was transferred to a naval museum in Piraeus in 1984 at the instigation of Minister of Culture Melina Mercouri, a procession of white-uniformed cadets marched in its shadow.

Beyond the Academy a small canal serves as another passage, separating Poros into its two islands: Sfairia, the small island on which the town is located, and the rest of the double island known by its ancient name Kalaureia. Kanali Beach on the right, broad and rocky with calm clear waters warm enough to swim in for eleven months of the year, is speckled in good weather with Greek families and tourists.

From the bridge the road forks north, east, and west. The west fork leads along the straits. It stretches to the stone ruins of the 1830 Russian naval base, now a beach, and farther out to an 1870 lighthouse. Development along this road reveals Poros's contemporary social, economic, and cultural conditions.

When I first walked, swam, and slept there almost four decades ago, old stone or wooden huts of local fisherman and peasants crowded this

Fig. 1.6. The Naval Academy, on the bay just across the canal, was a critical military base hosting international and Greek warships.
PHOTOGRAPH FROM THE HATZOPOULEIOS PUBLIC LIBRARY ARCHIVES

shore that creeps toward small, pine-shaded Neorion Beach. In their yards bronzed men mended fishing nets and black-clad women tended goats and chickens. On the rocky shore across from each hut, its tiny fishing caïques, painted green, red, or blue and peeling, bobbed against the rocks. During that first visit to the island in 1987, I slept in a local family's rented room for ten dollars a dreamy night.

Today fewer old islanders remain scattered and surrounded in the labyrinth of white guesthouses lining the quiet bayside road. Over the decades I have watched them sprout and spread. Once, a hut was unexpectedly separated from its ancient neighbor by a rare whitewashed rooming house or a getaway beach home for the newly affluent. Now conditions have reversed and there are more vacation houses growing like bleached mushrooms and crowding the remaining locals off this beach road that had been theirs for millennia.

Far more developed so that local life is almost gone, is the road to Askeli Beach that leads to the monastery. It is now crowded with modern guesthouses and resorts that line the beachfront. They cater to multitudes of summer vacationers that flock here, and lie empty, their vacant windows staring at the tranquil bay, during the long offseason.

Mornings and evenings in town and along the west road, fishermen put out in their small boats or gather along the shores as they have for millennia. They cast and wait, smoke and chat, pull in and recast. They haul in their squirming, gleaming catches, place them in buckets or tubs or dribble sea water on them to keep them fresh. They carry their catches home or sell them along the shore to residents or taverna keepers for their evening meals.

Today we see fewer fishermen. Now residents more commonly own or serve at the lantern-strung tavernas built along this road on platforms over the bay's edge, or in the food, rooming, and tourist services abundant in the harbor village. Hospitality, eternally good spirits, and delicious food, these qualities—part of Greek filoxenia,

Fig. 1.7. Askeli Beach, pristine and remote a century ago (1935), before modern tourist development.
PHOTOGRAPH FROM THE HATZOPOULEIOS PUBLIC LIBRARY ARCHIVES

guest-friendship—remain as strong and authentic expressions of the Greek spirit. You cannot leave without having eaten, along with the best food and wine, healthy verbal dishes of philosophy, ethics, history, religious and cultural teachings, and visit recommendations.

Elders still fish off the shore and are consulted for their natural wisdom. Do you want to know the day's weather prediction? Don't consult the internet. The fishermen, so they taught me, will observe whether the sea gulls are hovering and crying—meaning rain in a few hours—or placidly riding the breeze. They will observe whether the wind is blowing from the west—a short and gentle rainfall—or over the mountains from the south, indicating coming storms. If during the night the moon is surrounded by a hazy yellow-white circle like a soft halo of mist, it tells us that wind and heat are coming. As dawn stains the sky and awakens houses with early light, ask a fisherman along the wharf. He will stare up at the changeling sky for a few minutes, then accurately tell you what the day will bring, both soon and later.

As the day advances along the harbor front or the bayside porches, visitors are strung like chattering colored beads on invisible cords, sipping beer, wine, or coffee on sun-drenched porches. Nights transform Poros town. Colored lanterns click on along the waterfront restaurants as boat lights and reflections of the Milky Way dance on shimmering waters. Travelers and locals sit, happily accessible to meeting, at their chosen tavernas where they watch the scurrying waiters with loaded trays, listen to the knock of moored boats, and inhale the sweet breeze that drifts from the bay and the wooded hills. Meanwhile, all night long, water taxis plow the paths between the island and nearby mainland shore. The reflections of village lights and flaming stars dance on the dark waters. The two-horned moon looks down on all.

The night grows deeper, the starlight stronger, the lights of the tiny boats dance as they ferry late passengers across the glimmering narrow strait. One ferryman and one passenger with his small fare evoke images of the mythological Charon, ferryman of the dead, crossing the black waters of the River Styx to deliver his charge to the Underworld.

Early dawn light creeps up the strait and awakens the colors of earth, sea, and sky. With few vacationers around, residents emerge from hiding and the long shoreline speckles with fishermen. Some row or motor their wooden caïques through the strait or beat ink out of their catch of octopus or squid. Before development many sold their score of fish to taverna keepers from oil-soaked cloths spread under the sun. Now there is a small fish market selling the daily catch in a covered stall set back from the quay.

During recent visits, I met Greek women also fishing. I stopped by a dyad, shared that this was the first time I saw women fishing here and declared that I thought it was about time. "*Nai*! Yes! *Episis*. Me too!" they called back. Together we cheered, "*Opa!*"

Blacktop roads leave from the north fork above the canal and from the far end of the eastern canal fork. Both are steep and winding, cutting through green pine forests and silver olive groves as they lead to the two principal sites on Poros. Along twisting roads that circle the bay, past the resorts, and slowly rising up the mountain, we arrive at the Monastery of Zoodogos Pigi, the Virgin of the Life-giving Spring.[15] The monastery is dedicated to this special manifestation of the virgin. Throughout Greece Mary is worshipped as *Panagia*, the All Holy. Here she provides holy waters from her mountain that blesses people with healing. Her monastery sits in a glade two miles out along the east road, past overdeveloped Askeli Beach. The monastery is beyond, perched against the pine- and cypress-treed hillside. From here prayers of supplication are sent out to Mary. Though not deified as a goddess by the Orthodox church, Mary is deeply loved and worshipped all over Greece as the most important manifestation of the Divine. On Poros the city council and people have recently replaced St. George, protector of warriors, as the island's patron. In his place they elevated the Virgin of the Life-giving Spring to be their beloved protectress.

This monastery has practiced the ancient tradition of asylia, sanctuary, for centuries and into our modern era. James II, the Greek Orthodox Metropolitan of Athens, founded the monastery in 1713 after he was healed of kidney ailments by drinking the sacred waters flowing from its rock. A century later it provided the first orphanage in Greece for children of parents slain in the War of Independence. Since then and until today it has provided refuge for orphans, plague victims, the ill, infirm, and impoverished in body and spirit during troubled times. At times it sold off some of its land and holdings to support the poor and needy. It continues to this day to uphold the monastic ideal of retreat from the mundane and worldly to quiet the passions and devote oneself to prayer, study, contemplation, and good works.

Inside the monastery a twenty-three-foot-high series of gold inlaid panels depict the lives of Jesus and the apostles. Beside the altar is a painting of the Virgin by the Italian Rafaelo Ceccoli. It contains the face of his daughter who died of tuberculosis while in sanctuary at this monastery at age twenty-one in 1838. She is buried in the courtyard as are a few prominent Greek and British naval figures.

The monastery is also the home of the Icon of the Virgin of the Spring. It was painted in Venice in 1650 by the Cretan artist Theodoros Poulakis. It also holds other famous icons and trophies. On the altar stand icons of St. Gabriel, patron of messengers, and St. Michael, defender in battles, ubiquitous in Greece, somber and saintly in the dusky church.

Just outside the monastery stands a lion-headed fountain built into the mountainside. Depending on the season and the impact of climate change, cold, clear waters from the mountain either gush and gurgle or drip and dribble from the lion's stone mouth to splash in the catch basin below. Droplets coat the golden marigolds and purple petunias surrounding the catchment. They seem to promise that we too, if we take these waters, can be renewed, transforming from dry to wet, color-less to colorful.

From both monastery and canal, roads snake up into the rugged hills that wind through forests and then open outward on broad gulf vistas where islands float in the misty distance. Only the cackling of chickens, the braying of goats, the footfalls of the rare hiker, or buzz of a motorbike break the stillness of pine and olive boughs, the hot air thick and sweet smelling. The hills tumble away and far below the bright sea rolls against the brown and green island.

Fig. 1.8. An early twentieth-century photograph of the Monastery of the Virgin of the Life-giving Spring built onto a mountainside overlooking the bay beyond Askeli Beach.
PHOTOGRAPH FROM THE HATZOPOULEIOS PUBLIC LIBRARY ARCHIVES

Atop the Palati Plateau, the highest point on the island, stand the ruins of the Sanctuary of Poseidon. This sanctuary was the center of the Kalaureian League, a council of seven cities that met here and was one of the earliest federations in the ancient world, with origins in the Mycenean era around 1200 BCE. The small island of Modi, just off the east coast of Poros, where ruins have been recently unearthed, was its religious seat. Centuries later it was restored and developed as the sanctuary on Kalaueria.[16] Even today it may radiate mysterious energy. During a recent visit I had a dream in which a deep voice emerged from primordial darkness and declared, "The portals of Modi are open to you."

The Kalaureian League was called an *amphictyony*. There were others around the ancient world. Their purpose was to protect one of the major sanctuaries. Members of the Kalaureian League disregarded political and economic differences and conflicts and united for common religious and sacred matters and ceremonies, the purposes and practices of which are unknown. Library director Yannis Maniatis declares that the League "was like an ancient United Nations with its many committees for public service."

As a principal deity of the Greek pantheon, in addition to ruling as god of the sea, Poseidon was the protector of the endangered and conquered. This role and his tremendous strength were portrayed on a relief decorating the Athens Akropolis showing the god crushing an enemy with the island of Nisyros in the primordial war of the gods against the giants. Poseidon's mountaintop grounds located on the plateau provided sanctuary, the right of asylia, or asylum. To be in *asylon* was to be protected, safe from violence.* Poseidon's sanctuary originally provided this boon for refugees, the homeless, and shipwrecked. This tradition continued into historical times. The Athenian orator Demosthenes fled here and committed suicide before the altar of Poseidon rather than be taken captive by his Makedonian pursuers.

Today the sanctuary is a long stretch of knee-deep foundations scattered much of the year with sprouting purple, red, and yellow wildflowers. Old and heavy stonework demarks houses, dormitories, council rooms, and the once-grand temple of the sea god nestled near a cliffside and gazing out for millennia over his domain of sea and islands. From this sanctuary the Saronic Gulf opens in all directions. Islands dot the horizon and float in mist. Tiny farms freckle the hillsides below. A sea breeze climbs up the slope and mixes with trees, flowers, and vegetable crops to stain with sweetness. The pines seem to raise their limbs in praise. The sweet clean air rustles through their boughs like the breath of the god.

North and far below the sanctuary, where mountain meets sea, is Vagonia Beach. Here is the tranquil bay where in ancient times people seeking asylia put in to retreat in safety to the sea god's complex on the mountain above. Its ruins are now underwater and visible to swimmers.

Asylia is the right of asylum. *Asylon* is the safe place of refuge.

This sanctuary is the island's peak, center, and crown. Here, in the words George Seferis scribbled about his island retreat, it is "impossible to separate the light from the silence, the silence and light from the calm."[17] Here is the unadorned passage from the modern world to the ancient, from the quick to the dead, from the visible to the invisible, and material to spiritual. Here we find ourselves in the great sweep of time, nature, myth, and history. And here we may be, and return, restored.

2

COUNSEL WITH THE DEAD
Poet George Seferis on Poros

Heavy the task and hard, the living are not enough,
First because they do not speak, and then
Because I have to ask the dead
In order to be able to go further . . .

GEORGE SEFERIS, *POEMS*

A dead poet first brought me here. A dead ship, and the wars surrounding it, brought him.

Known to the world as George Seferis, his Greek name is Georgios Seferiades. He was a poet, essayist, translator, and diplomat. He was the first Greek writer to be awarded the Nobel Prize for Literature. His was a poetry of exile, longing, searching. He wrote simultaneously on the personal, historical, and archetypal levels so that his lyrics are both intimate and everyman's, of the present and the eternal. He is always voyaging and searching, never arriving and completing. To Seferis, Odysseus is our heroic role model, and we can only seek but never arrive home.

No wonder. George Seferis was born in Smyrna—now Izmir—Turkey, in 1900. In what Seferis called the "disaster" and the "catastrophe," he

COUNSEL WITH THE DEAD 37

and his immediate family fled to Athens in 1914, the remainder fleeing between 1922 and 1923, along with 1.5 million Greeks during the
compulsory population exchange with Turkey. As in ancient times and
throughout history, they were brutally forced to seek asylia.

After completing his education in Athens, Seferis entered the dip-
lomatic corps. He served in Albania and England before World War II,
in Egypt, South Africa, and Italy with the Free Greek Government in
Exile during the war, and in Turkey, London, Syria, and Lebanon after.
He finally served as ambassador to the United Kingdom from 1957 to
1961. This glosses over the events in Greece, victimizing and wounding
Seferis and millions of others—the world war and the civil war that
immediately followed, which he and other Greeks say was the worst of
all the catastrophes visited upon their homeland.

Exiled in childhood and rarely at home in Greece during his long
and busy life, Seferis survived expulsion, displacement, the world wars,
and civil war. He lamented, "We found dust and ashes. It remains to
rediscover our life now that we have nothing left anymore."[1] In his
poetry and inner life, he was forever seeking asylon, a place of refuge
and sanctuary in the Greece of history, imagination, and myth. He used
the Greek term *mythistorema*, mythic history, as the name for his first
volume of poetry. The term expresses his philosophy of survival and
composition—myth and history are one; we each and all live a mythic
history; we can best understand our lives by projecting them onto the
archetypal and poetic levels. In turn, these universal levels enable us, if
not to return home, at least to place our small struggles into a universal
context, making them more pregnant and tolerable and a small part of
the collective story.

George Seferis lived on Poros from 1946 to 1949. He lived and
wrote in Galini, the large reddish chateau facing Poros town from
across the deep waters. Among other writings, he composed his poem
series *Tsichla* there. It was inspired by the ship purposely sunken in the
Poros harbor during the world war to ensure it would not be used by
German occupiers. He visited the wreck. He seems to have had a strong
identification with it, as if he, too, were a wreck straining to endure the
lifelong painful history surrounding him.

38 ∞ COUNSEL WITH THE DEAD

Ancient wisdom and depth psychology both teach that we should follow synchronistic events that unfold in our lives as they are signs leading us to our destinies. It was a synchronistic event that seemed to come from natural powers by which I first encountered Seferis's poetry on a rough and rocky Atlantic shore far from his native Aegean Sea. It was 1986, and I was in my midthirties. I was sitting beneath the Fisherman's Memorial in Gloucester on Cape Ann, Massachusetts, a town once thronging with Portuguese immigrant fisherman, now like Poros both a disappearing commercial fishing and expanding tourist hub. Before me the blue-green-gray ocean rolled and heaved. Behind me the tall bronze fisherman strained at his wheel, eternally bending against the wind in remembrance of the thousands from this cape lost at sea since Gloucester's founding in 1642. I was in a solemn and pensive mood, facing midlife storms and challenges, seeking direction. Like Seferis, in my work with war veterans and the personal and American history I had lived through, I felt surrounded by brutality and exiled at home. I had just found Seferis's *Poems* in a used book loft on Gloucester's main street. Now it lay open in my lap. Poseidon, god of the sea and fair winds, seemed to visit at that moment. Like an arriving oracle, the sea breeze pulled and flipped pages, then stopped. My eyes fell where the breeze determined, onto "Stratis the Sailor Among the Agapanthi":

> *There are no asphodels, violets or hyacinths;*
> *How is one to speak with the dead?*
> *The dead only know the language of flowers,*
> *For that reason they keep silent;*
> *They go their way in silence; they endure in silence,*
> *In the city of dreams, in the city of dreams.*[2]

I looked up at the bronze fisherman honoring centuries of the dead who, we feel, demand something from the living. "The dead," Seferis wrote in his *Poet's Journal*, turning ancient belief into modern metaphor, "in order to speak, need live blood."[3] In ancient times the dead were offered the blood of human and animal sacrifices. Agamemnon sacrificed his daughter Iphigenia for fair winds to sail the Greek fleet to Troy. At an entryway to Hades, Odysseus slit animal throats and poured honey, oil, wine, and milk for "the numberless dead" so that their shades would speak to him.

We no longer live in an age of live human sacrifices, and animals are not sacrificed in mainstream or Western cultures. Instead, after flesh and blood are gone, we embody and enliven the dead by building statues and memorials, and writing poems, eulogies, and songs. These are honorific representations in forms that outlast us. We strain to give meaning to their sacrifices to assuage our pain and ennoble our losses. Seferis tried to provide that "blood" through the pain and labor it took to write his highly sensitive poetry. Do the dead receive our offerings? We cannot know. They may appear in dreams or visions. We may feel their spirits. But they do not answer us in a language many of us know how to hear or speak.

There is a vital connection between the living and the dead, often evoked or enacted through ritual. This is true for all traditional cultures. The shape, strength, rituals, songs, and music in response to this life-death connection help determine how tending, nurturing, supportive, or wisdom-making or neglectful is any community, culture, and country. Some of my own dearest dead are in massive and anonymous cemeteries stretched along the noisy byways of distant regions I cannot visit. I long to sit on my grandfather's grave during a lunch hour, afternoon siesta, or on holy days, as is done in some cultures. Many artists of preceding centuries wrote, sang, or screamed of the heart-wrenching loss of vital connections we have suffered . . . to ourselves, others, our communities, nation, history, the cosmos—to life itself. The Greek tradition practices *moirologia*, composing "words of fate," death songs for the departed that sing their memories and contributions after they are gone.

Seferis felt this modern and existential loss of vital connections to the divine, history, birth home, and community such that he was always deeply lonely. His sister said that he had "an open wound of sensitivity." His description of the poet Angelos Sikelianos could fit him; he had "a strength somehow wounded, yet ripe and mature."[4] Or as he said about himself, "I am almost sickened with sensitivity."[5] In contrast, his writer-friend Henry Miller, who stayed with him at Galini and traveled with him around Greece, described him as "a cross between bull and panther."[6] Seferis affirmed of our human potential that a person can at once feel deeply, act decisively, and live mythically. His connection to Greece and to Poros taught him that there was "the life beyond the statues." The statues are not only the marble works of art and architecture. The "statues" are anything frozen, unchanging, institutionalized, and codified so that it no longer lives but freezes us in dogma and fundamentalism.

Phil Cousineau, too, has written a masterful tome, *Who Stole the Arms of the Venus de Milo*, seeking the source of our experience of beauty and demonstrating how invisible energies, experienced as gods and goddesses, radiate from great works of art. "There is far more to a sculpture than stone or wood, more to a story than words or structure, more to art than canvas or paint. What's more is spirit, the ineffable vital force that an artist infuses."[7] Seferis's was, Phil's and mine are, searches for that force, that life beyond.

Seferis's music was haunting, somber, and heavy with accumulated sorrows. Yet like his countrymen past and present, and like the heroes of myth and history, he was determined to travel through ordeals personal and collective even to the land of the dead. We can connect to the spirits of the past. We can learn from them how to better steer our own storm-tossed lives.

Who was Stratis the Sailor of several poems? He was an ordinary sailor, one who "sailed for one year with Captain Odysseus,"[8] who went before the mast, as was said in the American tradition. He was not a king and epic hero like Odysseus, that great mythic traveler. He was an Everyman of the ever-restless sea and our postmodern baffling and blood-drenched centuries. His song and task, however, were not ordinary. In myth, visiting the dead, giving them proper offering so they could counsel the living, were tasks of Odysseus and Aeneas, heroes of the Trojan War, who needed to encounter the dead to find their way home. In Greek mythology Orpheus, Herakles, Pollux, Theseus, and Psykhe all undertook the Underworld journey and Persephone was taken there. Always the hero or heroine must make the Underworld journey, descend to the depths, confront mortality, overcome its terror, and undergo life-threatening ordeals to achieve transformation and finally return home with wisdom gained for living rightly. In Seferis, as in Dante, Alfred Lord Tennyson, James Joyce, and Nikos Kazantzakis, Odysseus served as a representative of the hungry human soul on lifelong quest, to paraphrase Kazantzakis, whose voyages were his native land. In Seferis, Odysseus captained Stratis, a commoner traveling the bloody century through its wars and civil wars, social and economic cataclysms and collapses, unto the threat of total annihilation, all the while seeking a way to finally be at ease, to arrive at the soul's long-sought home.

This was poetry for midlife, for the middle of the journey, for the years of wandering, weariness, and struggle, a time like Odysseus's on his journey home from the Trojan War. It is a time when our characters and the shapes of our destinies seem set, but we cannot yet clearly discern any path through the squalls or ahead to the distant island. It is a time during which we must find the strength, determination, and inspiration to travel and struggle on.

A year after first encountering Seferis's poetry I set out for Poros, the island that had been his favored retreat from his hectic and demanding urban life and duties in Athens during the turbulent post–world war era.

Poros is by far the smallest of the Saronic Gulf islands. These include the farther artists' haven and retreat island of carless Hydra, sea-blasted Spetses, home of naval heroes and site of a great sea battle, and Aegina, the island between Poros and Athens. Aegina is home to the best-preserved temple in all of Greece, the temple of the nymph Aphaia, identified with the ancient Minoan moon goddess Diktynna and worshipped since Neolithic times. Apollo and Artemis also have temples there, the three together known as the Sacred Triangle. It too provided asylon. Aegina was the retreat island for the great writer from Krete, Nikos Kazantzakis, where he lived with his wife, Eleni, for about a decade in the 1930s and 1940s during the German incursion. There he penned *Zorba the Greek* and much of his *Odyssey: A Modern Sequel.* Hydra was the retreat island of Leonard Cohen and other artist-rebels of the 1960s. In ancient times, the tragedian Euripides fled the turmoil of Athens to write in a cave on Salamis, the island closest to Athens and site of the great naval victory against the Persians.

Though feeling each island pull on me like a magnet across the waters, like Seferis forty years before, I boarded a ferry for Poros. During that first visit, I expected Poros would have the fewest tourists and least commercialism of the Saronic islands. I had read Seferis's pages on Poros in his *A Poet's Journal*. Like him, I was retreating to Poros to "scrape the rust off," to "dispense with things that keep me from seeing."[9] I was hungry for the light and landscape that, Seferis wrote, "threaten me seriously. I close the shutters so I can work." And like him, over the decades of my visits, I too have had to close my shutters against the glaring sunlight, penetrating beauty, and friendships so generous and warm that here, unless we impose it on ourselves, we cannot be alone.

My ferry chugged through the Saronic Gulf, past islands so small as to be mere resting places for gulls, others with mountains rising like purple statues into the clear sky. On the low, soft sea, I felt cupped and held, both relieved and expectant. From Seferis's "Mythistorema, VIII":

> *But what are they looking for, our souls that travel*
> *On decks of ships worn-out, crowded together...*
> *Shifting broken stones, breathing in*
> *Each day less easily the pine trees' coolness...*
> *We knew it, that the islands were beautiful*
> *Somewhere round about here where we are groping.*
> *Maybe just a little lower or a little higher.*[10]

My ferry docked, and I disembarked between yachts and fishing boats, hoping that Seferis's words, "This voyage is like a return to Greece,"[11] would be true for me.

Between whitewashed buildings on that first visit, I climbed wide stairways up to high winding alleyways. I strolled among bougainvillea and gardenias, citrus trees heavy with blossoms, flapping laundry lines.

At the top of the hill, I stood beneath the crowning clock tower to survey the wide harbor below and Galatas on the opposite shore.

I strolled past fruit and vegetable stands, trinket shops, a jewelry store, and tiny groceries. I picked my way through the clutter of chairs, only a few occupied in the afternoon heat, in the long, snaking waterfront line of tavernas.

On the small promontory at the harbor's northern end, standing in front of the old arsenal, I watched several dozen young naval cadets go through training exercises with rifles on their shoulders, caps above squinting eyes, exercises we can still view today through the surrounding barbed wire. Then I crossed the canal bridge and headed west.

On the long shore stretching back up the straits, I passed old wooden huts that today have been replaced by clean whitewashed tourist homes. Every so often, between the huts, a whitewashed tourist house sprang up. On some of their terraces, bathing suited vacationers, beers in hand, gazed absently off to sea. From a corner hotel, a strain of American rock music blared. Seferis wrote in "Mythistorema X,"

> *Our country is a shut in place. It is enclosed*
> *By the two black Clashing Rocks, and when we go.*
> *On Sundays, down to the harbor for a breath of air,*
> *We see, lit by the sunset,*
> *The broken timbers of unfinished ships,*
> *Bodies that know no longer how to love.*[12]

Poets, prophets, nomads through the ages have declared it—people get lost anywhere, especially at home. Seferis, like all of us and as I felt, was lost in the brutal modern world. He used his poetry and retreat to Poros to sift through the ruins of his culture to find signs or clues for some way back to its living sources or forward to some new life. I was traveling through Greece because I felt lost in America and modernity. I was also looking for the life behind the statues—and behind the poems and songs, billboards and screams of the modern world too.

As I was settling into my light-flooded room in a small international rooming house, I met a British couple on their way out. They noticed my book lying on my bed. "You read their poets? We came here to find the real, remote Greece. Maybe you can tell us where it is?"

"What's wrong with Poros?" I asked.

"Too many students with American rock music here," they said, already true in 1987. "Too much coming and going. We want old and slow. Can you suggest somewhere else?"

Their words set me to worry. I sat on my terrace looking westward along the waterway, watching the molten sun settle into and stain the purple hills and waters. I overheard travelers—common get-acquainted conversations in English, German, French, Russian, Swedish, Hebrew, and Arabic as well as Greek. I heard the virginal glee of a young woman from Indiana seeing the sea for the first time.

I felt surrounded, even here. But unlike the British couple, I did not want to flee any farther. Instead, I opened Seferis's journal to remind myself that he, too, had felt surrounded and in fact, we can feel that way anywhere. Seferis had come here to encounter again those people, gestures, moments, ways of life that still glowed with an eternal and authentic feeling; that in his words evoked "a ceremonial world." Modern intrusions indeed had marred the surface and traffic of Poros. Seferis reminded me to seek its soul.

Ancient philosophy thought the soul feminine. Poros's soul unveils herself when night falls on the town. Colored lanterns click on over water's edge tavernas. Travelers from all parts of the world promenade. Waiters swoop like laden sparrows or attendant butlers to serve their patrons lingering and jabbering into the wee hours. Lantern and boat lights reflect off the waters in a sparkling dance. The Milky Way above grows as thick as a cascade of tiny white pearls.

Seferis had celebrated Poros nights. "The lights of Poros are like candles," he wrote. "There's a feeling of enclosed space, of an empty church with the cold marble shadows in the dome invoking awe."[13]

From the bay before me and the woods behind came kala aura, the sweetest air I had ever smelled. It was a mixture of salt, sea, fish, pinewoods, flowers, and lemon blossoms laced together with a light airborne honey. Inhaling, I remembered that to the ancients and in their language, *pneuma*, or breath and spirit, were one.

COUNSEL WITH THE DEAD 45

I rose early in the golden mornings when only the fishermen were awake. I watched them row their green and blue dinghies along the shore, beat the ink out of their squid or octopi, hold up a specimen of their catch with a grin, market their score of fish spread out on oilcloths in the sun. Their daily round—for as long as fish and men live side by side; or until modern development halts this practice of the ages.

After several days life became simple. Rock music merely bobbed on the air, as did the boats on the water. Poros was taking me over, filling me with its smells, tastes, and personality. I began to feel moored. Poros was older, sturdier, and stronger than distractions the modern world could send my way. The ordinary things of life—meals, conversations, and the weather—were starting to gleam. On my first Poros day I wrote in my journal, "Here I want to be a man of no rank, among people of no note, in a place of no importance, for days without beginning or end." Poros residents declare this truth to this day, "Simple is all we need." Plato's eternal forms were beginning to shine through. Seferis, too, sensed this:

> *In this Turkish harbor*
> *Blood throbs in the pines*
> *And the rocks strain*
> *To relive the ancient embrace.*

"Summer Solstice," a late poem, reads in part:

> *The poplar tree in the little garden,*
> *its breathing marks your hours . . .*
> *Accept who you are,*
> *Do not cast it down under the thick plane trees;*
> *nourish them with the earth and rock you have.*
> *For better things—*
> *Dig the same ground to find them.*[14]

Seferis found that embrace, breathed that breeze, nourished the rugged ground here, on this bay. The Villa Galini was his retreat home around the sea-kissed inner curve of the bay and across from the town piers. Galini still stands proud and strong, looking like pink marble, surrounded by thick foliage half-obscuring its face. There he closed his shutters to block out the light and beauty so he could be in asylon and write.

Galini in modern Greek means "tranquility." Mention the word to a resident of Poros today and they twinkle and nod in affirmation. Dmitri Plakas, retired postman of Poros, smiles joyously when saying the word. Dmitri was a village postman for thirty-four years. He labored up and down the steep and winding alleys. He slaps his thighs to show how strong they still are. He invites me to poke their muscles. Though his upper torso is heavy and aging, those thighs remain marble hard. His last name *Plakas* means "tile" and indicates that his grandfather had been a floor tile layer, named for his profession as was common in traditional cultures. Dmitri, whom I sometimes call Big Dmitri because he is a large man and it differentiates him from the many Greek men who carry that name, declares that because of Poros galini, he needs to travel nowhere else. His eyes twinkle and his large hands rise to shoulder height. He pats the air gently as if he, like the god of this island, were calming the storm winds. Tranquility and more. Galini in ancient Greek meant that your ship—and your life—were safely anchored in calm waters, out of the storm winds. Classical scholar and translator Robert Emmet Meagher says of galini that it is understood to mean "calm," "tranquil," or "still" and "most often refers to the sea, that is, to calm or still sea waters, though it is also used for inner stillness or peace."[15]

It is why we come to Poros, and why residents who leave "for a better life" often return after encountering the modern world.

The sea was and is lifeblood for Greece. In Greek myth, in addition to the sea god Poseidon, the sea and its spirits are ever present. The Nereid Galateia was the goddess of calm seas who gifted galini. She was caught in a deadly love triangle. Polyphemus, the cyclops son of Poseidon, wanted her but she loved another. Polyphemus crushed his rival with a boulder when he found the lovers together.

Euripides addresses Galateia in a chorus from his tragedy *Helen*, calling her Galaneia and invoking her calming and safety-rendering powers.

COUNSEL WITH THE DEAD ❧ 47

> *Sea-swift Phoenician galley*
> *Fresh from Sidonian waters,*
> *You stir the sea to life*
> *With the labor of your oars,*
> *And lead the chorus of dolphins,*
> *As they leap and plunge in the still waters*
> *Of the unruffled sea.*
> *May Galaneia, serene daughter of the open sea,*
> *Her brine-blue eyes bright and gleaming,*
> *Speak to you with words like these:*
> *"Unfurl your sails."*[16]

Galini also occurs as a name in the Christian tradition. *Agia Galini*, St. Galini, was a woman from the Peloponnesos condemned by the Roman emperor Decius, who ruled from 249 to 251. She refused to give up her early Christian faith and was put to death by drowning in Korinth, north of Poros. The town of Agia Galini is named for her. It perches on the southern coast of Krete on the site of an early Minoan settlement and, later, of a temple of Artemis.

In the Catholic tradition, one of the cult names of Mary is "our lady of tranquility" (galini). She is appealed to for inner mental peace. Her prayer reads, in part,

> *Mother of Tranquility*
> *and Mother of Hope,*
> *look upon me in this time*
> *of disquiet and weakness.*
> *Still my restless spirit . . .*

This prayer declares that "the world cannot give" us the everlasting and gentle peace that can only be gifted by the divine.

Tranquility—a still blue windless bay safe from the world's wars and turmoil. Seferis found both asylia and galini here. Professor Meagher comments, "It is what every poet longs for, I guess."

On the morning of my last full day of that first visit, I set off on foot up the steep blacktop road that wound into the mountains, cutting through pine forests and olive groves until it reached the Sanctuary of Poseidon atop the high plateau of the island. I hiked the few miles from the low lime-washed harbor, then rested in a tiny wayside church. I gazed through its blue shutters, then stooped through its arched lintel. I whispered my prayer as I lit a lone candle in the sand-filled offering tray. Then I sat in silence on the nearest of the four wooden chairs in front of the wood-and-metal altar adorned with candelabra and saints' portraits.

Farther up this winding wooded mountain road, where it arced between stony goat fields, then opened to opalescent gulf vistas, I reached the sanctuary. I wandered between the foundations of old buildings and the bases of temple columns, imagining the Athenian orator and rebel Demosthenes's last moments on these steps erected against a dolphin-blue sky. I wondered at his choice to die here. What do any of us live for, what do I live for as passionately as he did? Would I choose to die rather than live in submission and captivity? What were my limits beyond which life was no longer worth living?

I walked softly toward the end of the sanctuary grounds farthest from the humble gate. Out of the piercing sun, neighboring the scattered and gnarled old olive trees, stands a grove of wind-twisted pines. I passed through low and tumbling stone walls that create a border around the sea god's archaic temple. The pines spread from the wall toward the temple's foundation stones. I sat in their shadows and smelled the pine breeze. Dozens of broken columns were scattered around my feet. I chose one—and have chosen that same one on every visit over the decades, every visit though years apart—the same altar stone, the same old shaped marble to hold my libations and prayers, mere yards away from the long-gone altar to Poseidon before which Demosthenes poisoned himself.

Before me the Saronic Gulf opened on blue sea and sky. Below me the slopes of Poros tumbled to the sea. From tiny farms below chickens clucked, roosters crowed. Every so often a sea breeze climbed the long hot slopes to rustle the pine needles over my head. Otherwise, it was so still I could almost hear the ant's footfalls on the column by my knee.

COUNSEL WITH THE DEAD ∽ 49

In some of Seferis's most urgent poems he searched through ruins to find "the other side of life." Sometimes he was rewarded for his efforts with a visitation. In "The King of Asine," Seferis wanders a ruined palace and lingers among its stone until finally,

> *Shield-bearing the sun was climbing like a warrior.*
> *And from the depths of the cave a frightened bat*
> *Struck upon the light like an arrow strikes a buckler . . .*
> *Could this have been*
> *The King of Asine for whom with such great care*
> *We searched as we went about this acropolis,*
> *Feeling sometimes with our fingers his very touch upon the*
> *stones?*[17]

And in "Engomi" an assumption occurs as Seferis watches men unearth the base of an ancient statue. They suddenly stand still,

> *And in their midst was a face ascending into the light . . .*
> *. . . the body*
> *Was rising out of labor, naked, with the unripe breasts*
> *of a virgin, Leader of Ways;*
> *A dancing but no movement.*[18]

For a moment the living stiffen like cadavers, and the dead woman returns to life through an artifact created to honor her. Then "the world becomes again / our world of earth and of hours." The dead return to the City of Dreams; the living breathe again.

But the living are now transformed. They have caught a glimpse of something eternal beyond the temporal, something radiant and everlasting beyond decay. Seferis's poem "Denial," was set to music by Mikis Theodorakis and is now one of modern Greece's most beloved folk songs. It tells us that our names disappear. We disappear. But *Orea,* it is Beauty itself, the Form, the Perfection, the Ideal beyond all appearances that is only known through its appearances, it is Beauty that births us and Beauty that devours us, and it is all terribly sad and wonderful.

50 ∽ COUNSEL WITH THE DEAD

Perhaps it was the marble stones and columns scattered around me. Perhaps it was the overpowering presence of worship. Or maybe it was what the ancients called the gods. Poros, they had said, first belonged to Apollo's mother Leto, then later by trade to Poseidon. This small island was god-loved. Sitting on that height, in the blinding sunlight that is yet only a shadow of the inner light of mind and spirit that first awakened in this hot, bright middle-of-the-world region, I felt the presence of Shades. Was it Seferis? Demosthenes? As dead and alive as shades, they might return to me for a moment just as that ancient virgin had returned to Seferis through the base of her statue. Stratis the Sailor had led the way. I was in their presence. In my very breathing of this ancient air, I could receive counsel from the Dead before returning home. And in the sweet breeze on Poseidon's mountain, I felt Beauty's breath.

I looked down the slopes and across the gulf toward the distant islands half-shrouded in mist. From the fallen columns around me crickets' clicks rose and echoed in the hollow of my skull. They reminded me that, like this sanctuary, I am only a temple of dirt and bone through which the spirit passes, and that I too would one day be abandoned by divinity that only dwells briefly in any chosen site.

I descended the mountain. I had heard. This island of asylon was becoming mine too.

3

THE GIFT OF THE SEA TURTLE
A Meeting in Poseidon's Sanctuary

Gather by me, tortoise,
Become my voice
— SAPPHO (AUTHOR'S TRANSLATION)

Almost a century ago, in these village streets, the wild and oracular woman called Elainie the Drunk declared, "You'll never find a miracle by looking. They come along if you wait; both miracles and fleas come of their own accord."[1]

Something else, wonderous and inexplicable, happened on my first climb to Poseidon's sanctuary almost four decades ago. I hiked and climbed through green pine forests and past silvery olive groves as Saronic Gulf vistas grew wider, bluer, and more expansive. About halfway up the mountain I rested on the steps of the tiny church, lime washed and tidy, not much bigger than a shed with a dome. Then I shouldered my pack stocked with water, oranges, tomatoes, bread, cheese, and wine, traditional foods from local farmers.

Fig. 3.1. Artist's rendition of the archaic Temple of Poseidon, nineteenth century.

PHOTOGRAPH FROM THE HATZOPOULEIOS PUBLIC LIBRARY ARCHIVES

I rounded a curved slope of the mountain. Ahead I could see a small and empty watchman's shed, a rough metal fence and gate that marked the opening to the sanctuary. Just as Poseidon's grounds came into my view, crawling through that unguarded gateway from out of the sanctuary and walking directly toward me was . . . a sea turtle. *Xionia,* the Greeks call them, and *Caretta caretta* is the scientific name of these endangered loggerhead turtles. It was long, large, and wide, a leathery green gray. It moved slowly but steadily toward me as its strong flippered feet pushed itself along the ground. I stared, blinked, and shook my head. Up here, on this waterless height a thousand feet above the sea, could I meet another sea turtle?

THE GIFT OF THE SEA TURTLE ⁓ 53

Another? A few days before this final retreat to Poros, I had been on Cape Sounion. Sounion is the tip of a long stone-and-sand peninsula about 40 km south of Athens that juts out into the Aegean Sea. It was the site, in mythic times, from which the Athenian king Aegeus awaited the sign that his son Theseus was returning home safely from Krete and his encounter with the Minotaur. The black sail, wrongly colored, flapped from Theseus's returning craft. Mistakenly thinking his son had died in the labyrinth, Aegeus jumped to his death from the promontory. Today the ruins of a grand temple of Poseidon hug the rough high Sounion rocks. Its tall and noble white columns rise from the rocky height to stand as guardians on this last point of land jutting into the Aegean. The spot is a favorite evening pilgrimage for Greeks and tourists arriving in throngs to watch the explosive colors of the sunset as the setting disc inflames the broad sea and sky with reds, golds, oranges, and yellows of every hue.

On my first visit there in 1987, I did not want to be around crowds. I wanted to hear, see, and pray to what is beyond the human. I circled Poseidon's temple several times, viewing the land, sea, and distant islands from all four directions through the columns. Then I climbed down the hill that is the temple's perch and walked northeast across the hard ground and scattered baked rocks.

I hiked to a lower hill, then stepped over scrubby bushes and sharp stones until I was alone before another, older ruin of a temple to a goddess. Athena and Poseidon had been the two most beloved deities of ancient Athens. In time before time, they competed before the original villagers to see who would become patron power there. Poseidon gifted the Athenians the wild horse and flowing spring—gifts from his primal earth powers. Athena responded with the bridle and olive tree. Athena won the people's vote. She triumphed because she offered wisdom, restraint, tools, and discipline to harness Poseidon's raw powers of nature to create and preserve civilization.

At Sounion, as at many other sites around the Mediterranean world, an older, circular temple to a mother goddess had predated a newer, more massive and rectangular temple to a god. I stood among the scattered low marble walls and columns in this small, unvisited sanctuary.

A fistful of dried flowers and a few sun-shriveled fruits lay in the center of the ruin site, offerings from previous supplicants. I was not the only pilgrim who came to pray here. I sat before the entryway stones, closed my eyes, and intoned a simple prayer, over and over, a chant, a mantra for us all:

Ancient Mother, return to us
Ancient Mother, bring me home

Still praying, I opened my eyes. At that moment a large sea turtle emerged from between the columns. The greenish turtle, moving on wide, silent flippers, pulled itself one slow foot at a time toward me. It stopped right in front of me. Its sharp dark eyes stared into mine. I stared back. We sat there a long time, this turtle and I, listening to each other's heartbeats. Then I thanked the goddess and only left to make the last bus back to Athens. On my ride, I told this story to a Greek woman who stared into me, smiled, and said, "I wish you many turtles."

Now on Poseidon's mountaintop sanctuary just days later, I stooped before this second sea turtle that stopped its slow walk right in front of my feet. I sat down in the dirt, cross-legged in front of it. As at Cape Sounion, we stared into each other's eyes for a long time. Was it the height, the heat, my tired or amazed condition? I saw, or felt, a Turtle spirit nodding to me, bidding me welcome. The first meeting at Sounion might have been chance, an accident; we were near the sea. It was not a long climb for a turtle. But follow the synchronicities. This seemingly impossible meeting on a mountaintop said something else. The ancients taught that the gods could take any shape they wished and often took animal form. Each deity had his or her animal messengers and spirits. Then who was before me?

Turtle and I looked intently into each other for a long time. Clock time dissolved. It seemed that the cosmos stood still. I entered an eternal moment, what the Greeks called *anagnorisis,* the thrill of recognition that changes the course of a single life, a drama, even history.[2] Turtle and I just sat and looked, sat and stared, sat and recognized something in this strange other. Something entered me. We were no longer aliens to each other.

When it seemed that the turtle was done with me, it slowly plodded around me on its flippers. I stayed still as it circled me and continued its downward trek, one slow flipper-foot at a time. When I was sure Turtle was done with me, I rose and stepped forward into the sanctuary. Soon I was sitting alone among the scattered foundations, columns, sunken rooms, and colorful wildflowers. I was in asylon from the modern world, as ancients had sought sanctuary from the violence and displacement of theirs.

My logical mind asked how long had it taken the turtle to climb the mountain? How long to descend? But among fallen colonnades beneath craggy old pine and olive trees, I thought that old Poseidon himself could have placed turtle on his mountaintop. Then again, we were in the mythic realm where deities, humans, and animals could exchange forms. Turtle might have walked or flown up here in another form. It might have been the sea god Proteus, the Old Man of the Sea, whom Menelaos, the Greek king and husband of Helen, wrestled with on his journey home from the Trojan War. Proteus could take any shape he wished and while wrestling with sea-roaming Menelaos turned into a lion, dragon, and tree. George Seferis had given Proteus these words:

> *I am your land;*
> *perhaps I am no one*
> *yet I can become whatever you wish.*[3]

Menelaos had to wrestle Proteus and hold him firm and fast through fierce and threatening changes to gain instructions for finding his way home from the Trojan War. This firm hold through the storms of life that wound and transform us was also what I was seeking, why I was here.

Then again, the turtle could be Poseidon himself. Turtle was messenger and totem spirit of Poseidon and Aphrodite in the ancient world. I felt Poseidon, as his hymn declares, "lord of the deep and true,"

56 ∽ THE GIFT OF THE SEA TURTLE

challenging and demanding me to be just that, no matter what, a servant of the deep and true.

Since my first encounters with Greek mythology in childhood, and for many decades in my imagination and travels since, I had studied, dreamed of, paid homage to the spirits of the land and sea dwelling here. Struggling to overcome my modern-day alienation and feeling of exile, I had begged to be brought home. In ways as mysterious, baffling, and illogical as any oracle, in ways just being revealed, in the eyes of sea turtle on Poseidon's mountaintop, my prayers were being answered.

4

POSEIDON

The Powerful, Unpredictable Protector of the Sea

Each god is the source of a world that without him remains invisible, but with him reveals itself in its own light.

KARL KERENYI,
HERMES: GUIDE OF SOULS

In ancient times, when Poros was called Kalaureia, the island was deemed worthy of the gods of both light and the sea. In his first-century BCE geography, Strabo wrote that Kalaureia belonged to the goddess Leto, the lover Zeus took in the form of a swan and impregnated. Leto traded the island to Poseidon for rocky Delos in the Cycladic island chain. There she bore her sacred children, Apollo and Artemis. She was afterward worshipped as a goddess of motherhood. About this trade an oracle said, "Kalaureia and Delos are equal."[1]

In his first-ever travel guide to Greece written in the second century CE, the Greek physician and traveler Pausanias said that Delfi originally belonged to both Earth and Poseidon, and they both gave the oracles there. Later, Earth gave her portion to Themis, goddess of justice and divine order. Themis then gave hers as a gift to Apollo, who gave Poros to Poseidon in exchange for the oracle.[2]

Whether from either source, Strabo or Pausanias, humble Kalaureia became the home island for the sea god and his sanctuary, and the sea god too gave oracles. This may be another reason the sea casts spells and calls people to it everywhere—if we are receptive enough, its nature or spirit can teach and guide us.

Who Was Poseidon?

Consider Poseidon's Homeric Hymn, dating to about 800 BCE. Mortals appeal to him, declaring that he is a great and invisible power. We moderns misunderstand "idolatry." Many hymns declare the gods "invisible." The gods were not their statues or representations; only fundamentalists of any age believe that. The gods were personifications of universal forces that were made accessible in beautiful physical forms that would attract the invisible powers to them and to which we could relate. They were intermediaries between the cosmos and the mortal, enabling humanity to seek personal and reciprocal relationships with them.

Poseidon surrounded and embraced the earth, as the sea embraces the land and as, in ancient times, it was believed great waters surrounded the earth in its center. Poseidon, like his tides, is restless, always moving, always changing. His is ceaseless energy, motion, and emotion varying in their manifestations from calm to stormy, gentle to raging, life-enhancing to life-threatening. As Heraklitos declared, *Panta rei*, "Everything flows."

Poseidon founded cities and protected those he favored. Sophokles declared that he oversaw the sacred site outside Athens where long-suffering Oedipus finally died. Here, as on Poros, he fulfilled the task of protecting the outcast.

This is sacred territory, all of it.
Dreaded Poseidon rules here
With Prometheus, the bringer of fire.
The ground where you tread

Is called the Bronze Way,
The threshold of Athens."[3]

Poseidon also lost cities to other deities. He sought to destroy those, like Troy, that offended him. He was utterly passionate and could not be deflected from his purpose. He loved or hated. He competed fiercely. He wanted rulership and often warred with Zeus for dominance. He resented Zeus becoming supreme ruler of the gods and may have been in that position in earlier ages. He knows the depths of earth and sea. He had a palace under the sea he favored more than Olympus high on a mountain. He fiercely inspired those he loved and sought to protect, and fiercely warred against those he resented. His realm is not the light of mind but the hidden depths of instinct and the unconscious.

As we have heard, the myth of Athens's founding portrays Poseidon as the source of wild, instinctual powers and Athena as their civilizing force. Athena's gifts made the sea god's untamed gifts from nature useful as tools to build civilization and won the people's favor. Since Athens was a sea power, Poseidon was second in importance to Athena, and a great temple was built to him overlooking the sea on Cape Sounion. Still, the sea god remained resentful and competitive.

Yet Poseidon, like Athena, is a source of what civilizes. He is savior and tamer. He saves when the seas are wild and destructive; he tames wild horses. This is one of his greatest, though often unrecognized, powers, for which he is a model. He restrains and controls the instinctual and natural forces that he also releases.

Finally, the god's hymn declares, salute and honor him. "His help was invoked by sailors before they took to the waves, and he was consulted before a colonizing expedition to make the journey as uneventful as possible."[4] He cups the earth. He is holy. Awaken friendship with the eternally dark, deep, and flowing. Appeal to the god-power to be kind and compassionate as we set off on his oceanic realm of natural and instinctual powers.

Poseidon, Neptune in Roman mythology, is popularly known as the god of the sea. Many myths and stories tell of his power, fierceness, vengeful behavior, and cruelty. And mythology is full of the

Fig. 4.1. Lightning, thunder, and fierce rains sometimes visit Poros, reminding us of the sea god's powers.
PHOTOGRAPH BY TASOS RODIS

hubris of mortals who foolishly set themselves against the gods and always fall. For example, in the *Iliad*, Poseidon fought on the side of the Greeks because he held a grudge against King Laomedon, father of Troy's King Priam, who ruled during the war. Poseidon was vengeful because he and Apollo had been disrespected and cheated by Laomedon when Zeus ordered them to serve the king for a year. In the *Odyssey*, though Poseidon had sided with the Greeks, he raged against Greek Odysseus for blinding his son the Cyclops and tirelessly attempted to destroy him on his long voyage home from the war. He holds grudges over generations and does not forgive or let go of his victims or their descendants.

Homer provides many passages of the storms that this fierce godpower provokes, the rages he inspires in his favored warriors, the destruction he wants to bring down on Troy. A few centuries after Homer, Pindar wrote,

I fear the assault of Zeus.
I fear the Earthshaker and his heavy stroke,
These once, with thunderbolt and trident,
Overwhelmed the earth and the host altogether."[5]

Poseidon is a repository of primitive, instinctual energies and passions, and these are of nature, the earth, and the "animal soul." This includes the parts of humanity, in holistic healing terms, that inhabit the lower chakras and ensure survival. We know him as one of the Olympian deities, but he was also an earlier chthonic god whose history traces back to long before their reign. The coming of the Olympians with their more complex and conscious characters represents the progressive development of civilization creating culture and order atop our primal origins and natures and out of chaos. Poseidon lived in both realms. So do we, and likewise must develop discipline and restraint.

Poseidon was not the sea itself but lived in and under it. The sea was mother earth's womb, the source of life. Poseidon's name may come from the archaic *posis da*, which meant "consort of Mother Earth."[6] One of his epithets was *Gianoxos*, meaning "holder or possessor of the earth," also indicating his marital relationship to the earth goddess.[7] Poseidon was the male cosmic power coupling with the great feminine source of life. Remembering, as Heraklitos taught, that the soul is fathomless, this god is "the archetype through which a psychological realm of great depth and beauty can be known."[8]

Poseidon imagery reveals his nature. In his fury he is portrayed as a fierce and stupendous power, often bringing wreckage. But in his maturity, he is pictured riding his chariot over the waves and steering his galloping white horses, whose manes are the sea foam. He had the kind of might represented by the ancient verb *krateo*, which meant at once to have power and the ability to restrain and control it for governance, rulership, the good. "He was a god of the old-fashioned ambiguous type who had the power to quell storms because he also had the power to raise them."[9] Greek philosophy and early spirituality taught that we must live in *metron*, or balance with natural forces, or they will turn against and destroy us. Sailors and horsemen sought to revere, respect, and be on good terms with Poseidon. This confirmed their belief about the gods—that the sailors' relationship with them was reciprocal, that they must appeal, express gratitude, live in humility and balance to receive the good. If not, the gods will be angry; that is, these primal powers would become imbalanced and turn against the people. In modern times, this eco-mythological understanding of nature emerges through the god-power influence on the rising levels and temperature of the ocean.

Poseidon appears in astrology in the guise of Neptune, his Roman name and the planet named for him. Astrological interpretations also help reveal his nature. His domain, the ocean, is associated with the collective unconscious. "Contact with the great ocean of the collective unconscious, that eternal storehouse of images and dreams, may . . . sweep us into the stormy realm of Poseidon." Psychic earthquakes, ecstasy, visionary longings and experiences characterize this realm and people who experience it. It is with the sensual, the symbolic, the mythopoetic, dreamlike and experiential that we perceive this god-power. "Perhaps because this archetype rules the ocean (the collective unconscious) where logic and rational processes cease to exist, one must look with other eyes to 'see' Neptune."[10]

Poseidon was called Enesidaone, Earthshaker; he was the god of earthquakes. This epithet confirms his chthonic nature and indicates that he may have also been an earlier earth god. Though identified with the sea, he was of the earth and caused it to rumble from its core. One of his totem animals was the bull, and this connects him to earlier Mycenaean and Minoan cultures as the bull was one of their totems. It was believed that Poseidon's giant bull lived in the deep earth under the sea. When humanity became out of balance or offended the god or the natural order, that bull kicked and raged; that was the source of earthquakes. So, fierce as he is, Poseidon was also a protector of the natural order. Balance, proportion, proper measure were key dimensions of Greek thought; countless myths and teachings warn of the dangers and destruction that occur when we exceed the measure. We see this crisis everywhere today in our world, environment, and political life. Heraklitos said that even the sun will not overstep its measure, or the Furies will seek it out.

POSEIDON 63

As the Homeric Hymn indicates, Poseidon was also the god of horses. One of his epithets was Hippos or Hippios. This may predate his connection to the sea as the epithet is found in very early records. Further, the breed of horse indigenous to Greece was originally too small to ride or pull a chariot. Larger, more powerful horses arrived with the invasions of the mainland by peoples from the north and near east.[11] Poseidon's power coupled with these. He guided his own powerful steeds over the waves. He became the "tamer," making raw instinctual power useful to humanity and the development of civilization.

Poseidon was also sometimes addressed as Pater, or Father. There are several meanings to this epithet, both light and dark. He had two daughters by his wife, the sea Nereid Amphitrite. But he had many children from many affairs and rapes. Some renowned offspring were Theseus, king of Athens, famous for slaying the Cretan Minotaur, and Bellerophon, who captured the flying horse Pegasus and slew the female fire-breathing beast the Chimera. From his darker nature he sired the sea monster Charybdis whose whirlpool swallowed ships and the Cyclops Polyphemus, who devoured some of Odysseus's shipmates and whom Odysseus blinded, awakening the god's ceaseless wrath.

Poseidon's lustful and equine nature were both expressed in his rape of his sister, the goddess Demeter. At Eleusis where she was grieving her daughter Persephone's abduction by Hades to the Underworld, Poseidon saw and lusted after her. She spurned him and, to avoid his advances, turned herself into a mare and hid among grazing horses. Turning into a stallion, Poseidon took her. Their offspring was the swift, black-maned horse Arion, who saved King Ardrastus's life in the war of the Seven Against Thebes.

In Poseidon we view the primal power of uncontrollable lust and its destructive potential. But the god also had the epithet Phytalmios, referring to "his role in providing 'growth' in agricultural practices . . . thanks to his connection with the 'sweet waters' of irrigation. . . . [His] multiple associations with natural features such as springs and clouds qualified him for a role in agricultural processes." Siring the horse and fertilizing the earth, he earned the title Pater at Eleusis.[12]

64 ∞ POSEIDON

Despite countless affairs and rapes with goddesses, nymphs, and mortals, Poseidon was married to the sea nymph Amphitrite. She was a daughter of Nereus, the Old Man of the Sea, who could prophecy and change shape at will. Poseidon saw her dancing and fell in love, but she was frightened of his power and fled to Atlas. Poseidon sent a dolphin to entice and fetch her. Gentle and graceful ways can provide a bridge to elemental power. Amphitrite returned to become his wife and bear children. Poseidon rewarded the dolphin by making it a constellation.

Losing the competition with Athena for patronage of Athens, Poseidon challenged the goddess to patronage of Troizen, the horse country and boyhood home of Theseus, across the strait from Poros. Tired of their competition, Zeus declared that they should share dominion equally. Still Poseidon hungered for patronage and competed with other deities for it. He lost Naxos to Dionysos and Aegina to Zeus and Hera. Poseidon appears to be a god-power often resisted and eternally frustrated with his portion. As an archetype of elemental passion, he demonstrates that our deepest hungers and yearnings can never be fully satisfied, and we exist in an eternal ambivalence.

Homer's *Iliad* is the source of the story of the three elder gods drawing lots for which portion of the cosmos each would rule. Zeus won the rulership of the heavens, Hades the Underworld, Poseidon the sea. In response Poseidon declared,

> *No one should think that I shall live one instant*
> *as he thinks best!*
> *No, let him hold his peace*
> *And power in his heaven, in his portion,*
> *Not try intimidating me*
> *I will not have it."*[13]

Though he ruled the sea, not the heavens, and though he was not the king-god as he might have been in earlier Mycenaean times, he would never agree to be subservient to Zeus. He was, in fact, his elder brother, and some sources say that he as well as Zeus avoided being swallowed by their father Chronos. The most well-known myth tells us that Zeus alone was saved from being devoured when Mother Rhea replaced him with a stone. Pausanias says that upon his birth Rhea laid Poseidon in a flock of lambs and told Chronos that she had given birth to a horse. Instead of the child, she gave Chronos a foal to swallow.[14] Again we hear his life-saving connection to the horse. It also hints that in earlier times he may have been more prominent as lord of the gods. In the early Liner B script "his name appears in the historical record . . . much more often than the name of Zeus."[15] And we hear how sibling rivalry seems built into the cosmos, each primal force in eternal clash and collision.

Fertilizing and destructive, lustful and passionate, married yet restless with numerous affairs and rapes, siring both heroes and monsters, seeking and wanting, gaining yet losing leadership and dominion time and again, vastly powerful yet eternally discontent with his portion of rulership, we hear Poseidon's dual and ambivalent nature. We appreciate the boons granted and curses imposed by elemental power and its expression through cosmos, nature, and mortals. Since the god-powers are personifications of *what is*, in both nature and psyche, we learn from Poseidon that everything in the natural and human worlds is ambivalent. Everything has its positive and negative traits, guiding and confusing, filling and emptying, blessing and challenging us at once. We learn that the nature of psyche itself is polytheistic in how the eternal, conflicting powers embody in us and in how we must grow to integrate and harmonize them—from the many to the one.

The Great Sanctuary on Poros

In ancient times it was said that Poseidon created the strait separating Poros from the Peloponnese when the god stamped his huge foot so that the sea sank then rose to flood the exposed plain. The ancients awaited the prophecy that said that someday the god would stomp again. Poros is in earthquake country and live volcanoes still breathe deep under its seabed. Indeed, he might.

Though very little is known about the religious practices in the sanctuary, which Pausanias described as "very holy," clues have been

Fig. 4.2. Greek members of a nineteenth-century Swedish archeological team directing excavations at the Temple of Poseidon, 1894.
PHOTOGRAPH FROM THE HATZOPOULEIOS PUBLIC LIBRARY ARCHIVES

uncovered from archeological research by Swedish research teams. Locally, in addition to Poseidon, there were cults to other deities including Zeus Sotar (Zeus the Savior), Artemis, Aphrodite, and possibly others. Further, at least a few significant practices are known.

At the sanctuary, "a virgin priestess served until the time of her marriage."[16] Animal sacrifice followed by a ritual meal was central to all Greek cults. Professor Meagher explains its importance:

> The act of ritual sacrifice was, quite simply, the central cultic act of ancient Greek Religion, the sacred experience *par excellence*. In it the essential order of the universe was acknowledged and reinforced. The proper performance of sacrifice was seen as a stay against chaos rather than as a collapse into it.[17]

At the ritual meal supplicants experienced themselves as eating together with their deity. Refuse from Kalaureia has revealed that fish as well as pigs, sheep, goats, and cattle were sacrificed. Individuals or groups brought these to the sanctuary where they were boiled and mixed into a stew with legumes. Since lamp fragments were found, the meals might have taken place at night.[18]

The first antiquity that began the collection of the Poros museum was a giant marble left foot found by a schoolboy in 1956. He believed that the sculpture had been the foot of a god, and it had blessed his family orchard. With this antiquity, the schoolmaster Christos Fourniades founded the island's collection.

This schoolboy's discovery was a modern replication of an ancient belief. Poseidon was here and worshipped for at least three millennia. Whether in earthquakes, artifacts, or turtles on his mountain, he may appear again. I imagine what that boy might have thought and felt when he uncovered the foot on his family land.

> *Father! Teacher! Come!*
> *See what my plow has uncovered.*
> *There is a giant foot in our orchard.*
> *It must have been left by a god.*
> *Now I know what makes the olives ripen.*
> *Now I know why our oranges and lemons*
> *smell so sweet they make me cry.*

Athena, Apollo, Demeter, Asklepios—their major sanctuaries are world renowned. The Akropolis of Athens with its Parthenon, Eriktheon, and Temple of Athena Nike; Delfi, home of Apollo and his oracle; Eleusis, site of the Mysteries of Demeter and Persephone; Epidauros, the healing sanctuary of Asklepios and home of the great tragic theater— these were major sanctuary sites where rituals and ceremonies to honor the Divine and facilitate transformational experiences connecting mortals to the cosmos, their souls and destinies, were practiced for many centuries. These sites are significantly restored with accompanying museums to display their related artifacts. The public associates these with their deities; countless tourists from all over the world and throughout the ages have visited or made pilgrimage there, and they have developed into major tourist attractions on which the Greek economy now depends.

68 ∽ POSEIDON

What about Poseidon, one of the chief and most important gods of the ancient world, perhaps a king-god to the earlier Mycenaeans, and a necessary archetype for a seafaring people? People commonly think of his major site as the great temple at Sounion, on the peninsula south of Athens, standing vigil as its tall columns gaze out over the blue Aegean Sea. But Sounion was a temple, not a sanctuary. A temple is a place of worship and often is beautifully maintained with surrounding grounds and gardens meant to please the divine and soothe the populace. In contrast, a sanctuary contains temples but is larger and more developed. It serves as a site of safety, protection, and refuge as well as ceremony and worship. Sanctuaries are sometimes found in wilder, more remote places. Sounion was Poseidon's temple and as Athens was a sea power, after Athena he was second in importance to the Athenian people. Hardly known to most people, not mentioned in travel guides, sparsely visited, the sanctuary on Poros was Poseidon's major site in the ancient Mediterranean world.

We do not know what the sanctuary looked like as only sparse ruins and few finds remain into modern times. What we know of its greatness and expanse is recorded in the writings of Strabo, Pausanias, and Plutarch. They each visited and described the site in detail. In recent centuries, based on their records artists have made imaginal drawings and engravings of the sanctuary, sometimes locating it in the wrong place. These later nineteenth century artistic renditions created long after the sanctuary was gone, library director Yannis Maniatis declares, "are fantastic but inaccurate."

Sanctuary literally means a holy place, consecrated, "the holy of holies." It is a place where we are promised protection and can be reconciled with the divine. It is built as a sacred site set aside, as the Bible declares, for the divine to dwell among the people. In Biblical, Greek, and Roman times, sanctuaries were especially welcoming and protective of the oppressed and fugitive of all kinds. It was so with the great sanctuary on Poros. But since Poseidon's worship was so ancient and important here, and his sanctuary was a holy center of the archaic world, why does little remain and why is little known and developed in modern times? There seem to be both archaic and contemporary reasons.

The historical explanation is that little remains due to the invasions, pillaging, and natural disasters of the region. In 395 the Visigoths intended to attack Constantinople. Under their leader Alaric they redirected their strategy south to raid the sanctuary treasuries. They looted and destroyed Delfi, Akrokorinthos, Epidauros, Kalaureia, and Sparta farther south on the Peloponnese. They took all the gold and destroyed all the statues they could.

The second regional cataclysm occurred only a decade later. In 405 a severe earthquake destroyed the remaining buildings. In the ensuing centuries local inhabitants stole remaining stones to use for building their own homes and churches. Today many such stones can be seen buried in the architecture of various buildings. Poros stone is a pale and coarse limestone found on the Peloponnese, highly porous and full of perforations so that it absorbs liquids. The ancients used it extensively as a building material. Subsequently it was pillaged by more modern people and used instead of marble because it was already shaped and prepared for construction. The English word *porous* comes from this lightweight and air-filled stone.

There are likely modern political and economic reasons, as well, as to why this sanctuary has received relatively little recognition and attention. Classical scholar and translator Robert Emmet Meagher offers this interpretation: "Tentatively, I suspect it has a great deal to do with politics and finances, which have always been intertwined and whose tentacles have so often reached into religion."

Meagher affirms that the temple of Poseidon at Sounion would be its obvious competitor for recognition. He analyzes the political importance of that structure.

The temple of Poseidon at Sounion was a crucial part of Perikles' imperial building campaign in the mid 5th century. The Athenian acropolis was the focus of this effort, but Cape Sounion was also crucial, as was Poseidon. The Athenian empire, of which Perikles was the architect, was a thalassocracy. The temple of Poseidon at Sounion announced to the world that Athens controlled the seas. Piety had little or nothing to do with it. The gold-plated cult

70 ∽ POSEIDON

figure of Athena in the Parthenon was created in such a way that the gold plates could be removed to fund Athens' war efforts if needed. It was, as it were, an investment in the empire. A panhellenic cult center of Poseidon on Poros served no purpose in Athens and was perhaps competition. Besides, it was in Spartan territory and Sparta was the archenemy of Athens and its own assembled imperial allies.

Meagher brings his analysis into modern times.

Flash forward 2,500 years. Apart from Crete and Delphi, Athens and nearby sites and the islands that made up the Athenian allies, mainly the Cyclades and the Dodecanse, today remain the core focus of Greek tourism. Ancient invasions, pillaging and neglect do not justify the investments necessary to attract tourism. Thus, the neglect continues.[19]

Add to this sad story Yannis Maniatis's testimony that municipal plans and monies do not prioritize cultural restoration. There is a large, decrepit building behind the Poros museum that could house the larger collection of antiquities that have been found and are in storage awaiting display. Local personalities and politics have thus far not enabled the municipality to acquire the building or expand the museum for the good of all and the honor of the island's ancient traditions.

Poseidon in Our Lives and Characters

Steven B. Katz is a retired professor of rhetoric, poetry, and technical and scientific communications. He is a scholar of the classics and distinguished teacher and author. We have been friends and colleagues since meeting in graduate school forty-five years ago. Honoring each other's legacies, he calls me Odysseus for my travels, and I call him Cicero for his rhetorical expertise. We will hear his personal encounter and wounding by the god-power. Now he reflects on the presence of this archetypal power in our lives, cultures, and history.

Poseidon exists and is disguised and powerful. I have encountered him and his trident spear again and again, in recent years in Venice, the Italian city of canals and lagoons that, whether they know it or not, still worships the god they call by his Roman name: Neptune. Neptune is omnipresent in a city that owes everything to the sea—its role in history as major military power in Italy, and the riches of silks and spices that slid in from the sea. Poseidon's three-pronged spear graces every light post that always points heavenward; those trident lamps cast light and shadow in equal measure on the stoned-over streets and bridges that run over marshland. From its beginning as a few houses, then palaces and waterways, the whole city is built and rests on thick-bundled stilts buried beneath that reach all the way through the soft mud and water to the clean sand below. As a reminder, he occasionally floods the entire city that he upholds and can also destroy all.

From Venice and human history to a cosmic view of the earth as if from the Olympian heights that look down with their god's-eye views, Steven reflects,

Throughout the Earth, Poseidon's presence is manifested in the waves that mercifully wash each other, and the ripples of water that gently drown themselves; the deep rumbling of the seven oceans that fill most of the watery world, the indecipherable chatter between the animals that have dragged themselves up from the sea, and the mysterious creatures that remain on unexplored ocean floors. Poseidon can be wrathful and magnanimous, indifferent and kind. Often, we do not know which we feel, and given that emotions are multidimensional, it may be all of them at once.

Since Jung we have understood the Greek deities to be archetypes, representations in psychic imagery and myth of the universal characters, stories, energies, and traits that unfold in each of us individually, collectively, and throughout time. How did the Poseidon archetype survive and transform into modern times?

Panagiotis Milonakis operates a small traditional taverna on the narrow back streets of Iraklion, Krete's capital. He tells this story, told to him by his grandfather and carried as family legacy.

Grandfather loved to fish. One day, in calm, sunny weather, he and several men went out to sea in their long boat. Without warning a fierce wind arose and the boat rocked dangerously in the waves. The storm grew worse, the wind more violent. The men tried to protect their ship, but it was out of control in the tempest, and they all expected to die.

They knelt in prayer—first to God, then to the Virgin Mary, finally to St. Nicholas. Only after the saint's prayer did the wind begin to die down. The men got their boat under control and landed on a tiny island called Thea, "mother goddess", with a small church of St. Nicholas. They promised the saint they would do all they could for him.

After two days the fishermen returned home to families that had given up hope for their return. Grandmother, too, had been praying to St. Nicholas. They gave thanks and named their first child Nikola. The men regularly returned to the island with giant candles for the saint. Nikola became an icon painter and is the mother of Panagiotis.[20]

In the Christian tradition, Poseidon and his powers were transferred in symbology and iconography to St. Nicholas, the patron of ships and sailors. Numerous miracles like Panagiotis's are attributed to him and other saints all over Greece. There are also many churches to this saint throughout Greece, but only two on Poros. One is his church, appropriately, at the Naval Academy. Sailors and ships to this day carry his image on their vessels. The other is a tiny church of the saint that stands at the top of the stone-lined alley beyond the Center for Ancient Healing. A large and heavy ship's anchor, painted bright red, leans on the narrow stone sidewalk opposite the church's entrance. The church has only nine narrow wooden chairs and no iconostasis, but icons and images of holy figures cover its whitewashed walls.

Icons are ever present. A picture of the saint once hung inside that showed him crowned, dressed in clerical robes. His left hand hugged a Bible against his heart and his right raised in blessing, radiating protection over a modern ship, laden with panicking passengers, floundering and half-sunken in a sea storm.

Recall Poseidon's hymn addressing him as "savior of ships." St. Nicholas and Poseidon are the same archetype taking different forms in different Greek eras and religious traditions.

> Nicholas is the saint of the sea, or, if you prefer, he is Poseidon under another name. The early Christian fathers interfered with him as little as possible in making him a saint. . . . The Orthodox icons carried in ships and boats pictured him clothed and stiff in clerical robes, but sailors still think of him as having power over the sea, as the maker and calmer of storms.[21]

Expanding and popularizing Jungian archetypal thought, but with, perhaps, a loss of the sacred dimensions and practices, modern psychology speaks of gods and goddesses in every man and woman.[22] Growth and healing are achieved, in significant part, by determining the dominant and submissive archetypes active in each of us, depathologizing our conditions, working backward, as it were, to discover the god in the disease, to reveal our "bio-mythic narratives." Determine which of the god-powers are acting in us and we can restore and heal the troubled archetype.*

As an archetypal or psycho-spiritual presence and pattern, Poseidon was a powerful, life-shaping force expressing itself in my family of origin. Through several generations of my family, Poseidon was pater, father.

My maternal grandfather, Irving Sobel, lived much of his life on the seashore. He walked, swam, sunbathed every chance he could. He grew up on the New Jersey coast where his early widowed mother moved him so the ocean air would restore his health after a severe attack of measles.

---

*My work with veterans and warriors is shaped by this philosophy wherein we seek to restore a noble and healthy warrior archetype from its traumatic distortions caused by modern military service and warfare.

The sea and its breezes—Poseidon—healed him and he became a life-long lover of the sea. In his senior years he returned to live by the sea to spend the remainder of his life near the element he most loved.

When he was ninety, we swam together off Long Island beaches. Though I was in my thirties, he warned me, as if I were still his young grandson, "Don't go too far out. Stay in front of me. The tides can be strong, hidden, and carry you away. I know the ocean. It can be calm or cruel. I'll protect you." He was a gentle and kind patriarch. The ocean was in his blood and spirit, and he was a tamer and guardian.

I hardly knew my paternal grandfather, Izzy Tick, as he died just before my fourth birthday. But from memories and family lore, he was indeed a Poseidon. Surviving pogroms in Poland and laboring hard to establish himself in America, he was determined, hardworking, and loyal, but also angry, morose, stubborn, explosive. He spoke little. He was apparently hard on my father growing up. After World War II, when my father entered college on the GI Bill, he demanded that his son give up his education to work in the family delicatessen. My father could not resist his intimidating and overpowering rulership, but was cowed, subservient, and developed his own brooding rage.

A heart attack is an earthquake in the body when the heart finally explodes from too much accumulated or repressed stress, rage, or sorrow. My grandfather died suddenly of a massive heart attack, stricken at age fifty-four on the threshold of his deli as he was opening for the day. God in the man—this grandfather had the character and suffered the fate sent by Earthshaker.

My father was a Poseidon. Like his own father and the god of mythology, he labored hard and was fiercely devoted. But he was controlled by Poseidon energies. Like the sea, he unpredictably went from calm, serene, and approachable, to angry, raging, explosive, and violent. Like visiting the seashore, I never knew from one day to the next whether I would encounter calm or stormy weather. Like Odysseus on his raft with Poseidon tracking him, I sometimes felt in danger of being battered and destroyed. Like a god's supplicant, I did everything I could to appease, calm, understand, or resist him without engendering more rage.

Another characteristic of the god was his competitiveness and jealousy toward Zeus and other deities. In some sources we are told that he was born before Zeus and escaped being swallowed by their father Chronos, or Time. In the story of dividing the cosmos between the three brothers Zeus, Poseidon, and Hades, he received the sea. But that story first appears in Homer's *Iliad*. Centuries earlier, during Mycenaean rule, he may have been the king-god and Homer's story is also the story of his displacement from supreme power to be, no matter how strong or worthy, Zeus's underling among the Olympians. We also have stories of his losing the patronage not only of Athens, but of other city-states and islands to other deities. In Poseidon's essential character is the condition of being dispossessed and displaced from his rightful station and power, living instead with a broiling but ineffective resentment toward other powers.

This was an essential component of my father's character and story. He was a highly intelligent man and wanted to be an engineer or history teacher. But his Poseidon father yanked him from college to work in the small family delicatessen. He served that role until—another cosmic cataclysm of elemental power—the store burned down on my tenth birthday. Though it brought financial ruin and lifelong hardship to the family, on his deathbed my father finally confessed to me, "The fire rescued me." It took a Poseidon-like conflagration to violently release him when he could not do it willfully for himself.

As a boy and teenager, I saw how frustrated, resentful, and unfulfilled he was, and I implored him to return to college or seek better employment. He never did. My mother and his own childhood friends said that he was highly talented and intelligent and should have done the best of them all. But again, he never did. In his employment history, he always just "slugged it out," taking responsibility when bosses did not, filling in for lazy or incompetent coworkers, giving guidance to others who could not work out problems, but never getting credit, position, or salary commensurate with his contributions. He was a good sergeant but never an officer and always frustrated. Like Poseidon under Zeus, he always felt dispossessed from his rightful rulership and never found a facilitative way to use his own instinctual and emotional powers or position.

76 ∽ POSEIDON

I have inherited Poseidon's character and spirit through birth, inheritance, and transgenerational transmission. I was born in April under the astrological sign of Taurus, the Bull. Our astrological signs are psycho-spiritual indicators of our innate and inborn natures, what was called *phusis*, "the essential character of a human that the Greeks believed was marked from birth."[23] Taurus personalities are intelligent, earthy, sensual, passionate, powerful, loyal, tenacious, determined, affectionate, and trustworthy. They are also "bull-headed," stubborn, resistant to change, patient until aroused, but then their anger can take over and dominate them. They work hard at their tasks and endure hardships and sacrifices but feel unfairly treated when they are not recognized or fail to reap the rewards of their efforts. We hear how bull-like Poseidon's personality is.

I am a Taurus. The bull is my "animal soul," my *phusis*, the character and spirit I was born with. Heraklitos taught that character is destiny. I was birthed into the universe to seek a passionate connection to the god-power who was of the bull. I stood in front of the charging bull fresco from the Minoan palace of Knossos on Krete. I heard the words spoken aloud, "*Eimai o Tauros.*" I am the bull. I felt deeply and immediately at home on Poros on my first visit. Taurians and bulls love their home territories, their pastures. It was as if that bull spirit in me found mine.

My one grandfather and I loved the sea together. My other grandfather labored until his heart exploded. My father and I often butted bull-skulls in our passions and disagreements, like Poseidon and Taurians, never yielding when we believed we were right. We all were good, loyal men working hard for others, and we all felt unappreciated and under-rewarded for all that we gave. Yet, like Poseidon, like his bull, like his turtle, we endured.

In his maturity, Poseidon is pictured as a regal charioteer steering his galloping steeds over the waves, their blowing manes, the sea froth. Those with Poseidon natures are intense, passionate, receptive to deep unconscious influences and powers. Many of his myths sound warnings of the consequences of these powers unleashed without balance or guiding reason. Poseidon natures are challenged to learn moderation, integrate these powers, guide rather than be controlled by them, and embrace "the deep and true" with courage, strength, honesty, alone if necessary, and without flinching.

The Gifts

Dmitri Plakas, the retired postman, lives on a farm on the northern side of Poros, away from the village and among uneven hills, rolling valleys, lemon and orange trees, surrounded by pine-forested mountains, about a half kilometer below Poseidon's sanctuary. Like Poseidon, he is a big man. Like Poseidon, he is passionate and of a complex and ambivalent nature. We sometimes sit together at Rota over dinner and often for late-night tea, wine, and talk. He greets me as *Eddiemou*. He smiles gently and affirms our many years of friendship. If I miss a day's visit, he asks where I was and declares that he missed me. He talks to me with affection and respect and quietly confesses things that bother him. But political news or a soccer match may be on a nearby television screen. He will suddenly turn to the screen, argue, shout, protest, and verbally correct what he sees, whether it is a politician's faux pas or a bad soccer kick. But when I left a gift for him in my hotel room and wanted to run and recover it, he patted the air gently and said, "Galini. Galini. Avrio." Relax. Be calm. Tomorrow.

One evening at dinner, he played sad, moving Greek music on his cellphone for me. It was a video showing beautiful vistas of the sky, a Greek military jet flying its maneuvers, and several portraits of the pilot. As it played his eyes reddened and tears dribbled down his face. He made a gesture with his big hands of flying through the air, then suddenly sinking toward the earth.

I understood. "Moirologia?" I asked. Moirologia are Greek "songs of fate" composed in honor of one deceased. "Thanatos?" I asked. Dead?

Dmitri nodded his scraggly and balding head and said in English, "Only twenty-eight." He wiped his eyes with a napkin and sadly said, "No more!" He tapped his heart with his large hand and said, "*Problema*. Feel too much. Not for myself, for the world."

78 ∽ POSEIDON

Standing behind him, the owner Giorgos declared, "You are a very good man."

Dmitri said, sadly, gently, "Good men always make problems—for themselves."

Dmitri has other connections to the sea god of this island. He served for thirty-two months in the navy and was stationed in the 1970s on Cyprus during the troubles with Turkey. He has been to war and about that he also declares, "Enough!" Now, when only twelve months of military service are required, he grunts, "Eh! *Efkolo*!" Easy!

Dmitri lives alone on his small farm down the slope from Poseidon's sanctuary. He grew up there, long before there were modern roads. His father's family had been on Poros for many generations. His mother came from a village on nearby Methana. She was raised on a volcano and Dmitri reports that she was intelligent and strong, as if she carried the mountain's energy. From age five until he left for the navy at eighteen, every Saturday he and his father, guiding their donkey, threaded the narrow pine-lined trails down the mountain to the sea. It was a three-hour hike. They fished for Poseidon's children the salmon, loaded their catch on their burro, then climbed the three hours back. At home they feasted, then fell into a deep, exhausted but fulfilled sleep.

Dmitri often pulls out his cellphone to display a photo of a broad and sleek white horse. Poseidon's animal is his only companion. Her name is Dora, which in Greek means "gift." He loves Dora and tends her every day as his retirement chore. He used to ride her but in his elder and heavier years no longer can. Still, she is his dear friend. Dmitri laughs gleefully when I address him as Dmitri Hippos.

At one dinner together, he greeted me with two huge lemons, bigger than elongated, sun-yellow tennis balls. He scratched the skin. We both inhaled the pungently sweet perfume. He waved his hand for me to take them—his humble and generous gift from his farm.

Big Dmitri is serene, kind, gentle, compassionate, and tender, and loud-mouthed, passionate, opinionated. He argues and embraces, barks and cries, sings and praises, like the god of his island, like the sea. His horse Dora, his gift, his dear friend, is Poseidon's totem. And our friendship on the god's island is a gift to us both.

The wisdom literature of the world testifies to humanity receiving, in some tangible form, precious and life-sustaining gifts that seem to come from eternal and invisible sources. We have heard stories of miracles, oracles, prophecies, synchronistic experiences, meetings, dreams, visions that carry us beyond the ordinary and expected. In these ways we may receive and develop love, wisdom, faith, healing, friendship. In these ways we are gifted. As Heraklitos taught, "expect the unexpected" if we wish to discover truth.

5

GREEK MYTHOLOGY ON POROS
The Naming of an Island

The god only inspires his own.
　　　　　MARY RENAULT, THE KING MUST DIE

In Greece every step is suffused with mythology and history, beauty, passion, and urgency. It is as if the very dust and rocks are vital, alive, dancing in the brilliant sunlight, carrying the sweat and imprints of the mythic and human strivings and struggles that unfolded here over millennia. We relate their myths to the stories of our own lives and struggles. We sometimes see great or simple ancient personages in dreams, visions, and embodied in modern Greeks. Or we see ourselves in their times, as if in past lives. We feel ourselves with them as we walk in their footsteps, breathe their air, feel them beside and deep within us. We sense the eternal life of the archetypes unfolding in the temporal and in us.

Especially on Poros, the passage between the eternal and temporal seems so thin that the mythic, ancient, and modern worlds interpenetrate. All at once, we are in mythistorema, mythic history. We settle into a new consciousness in which soul and ultimate matters truly come first—the top rather than the bottom line. We live mythically.

When Theseus Was Here

This region of the eastern Peloponnesos, its mountains and valleys, forests, and waters, was the birthplace and childhood home of Theseus. He was one of the most important and beloved figures of the ancient world, renowned as the slayer of the Kretan Minotaur and an early and transformational king of Athens. The animals that roamed and deities that dwelt here were his early companions or prey. His birth in Troizen, near Galatas, his relationship to Poseidon, and his times serving the mysteries on Poros all stamped his character. From a childhood here roaming, hunting, participating in the sacred and secular life of his community, mentored by the king, his grandfather, he went on to become king of Athens and hero of many adventures.

Pelops was an early king of Pisa who gave his name to the Peloponnesos (or Pelop's Island). Pittheus, his son, was the king of Troizen. Pittheus was considered to be especially strong and wise. He had two daughters, Aithra and Henioche, by Hippodamia. He had won her hand in a chariot race thanks to his appeal for aid from Poseidon and divine help from his charioteer and friend Sfairos. Sfairos had died on the way to the race. He appeared in a dream standing over the king requesting a funeral. This was a founding myth of the chariot races at the original games at Olympia on the western Peloponnesos. Sfairos was granted his spirit's request and buried on the smaller of the double islands that now bears his name—Sfairia.

Aegeus, the king of Athens, was childless and in grief that he did not have an heir to whom to pass his throne. He had consulted the Delfi Oracle who instructed him to "loose not the wine-skin's jutting neck," that is, refrain from intercourse until he returned once more to Athens. On his way he visited Pittheus. They discussed his conundrum. Pittheus got Aegeus drunk, and he ended up spending the night with Aithra. But Poseidon had slept with her first.

Sfairia and Kalaureia were both across the strait from Galatas. At age seventeen, Pausanias tells us, "because of a dream from Athene," Aithra had to bring libations to the tomb of Sfairos on the small island, where his memorial stood. The poet Bacchylides, around 470 BCE, put these words in Theseus's mouth, "I myself / come from the daughter of wealthy Pittheus / when she lay with the lord of the sea."[1] And Pausanias records, "While she was over there, they say she slept with Poseidon."[2] Whether by Poseidon, Aegeus, or both, Aithra became pregnant, and her child was Theseus. Pittheus put out the story that he was fathered by Poseidon. Aegeus returned to Athens, leaving his sandals and sword beneath a boulder that Theseus would have to lift and recover to learn and prove his identity as prince of Athens. The massive gray boulder is honored to this day where it stands before the entryway to the ruin site of ancient Troizen.

Aithra, a priestess of the goddess, founded a shrine to Athena Apaturia, or Deceitful Athena, and changed the island's name to Holy Island. It included Sfairos's tomb. The name derives from the ancient word *apati*, which means "trick," "fraud," "deceit," or "treachery." It was given in honor of the illusory dream the goddess gave to Aithra that it was Poseidon who slept with her, and the god would be considered Theseus's father. Athena, patron of Athens, determined that Theseus should be born of Aithra and, like many saviors and heroes, believed to be born of a god and a mortal woman.

In ancient times, honoring this myth, there was an annual procession from Troizen to Sfairia called the Apaturia, during which youths were registered in their list of relatives. Theseus later transferred this ceremony to Athens. Pausanias says that Aithra also established the ritual "of Troizenian virgins dedicating a girdle to Athena before marriage."[3]

The temple of Athena Apaturia on Poros, once sacred to the goddess, is now the site of St. George's Cathedral, the island's main cathedral. Built into its ornate structure are several archaic columns and stones from Athena's and Poseidon's temples. Stones from Athena Apaturia's original temple were used in building five parish churches. The lives, stories, and holy sites of the old gods are always the foundations of the newer.

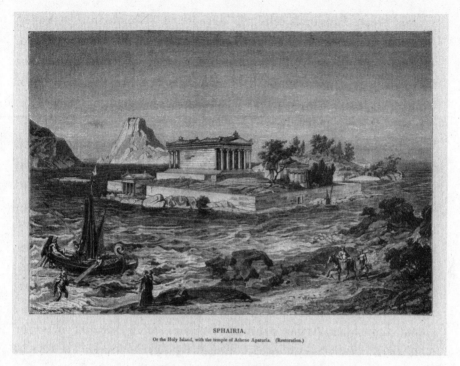

Fig. 5.1. Artist's rendition of the Temple of Athena Apaturia, nineteenth century.
PHOTOGRAPH FROM THE HATZOPOULEIOS PUBLIC LIBRARY ARCHIVES

British author Mary Renault is famous for her novels depicting life in ancient Greece, effectively bringing myth and history into one united story of how "it" might have happened. *The King Must Die* gives the story of Theseus from birth in Troizen through his defeat of the Minotaur and return to Athens. In her telling, Aegeus swims the strait at night and comes upon Aithra, as foretold by Athena, awaiting the god in the dark. Theseus is conceived and the two kings—of Troizen and of Athens—agree to keep the prince's birth and lineage a secret until he is old and strong enough to claim his kingship.

Later Renault has the boy Theseus spend one month out of every four at Sfairia for three years, serving an apprenticeship to his god and learning of their sacred relationship and his proper practices. Of the island and its sanctuary, he says, "When you serve a holy place, you can never forget, even in sleep, that the god is there."[4]

Theseus discovers his birth origin, travels to Athens by land and along the way cleanses the overland travel route of brigands. One was Sinis, according to the poet Bacchylides, "once the greatest in strength, being son to . . . earthshaker Poseidon."[5] Two sons of Poseidon, both supreme in strength as inheritance from their common father, fight to the death. Theseus conquers. Poseidon's good son overcomes his bad, as our internalized conflicting powers must. Here again is the ambivalence and balance built into mythological thinking. Theseus reunites with Aegeus and finally goes to Krete with the other sacrificial youths to become bull leapers and eventually defeats the Minotaur and causes the downfall of the Mycenaean power base.

Theseus's tragic family story continues to unfold across from Poros at Troizen and along the strait. He had a son Hippolytos by the Amazon queen Hippolyta. After her death he married Phaedra, a princess of Krete. Phaedra developed an obsessive love for Hippolytos, which he rejected because he was sworn as a celibate priest to Artemis. Phaedra hung herself, leaving a note accusing Hippolytos of rape. In a rage Theseus called the curse of Poseidon down on his son. As Hippolytos was galloping away from Troizen in his chariot to escape his father's misplaced wrath, Poseidon sent a tidal wave to flood the Peloponnesian shore. Father conceived and son doomed by trickery from the same god on the same sacred ground. Euripides's play *Hippolytos* tells of the ritual practiced in ancient times to honor the youth and his tragic fate; before their marriage day unwed girls cut their hair and sang songs in honor of him and of Phaedra's love.

The myths indicate that god-powers have our fates and destinies in their greater minds, and shape events, including by dreams, trickery, and deceit, to make their plans come true. Human passions drive us to mistaken or unworthy deeds. Human pride defies the gods. Even devotion to gods is no insurance against a tragic fate. Loves may be false or true. Heroes are complex, ambivalent, tortured, mistaken, causing themselves and others much harm as well as good. Our mortal task seems to be to do all we can to discern the will of the cosmos, shapes of our destiny, myths we are living, attune ourselves to that, and cooperate rather than harm its unfolding. These themes are found in the myths from Poros and environs. All were enacted here in mythic and historical times and re-enacted endlessly in the eternal human story.

Archaic Gods Named Poros: A Digression

"What's in a name?" Shakespeare famously asked in *Romeo and Juliet*. Humanity has been pondering the question ever since.

As mentioned, the word *Poros* in ancient Greek, as in modern times, referred to a ford, passage, strait, a thoroughfare for ships. This is the realm of Poseidon, "savior of ships." Poros was also the name of two little-known gods. The name of the island is modern, only about six hundred years rather than millennia old. Historically the island and god names are unrelated.

The double island was renamed Poros in the 1400s for the strait that separates it from the mainland, and the word *Poros* itself is decidedly geographical and was used that way in classical times. However, archetypally and poetically, through metaphor, analogy, the imagination, and in the mysteries of language to evoke the unseen, we can use mythology to help us enter the island's spirituality. As Prof. Dennis Patrick Slattery observes, "Myths use the language of metaphor for their energy and durability. . . . A metaphor, like a myth, is 'a transport vehicle' that encourages us to move out of the boundaries of the known. . . . Mythopoetic thinking relies on the power of analogy."[6] Though not historically related, the analogy between the names of the island and the archaic gods reveals hidden dimensions of the island's character and powers.

There were more, earlier god-powers and their myths than we commonly know from the popular Olympian pantheon. Before reason and modern technologies, mortals were more in tune and in touch with, dependent on, and victim to the natural and cosmic forces. These were considered living and divine. They were named, evoked, and offered prayer and sacrifice. Stories told of their origins, purposes, and relations to the other forces and to us. Modern thought judges these practices as anthropomorphism and projection resulting from superstition and

86 ᴄᴏ GREEK MYTHOLOGY ON POROS

ignorance. It may be closer to the truth to say that prerational people were ensconced in an embracing religious mythology and not separated from the cosmos by intellect. Instead, they experienced these powers as living, suprapersonal forces and sought to be in a right relationship with them. This brought them experientially closer to the divine than most modern people are today.

What we call personification for the ancients was the experience of living cosmic forces made personal. "Person" in Greek is *atomon*. It derives from the ancient Greek *atomos*, meaning "indivisible." The "person" of the original gods were "atoms," indivisible and basic units of the cosmos. Their "personifications" were experienced as indivisible powers alive in the cosmos. Might and Violence, for one example, are both gods given roles and voice in Aeschylos's play *Prometheus Bound*.

Poros was the name of two barely known early gods. They were birthed into the cosmos and the human imagination long before the Olympian deities with which we are familiar. Though the island was not named for them, through analogy, mythopoetic thinking, their stories and meanings help us appreciate the character of the island.

Plato reports some of the mythology of Poros the god—ancient sacred history—in *Symposium*. These stories were well known and oft-repeated in ancient times. Poros was the god of Plenty. He was the son of Zeus and his mother the goddess Metis, or Discretion. The ruling cosmic patriarch mated with the primal power of balance, reflective thought, and choice to give birth to Plenty, Resource, and the means of achieving them.

Poros was at the deities' birthday party for Aphrodite, goddess of love and beauty. On this festive occasion, he did not practice moderation but got drunk on nectar and fell deeply asleep in *o kipo tis Theas*, the garden of gods.

Meanwhile, Penia, the goddess of Poverty, arrived. From her we derive the English word for the poor coin, the penny. As was common in early days, when a celebration occurred there would be excess and generosity of spirit. She arrived at the door to beg, as she commonly did. Seeing Poros asleep, she plotted to have a child by him to transform her own circumstances. As Plato tell us, "She lay down by his side and conceived Love . . . and as his parentage is, so also are his fortunes." Love is always poor, "rough and squalid . . . always in distress." And like his father, Love is always plotting and intriguing, a philosopher, enchanter, magician, and sweet talker. Neither mortal nor immortal, Love "is alive and flourishing at one moment"— Poros—and dead at another—Penia. Plato declares, "that which is always flowing in is always flowing out . . . [so Love] is never in want and never in wealth."[7]

Poros, the early god, the power of wealth, is the father of Love, half its parentage, giving Love half its essential character. Modern misinterpretations, psycho-spiritual afflictions, and imbalanced cultural expectations wish Love to be all giving and resourceful. We ache for the flowing in. We resist and grieve the flowing out and think something wrong. But on the island, wise people understand this. Rota's Giorgos Dimitriadis declared, "We can never have everything we want," and "no matter what we wish, we cannot do everything." He echoed Heraklitos, who taught that even if we got all that we wanted, it would not be for the best. Like Penia, the island and its people are poor and simple, but like Poros many are wealthy in wisdom, kindness, and character.

There is another barely known god named Poros who also provides insight into the meaning of the name. Alkman was an early lyric poet from Sparta, active around the seventh century BCE. He composed works especially for choirs to be sung at festivals to the deities. Like Hesiod, he wrote a theogony, a history of the gods' origins and stories.

In Alkman's account, Thetis was the first goddess, one of the primordial beings representing the foundations of the cosmos. On the trackless void of primal chaos, she produced three divine children who appeared immediately after the creation. Her children were Tekmor, which means a goal, boundary, or fixed mark, an end, object, or purpose, and is associated with limits and death. She also had Skotos, which is uncharted darkness or gloom. And she had Poros, which means the path, the track, the way of getting somewhere or of providing or achieving something.

Though not originally a reason for naming the island, Poros as a narrow strait, a sea passage, and Poros as a way of getting somewhere as we move toward our purpose or goal, can be seen as related in meaning. The island too has this meaning; it is a way of getting from the mundane to the significant, from the worldly to the divine, from the poor to the rich in spirit. In its mythology and linguistic etymology, the resonant meanings of the name Poros carry us into the archaic world and provide a passage from our modern impoverishment of spirit to its resurrection and richness. Birthplace of a great king and named for both the passage to and richness of our ultimate purposes, in myth and name, Poros promises all this.

Finally, what's in a name? In his library office, thick with books about Poros and Greece, walls covered with posters of cultural events he has facilitated, I ask Yannis one last time if Plato's story of the god Poros has anything to do with the name of the island.

Yannis is a historian and public servant of impeccable integrity and devotion. The elder "encyclopedia" throws his arms wide and laughs heartily at my question. "Absolutely no relation," he exclaims. "The meaning of *poros* is clear in ancient Greek. It meant a passage, something decidedly local." Yannis then recites a litany of ancient writers—Homer, Herodotus, Aeschylos, Pindar, Aristophanes, Euripides, Xenophon— who used the word with its strictly geographical meaning. "I do not support the idea that the island's name is related to the name of these archaic gods. There may be metaphorical connections as you suggest, but it is we modern people who discover those; they were not part of the original naming."

Poros invites discovery and expansion. We travel our passages and straits in search of wisdom.

6

A History of Asylia (Sanctuary)

Stories from Refugees through the Ages

> *Blessed is the one who slips free*
> *Of the storm's mouth*
> *And rides the sea*
> *To safe harbor.*
>
> —Euripides, *Bakkhai*

Tiny Poros has stood throughout history as a place of safety, refuge, and resistance, beauty, hope, and spiritual presence. From mythic into historical times, and from the ancient world to the modern and today, Poros as a place of asylum has granted protection and galini to countless refugees, wandering souls, and its own residents who have needed home or safe port during times of personal or historical crisis and loss.

Demosthenes on Poros

The orator Demosthenes, 384–322 BCE, is best known for training himself to eloquence. He was not able to pronounce the rolling Greek letter sound *rho*. So, he famously practiced oratory with a mouthful of marbles. He was an exceedingly influential orator, of fierce and unbending opinions, devoted to carefully preparing his orations, then giving moving and powerful deliveries that impelled political action. Plutarch described him as a person who believed "that the good is the one thing to choose for its own sake."

Demosthenes was prominent during Makedonian supremacy. As Plutarch retold it, "he allowed no act of the Makedonian to pass uncriticized and seized every opportunity to arouse and inflame the Athenians against him." Like Sokrates he insisted that honor and duty must come before safety and security.[1] With these values Demosthenes prodded his city-state and others until Athens and allies finally rebelled against Makedonia. He continued to inflame them throughout a sustained war. Plutarch reports that his oratory was supreme and had he also been a man of incorruptible honesty, and a courageous rather than a meek soldier in the wars he initiated, "he would have deserved to rank" as one of the great souls of the ancient world.

Makedonia defeated Athens in 323 BCE, and Demosthenes fled to the Poros sanctuary, among the most inviolable at the time. He had once preached that life without freedom was not worth living. Now, surrounded by his pursuers, he begged a few last minutes to write a farewell letter to his family. His foes watched from outside the grounds; they would not risk the curse levied for killing a suppliant in sanctuary. While they waited and taunted him for cowardice, Demosthenes chewed a poisoned pen. He sickened before Poseidon's altar and asked his captors to support him as he staggered out of the sea god's temple so as not to profane it, then fell dead upon exiting.[2] He chose to die free rather than be taken captive.

Pausanias declared that "heaven has never shown its jealousy more terribly than . . . when it sent to Demosthenes in his old age the experiences of exile and a violent death."[3] But Plutarch judged Demosthenes's suicide as admirable in planning and execution. "For when the god no longer granted him sanctuary, he found refuge . . . at a greater altar, removed himself out of reach of arms and soldiers, and laughed to scorn the cruelty."[4]

Twentieth-century Greece's prolific poet and radical Yiannis Ritsos also courageously raised his voice against oppression and tyranny. As with Greek poetry and culture in general, past and present, fact and myth blend into one unified vision. Ritsos contemplated Demosthenes's suicide in his 1969 poem "Requiem on Poros." He declares that "we keep forgetting the gods" but that Demosthenes's act "in the pine-covered spot" makes us remember Poseidon. He praises "the stammerer" who became Greece's greatest orator, then reflects: "condemned by the Makedonians and the Athenians, learned, in the course of one night, the most difficult, the greatest art of all: to be silent."[5]

Demosthenes remains a fascinating and ambivalent character. He was honored as a great orator but reportedly was a mediocre warrior. He inspired his people to resist invasion and tyranny and live by high ideals. But beware: the consequences of our ideals can lead to disaster. Demosthenes is honored as a role model for dying as a free man rather than consenting to capture. The Greek people are passionate about their freedom, and he serves that paradigm. Yet we must also be able to defend and develop our ideals. On the personal level, many of us feel as if we have marbles in our mouths and must practice assiduously to learn to speak openly and truthfully. Demosthenes is a role model as he shows that we can evolve from stutterers to leaders. His final choice inspires us each to ask ourselves—when might life become so unbearable that we would choose to die?

Refugee History Through the Ages

We have heard of the wreckage caused to the island by the invasion of the Visigoths in 395 and the earthquake a decade later. Poros and the surrounding region, sacred and thriving in ancient times, were reduced to ruin and waste. From the fifth century through Alaric's invasion, everything was destroyed. The sanctuary and its supporting villages

92 ᔡ A History of Asylia (Sanctuary)

and cities were wrecked, treasures and artworks plundered, inhabitants slain. Survivors fled. The island did not then recover. Bereft of its population and resources, it became a lair for pirates raiding the gulf and the Peloponnese. Imagine this small and beautiful island nestled quietly in the Saronic Gulf, forgotten by history, avoided by humanity, as though the flames and pains of conquest were still fresh and the land unsafe and unwelcoming. For a thousand years, Poros was nearly uninhabited except by a few shepherds and farmers and the pirates operating from its shores.

Poros became the island we know by this name at the end of this period of isolation. Again, the Ottomans influenced its history. Again, refugees fled from the lands they had previously settled and found sanctuary on Poros.

The Arvanites are a bilingual cultural group in Greece who came from Albania or the borderlands between Greece and Albania. They speak Arvanitika, an Albanian dialect that today through lack of use and speakers is one of the world's disappearing languages. During wars of expansion in the 1400s, as Albanians spread south to the Argoloid, Arcadia, and the Peloponnese, this population fled Albania and moved across the border. For safety they spoke their own language but kept their Greek religion and identity. As the Ottomans advanced, these refugees fled to the Saronic islands, sparsely inhabited at the time, seeking safety as Ottomans conquered parts of the Peloponnese. On Poros they created the medieval settlement called *Kastelli*, or the Castle, on the height today occupied by the clock tower. It was a fortified village surrounded by steep and tall cliffs that protected them from pirates. This group of refugees first dubbed the island "Poros" after the strait.

Over the centuries Greeks and Arvanites found their way to the island and created a peaceful mixed population. Poros continued throughout history to be a place of refuge. Some Albanians arrived during these ensuing centuries, and especially during the Revolution, to fight the Turks and remain to settle.[6] A century ago, in 1923, during the crisis with Turkey and the forced population exchanges and relocations of more than 1.5 million people, the Greek nation did all it could to rescue, support, and reintegrate these refugees into their homeland.

The old ship *Averof* was part of the rescue convoy. The Saronic Gulf islands received as many of these homeless as their small communities could absorb. Poros accepted about twelve hundred.

To give these refugees a home, a model community was built on the Kalaureia side of the canal, above the island cemetery where

> Tiny lanterns burn on the new graves . . .[and] during summer nights the place is alive with lantern flames and large sluggish fireflies. . . . [T]he refugees settled peaceably in their new homes, giving to that part of the island an Asiatic flavor with their wailing Turkish songs, their voluptuous dances, their slower heavier tempo, their sadder gaiety, and their drearier and crueler acceptance of fate.[7]

The last survivor of this exodus arrived on Poros as a five-month-old baby in his mother's arms. At his death on February 7, 2023, he had reached the age of over one hundred years and lived in the old neighborhood with a clear mind that remembered his tale.[8]

Michalis Hatziperos lived a hundred years. He was the longest-lived, first-generation refugee who came from Asia Minor and through great difficulties grew up and created his life on Poros. Born in Asia Minor in 1922, he died on Poros at one century old on the island that hosted him and gave him a new home.

On Poros, Michalis found asylum and hospitality. The island not only hosted hundreds of refugees in the first years of the Disaster, but it was the only place among the Saronic Gulf islands that kept them and helped them build a new life through the ashes of destruction.

During the expulsion from Turkey, more than 150 families arrived, according to library director Yannis. Most of the Asia Minor refugees settled in the area of Synoikismos, where even today several habitable refugee houses are preserved, with shady courtyards, as a monument to this large part of Poros history.

Michalis's story began with the disorderly retreat of the Greek army in Asia Minor, which found the family of Panagiotis and Maria Hatziperos from Vourla welcoming their seventh member on the day of the Annunciation, March 25, 1922. In the midst of the war, Michalis's birth personified hope for tomorrow, which would find the newborn child in bundles, his family building a new life on hospitable Poros.

"These are our places." Michalis showed color photos from his 2003 trip to Vourla, also the hometown of George Seferis. "These are Turks," he said, showing a photo of him with a group of people. "The Turks had no hatred for us," he declared. "To give you an idea, as the jihadists are today in Syria, there in Asia Minor, as my mother used to tell me, they were the Chets, fanatics who brought hatred, brutality, and the destruction of peaceful people."

Michalis's father, Panagiotis Hatziperos, was originally from Naxos, its immigrants in Vourla the majority among the Greek community. They immigrated there in the period 1830–1897 with the development of viticulture. "My father was a raisin merchant and had a grocery store in town," he said. "We had no problems with the Turks, as long as we paid the taxes."

In the summer of 1922, disaster came. The seven-member family left their lives behind and set off for the port of Vourla, Michalis only five months old and in bundles. Confused and terrified, the baby was left alone on the side of the road. His mother turned in her tracks to recover him while his father pretended to be crippled to save his family and board the ship with them.

From Vourla, they boarded a cargo ship with hundreds of other hungry refugees. As the ship passed the islands and major ports, refugees unloaded a few at the time. The ship continued to Volos and Chalkida, then to Piraeus and the Saronic islands. Poros was beautiful and close to the Peloponnese and Athens. Arriving there, Michalis's mother said, "Panagiotis, we will go down here."

The family disembarked, ragged, hungry, and suffering. The locals welcomed them with love. After all, soldiers from Poros had given their lives in that war. "We were hosted by people of Poros. They took us into their homes and helped us," Michalis said in tears. Indeed, compared to other places in the Saronic Gulf, Poros hosted and affectionately embraced a large community of refugees.

Michalis's father, Panagiotis, together with another refugee Chatzikyriakos, opened the first grocery store on the Poros seafront in 1922. Later, Chatzikyriakos left for Athens. The family, in turn,

Fig. 6.1. Before the modern era, grocery boats lined the waterfront marketing local produce and supplying the island's additional needs.
PHOTOGRAPH FROM THE HATZOPOULEIOS PUBLIC LIBRARY ARCHIVES

opened grocery stores in different neighborhoods. One of them displayed a large sign that read "Hospitable Poros."

Since then, the food business has passed through the hands of the men of the family, from the father to the older brother Nikos and then to Michalis. Today, the business is run by Michalis's children. The same store has been in operation for a century.

"The refugee was an investment for Greece," Michalis said. "Many refugees were artisans, traders, and even industrialists. They helped develop the entire country." He remembered merchants and artisans who contributed to the development of Poros. He gave as an example Babis Kanatsidis's own ancestors, who were quilters, a profession with a tradition from Misti in Cappadocia.

Η πρώτη δοξολογία στο θωρηκτό ΑΒΕΡΩΦ στις 6 Δεκεμβρίου 1958 (Αρχείο Γ. Αθανασίου).

Fig. 6.2. The much-storied flagship of the Greek navy, the *Averof*, ceremonially docked in Poros Harbor, 1958.
PHOTOGRAPH FROM THE HATZOPOULEIOS PUBLIC LIBRARY ARCHIVES

With a clear mind to the end of his life, Michalis recalled important periods of modern Poros history: the reconstruction of the refugee settlement on Poros; the difficult years of the German occupation. He remembered October 14, 1944, when, upon liberation, the battleship *Averof*, together with other ships, sailed into the strait. At twenty-two years old Michalis took his boat out to meet them. "They threw cans of food at us. An Englishman threw an ashtray of cigarettes. He hit me in the head, and I was bleeding. They took me to *Averof*'s clinic where they stitched me up and wrapped me in bandages." Michalis was the only "casualty" of the celebration.

"Those were very difficult years then," he reflected, "but there was optimism for tomorrow. Possession then was misery, but after four years our struggles passed. Today's economic war is worse. We don't know how long it will last. Young people today are unhappy. There is no optimism," he said, distressed. Vasiliki, his tireless life companion who comes from Trizina, agreed. Since childhood they have been side by side on Poros and shared more than seventy difficult and wonderful years. Together they had three children.

Michalis opined on what is happening with refugees from the Middle East. "What our people experienced a century ago is happening today. Didn't the same thing happen in Syria, Palestine, Cyprus? And in Iraq and Serbia the same. But who should you tell these things to?" he said, sadness in his eyes. "They tell you to leave in the clothes you're wearing. To leave the labors of a lifetime behind. Being a refugee is a bad thing . . ."[9]

Many family histories originated elsewhere around the Mediterranean world to arrive on Poros only a few generations ago. Some contemporary families remember these origins of migrations and military service.

Journalist Babis Kanatsidis came from a refugee family. His ancestors were from Cappadocia in central Turkey. When the Turks gave his family their choice between their language or their religion, declaring they could not keep both, the family fled north, then eventually reached Poros. His grandfather carried an ancient craft and practiced it on Poros; for forty years he made cotton and wool mattresses by hand. Babis affirms that his family and other refugees happily settled on Poros and nearby Salamis because they were so welcomed and absorbed by the islands that they did not need refugee communities.

Alexandros's family emigrated from Kriti after his grandfather fought in three wars: the revolution against the Turks in 1897, then subsequently in World War I, and the Greek-Turkish War of 1919–22. Though Alexandros is a humble and undistinguished resident of the island today, he proudly lives in and works to restore his grandparents' old house and garden and tells stories of his ancestors' deeds. "His grandfather was a genuine military hero," his neighbors say and honor Alexandros for his relatives' contributions several generations back.

In spiritual and religious traditions worldwide, sacred sites have provided sanctuary—safety and protection—from the forces of oppression. Providing sanctuary is living by spiritual values—we all need help,

Fig. 6.3. The mid-twentieth century harbor front of Poros is its most crowded feature, attracting locals, tourists, navy personnel whenever boats dock.
PHOTOGRAPH FROM THE HATZOPOULEIOS PUBLIC LIBRARY ARCHIVES

safety, comfort. Life is sacred and must be preserved. Those who provide sanctuary are "doing God's work"; world spiritual leaders model, practice, and teach it. Religious values of generosity, compassion, friendship, healing, humility, equality are all modeled by sanctuary. The people and history of Poros embody these values and declare that at base, we are all the same and need each other.

Asylia in Modern Times

Refugees find their way to Poros today as they have for centuries.

Aris was born and raised on Cyprus. His family home stood on the street that was the very border between the Greek and Turkish territories. Through his windows he looked on Turkish Cypriots. One night in July of 1974 Aris was suddenly awakened by gunfire, explosions, and shouting. "Grab some clothes and let's go," his father shouted. "We are being attacked." The Turkish invasion had begun. Troops were entering their neighborhood as civilians screamed and fled. "We need to get to safety," his father said. "But don't worry. We'll be back in a few days."

The family escaped while the father remained to defend their home and neighborhood. Aris declares that he was like a guerilla fighter—inexperienced, untrained, without equipment, but with his comrades fiercely defending their homes as long as they could. "The common people are never honored," Aris complains. "The world celebrates the 300 Spartans. But they were the special forces of their times, highly trained, supported, and ready to die. No one celebrates the 700 Thespian militia—ordinary farmers and artisans fighting with their farming tools. They are the real heroes. Like my father was in our times."

Since he and his family suffered so much loss due to military and political movements, Aris is analytic and critical regarding military history. He wants the ordinary people recognized for their contributions and resistance. He declares that Alexander the Great was "like Hitler" in his conquering strategies, killing the elderly and weak, forcing men to join his forces as he advanced. "He only gave freedom as a settlement surrendered and their men joined his army." About world politics he observes, "The United States is the Agamemnon of today. He didn't care about Helen. He only wanted Troy's gold. It happened on Cyprus. The U.S. supported Turkey to split Cyprus so they could have military bases there. The Trojan War or our modern wars—it is always the same."

Aris and his family found their way to Poros and made a home there. The "few days" before returning to their family home on Cyprus stretched and stretched. He was only able to revisit his birth and childhood home thirty years after he and his family had fled it in terror. Poros has been a good and safe second home for Aris, but his wounds are only decades old and historical and transgenerational. Like a traumatized veteran, horror stories flood from his mouth. He feels resentment toward the world powers for transforming his home island into a political and ethnic battleground. Yet he carries his history and built and runs his store without collapse. How? I inquire. "Because I am not a storekeeper; I am a philosopher. Only *nous*, 'mind,' enables us to rise above our sufferings."

After so much early turmoil and loss, in search of inner peace, Aris went to Mt. Athos. Mt. Athos has been a "holy mountain" and center of Eastern Orthodox worship for over a thousand years. The monks of the approximately twenty monasteries on Mt. Athos live a strict and austere life and are respected all over Greece for being especially sincere.

Aris visited Mt. Athos, seeking healing from the pain he still carries about his traumatic history. As he works to heal and live a good life in the present, he reclaims the lessons monks spoke to him to give him hope and future direction. "Beside the cradle is the coffin," one advised, urging him to take our short life seriously and live it well.

Aris handed me a pen labeled "Poros" and a deck of playing cards with photos of sites around the island. "I cannot let you leave without gifts," he said. "I am sorry I cannot afford more." I still carry and value these simple remembrances of Poros that contain a promise of friendship and the message to endure.

Strong, slender, upright Oli was my waiter at Rota over many visits. He was in the wave of a million Albanian refugees who arrived in Greece in desperate conditions two decades ago. Oli says that many were hungry migrant workers who were only looking for work and moving on. He arrived in Greece at age seventeen, speaking only Albanian, and made his way to Poros. Giorgos gave him a job at Rota, and asylia. He worked there about fifteen years, became fluent in Greek and English, married, and has a young son with an Albanian name.

In 2019 there was a severe earthquake in Albania, causing significant loss of life and destruction of property. Sadly, Oli said, "It happened. Now everything is different forever. Again and again. That is what refugees learn to accept. But so many families . . ." Finally, he declares, "I am happy and peaceful on Poros. I feel safer here than anywhere. Here I am successful and blessed."

Mimoza is the friendly and generous waitress at Rota, happily serving customers early in the morning or late at night. She has an infectious smile that projects good will even when she is tired or worried. Along with approximately a million other refugees, Mimoza's husband Mir left Albania when the Communist regime collapsed in 1991. He lived and worked in several different countries before settling on Poros. Mimoza joined him a decade later. They had had to emigrate one family member at a time, but now "we feel extremely lucky to be here. This is a good place to live." The family is in another tradition; Albanians have

A History of Asylia (Sanctuary) ～ 101

been emigrating to Greece since the thirteenth century. They are fully assimilated and today make up the largest expatriate group in Greece. Mir and Mimoza's children were born in Greece and their daughter is presently in college in Patras. "My children are not Greek or Albanian," she declares with a smile. "They are both together."

As Mimoza and others affirm, in sanctuary ethnic and historical differences dissolve as we become one people striving together to right the difficulties of life and history. Providers and refugees alike grow, mature, and develop bonds that replace loss and fear with peace and friendship. In our modern times and in response to international crises, we practice the ancient rite of filoxenia, and it is sacred.

Asylon Today

To this day, refugees find their way to Poros to seek the inviolable safety promised by the tradition of asylum and live among people who still practice it. During the recent Israel-Hamas War, as terrorists invaded Israel, and Israel struck back in Gaza, Israeli civilians, some affluent enough to escape and support themselves, some with children in tow desperate to preserve and protect their families, arrived on Poros in increasing numbers. As in previous centuries, these refugees too seek to escape from the horrific war zone they are trapped in. Poros continues to beckon to people the world over, seeking such safety and serenity for themselves, their families, and the hopes for a good life.

Why Poriotes Return

Many natives of Poros, from the distant and near past and into the present, leave the humble island for the bigger world. It is often to Athens. But it may be to London, Australia, the United States, or elsewhere. They seek education, adventure, better employment opportunities, escape from what to the young seems like boredom and quietude to an exciting larger world. And they might roam the world and be found anywhere. Boating down a small estuary of the Mekong River in Viet Nam, I called out to a passing sampan with a lone passenger, *"Xin chao!*

Hello!" He called back, "*Yiasou! Kalimera*!" (Greetings! Good day!) As our boats floated past each other up and down stream surrounded by jungle, we each stood up and cried out a brief Greek conversation, with our final "*Eimaste kala*! We are good." As in ancient times in myths and life, Poriotes and other Greeks may be found sailing the waters of the world.

They leave. They often discover that in the wider world they cannot find what their souls sought or their health needed. They return. This is spiritual asylia.

Nikos Kollias was born and has spent his life on Poros. About a century ago, his great-grandfather had migrated to "Salt City," Utah, seeking opportunity and a better life. But later, with his family and young son, they returned to Poros. They discovered that the good life was not found in money or the American lifestyle, but back home on their humble native island.

Nikos's grandfather was born in Salt Lake City on the same day as Nikos decades later. He owns his ancestor's birth certificate and felt his grandfather's spirit with him as he turned a half-century old the day after *Pascha*, or Easter. Born and reborn again on Poros.

Christos Drougas is a sweet, kind, and friendly man. He is short, trim, with clipped grayish hair. He walks with a rocking limp. One arm is slightly and permanently bent. His voice is always tender and welcoming, his smile and hugs melting.

Christos works at Taverna Sti Rota as host, waiter, and accountant. His "office" is a table along the walkway between Rota's inner room and outer seating areas. There Christos sits, sips his coffee, manages the books, and exchanges the news and gossip of the island with passersby. When Rota's owner is away, Christos stands in as manager. They make long business trips together, sometimes driving three hours across the Peloponnese to Patras for supplies and returning the same day.

Christos was born on Poros in July 1961. Today there is a small supermarket, Kritikos, toward the end of the waterfront street. In 1961 it was a clinic where the island women had their babies. Early one morning, the sun peeking over the strait's waters, Christos's mother felt it was time. The infant arrived with the bright dawn.

A History of Asylia (Sanctuary) ∾ 103

When Christos turned fifteen, he left the island to attend a technical high school in Athens for his last three years, 1975–1978. After graduation he returned to Poros to serve his required military service. From 1981 to 1983 he served at the Naval Academy as personal assistant to the navy chief—just like he is in Rota now.

After the service he followed his father to work in his small restaurant here, which Christos inherited upon his father's death. It was called "The Halfway House" because it stood halfway between the village and Askeli Beach. Coming home from work, people stopped for a drink or a meal. Later Christos redesigned the restaurant, had a local painter decorate it, and named it Bacchus, the god of wine. Because the business was seasonal, in winter he went to Piraeus to help in a large restaurant called Ippokampos (The Seahorse), which he ran for five years. Then in 2013 he developed multiple sclerosis, causing the limp and deformations he carries today. He was forced to sell his business.

Seeking health, work, and a place to belong, Christos returned to his native Poros in 2013. He still owned Bacchus. For five years he wintered in Copenhagen with a butcher friend, learning about meats. His ownership and travels ended in 2013 because of his multiple sclerosis, but for six years he helped friends in their restaurants.

Rota's Giorgos approached Christos looking for reliable year-round help. Part of Giorgos's ministry was hiring refugees and others in various states of need. Rota provides asylum, and Giorgos granted it. Giorgos and Christos had been friends for many years. Giorgos sought Christos, and he has been working at Rota since 2019. Though he limps and one arm twists, he deftly weaves between tables to give customers his warm welcome and attention. When at dinner Christos saw me picking at my grilled snapper to avoid the bones, he walked over to me, put his hands on my shoulders, bent over and whispered in my ear. "I tell you a secret, Eddiemou. We eat the fish skin. Don't pick at it like a chicken." We both laughed. Describing the catch of the day to my visiting pilgrims, he speaks like an eloquent ancient orator. And when I stand to help clear my table, he smiles and says softly, "Don't do that. You are our friend and guest. That is my job."

"Working at Rota is my medicine," Christos declares. "I can

maintain myself and my MS in a steady condition instead of rotting away. Here I have friends of many years. I love my work. It gives me life. It is how I maintain. Here there is no stress in my life. That is what kills us." Humble and kindly Christos quietly made a significant contribution to Greek cuisine. *Feta me meli,* feta cheese wrapped in filo dough and drenched in honey, is a Greek delicacy. It was invented by a famous chef whose son taught it to Christos. Christos brought it to Poros, and it became so popular it spread all over Greece.

Rota is Christos's asylon. Giorgos affirmed his special talents and needs, and by employing, befriending, and relying on him, created the boon in our times. In this instance and many others on this island, the practice of asylia is not official or ecclesiastical, but practiced every day by ordinary people with hearts full of compassion. They demonstrate how we, by our own efforts and creative daily practices, can deliver sacred boons to those in need. As Sokrates taught, by doing the good, our souls deepen and grow.

Tasos Rodis was born in Piraeus in the 1970s and raised on the island of Poros. He had what he describes as "a quiet, normal childhood life." Because Poros was a tourist destination, "I used to have my winter and summer friends. I had the luck to always play outdoors with my friends, without caring about weather conditions."

Tasos was an average student at school, not putting much effort in, but "directing all my energy in sports." At age eleven, he started training in track and field.

I was fortunate to have a great athletic coach next to me and a band of friends who transformed that part of my life into an amazing and fun-filled period. I was good in athletics, wining national championships several times. Athletics is an individual, very demanding sport, where each result depends completely on your performance. I learned to work hard to achieve my goals. At the same time, I was lucky enough to possess athletic intelligence. One example is that we should always compete against ourselves and not against opponents. Psychologically that provides control and reduces anxiety and stress. Then we have a higher probability of achieving our goals and winning.

A History of Asylia (Sanctuary) 105

Tasos decided to study the science of sport. At age eighteen he left Poros to live, study, and work in several European counties, as well as elsewhere in Greece and the Middle East, eventually becoming an expert in his field. While his profession was a priority, it was equally important to him to learn new cultures. Since he had left the island when young, he felt hungry to explore the wider world. Further, at the time, he could not see himself living on a small island because of its limited opportunities.

"Chasing my profession," Tasos says, "led me to places far away from Poros, like Australia, Canada, and the Middle East." He reflects on his world explorations:

> I enjoyed every place I lived. I made things easy for myself by keeping mostly positive people and vibes around me. I could also call some of the places I lived "home" even though there was an expiration date. However, there was always a missing element inside me that I couldn't clearly see or recognize. That missing element made me lose my internal balance from time to time. I always considered this to be part of my character without paying much attention to it. However, in 2019 that element hit me again, but that time it was a thousand times stronger than before. That last hit led me to lose my internal balance.

The world challenge that arose during the Covid-19 pandemic plunged Tasos into an internal crisis. He could no longer avoid what was bothering him and missing from his inner life.

> During the unknown, unclear, and tough times of Covid-19, I was away from Poros, but this time found myself struggling with important questions and concerns about my life. That feeling became more intense when I had to face a health-related issue for one of my family members. It was then that I decided to return to Poros without even having a plan for my future. I wanted to return to the only place in the world that could offer me the feeling of safety in difficult times.

Tasos returned to Poros. His first few months back were difficult because,

I had stopped chasing what I had chased for so many years. But slowly and naturally, I started becoming part of the island again. I started seeing the beauty and peace of the island with the eyes I had had as a youngster. But this time my vision was clear and much richer. Now, I could see these qualities through the experiences and knowledge I had gained all the years I was physically and mentally away from Poros exploring the world. This perspective helped me find my role in this small islandic society again. I slowly recognized the missing element all these years. It was simply the feeling of being in a place you belong, a place that is familiar to you, where you feel safe, where you can live without putting any effort to make it yours, since you already belong there.

Tasos generalizes from his story to life wisdom. "From my youth, I wanted to travel the world, to see and live in different places, meet different people, and explore various cultures. I wanted to live my own Odyssey, and I did. I learned that even if you finally manage to find your Ithaka, the journey must go on."

Now Tasos works for the local organization Katheti, opening new offices on the waterfront and creating programming—dance lessons, art exhibitions, public education against commercial fish farming—to protect and restore culture to the island. Among other contributions, as an experiential introduction to the village, Tasos invented a group game called Sokaki after the alleys. He distributes street maps to teams of new visitors and sends them climbing the steep back streets seeking hard to find local landmarks. He explains,

Katheti is a cultural and educational center serving the Poros, Troizinia, and Methana region. It supports local artisans and entrepreneurs, students preparing for their futures, and all those who seek to expand their horizons, learn new skills, share knowledge, and celebrate the richness of our culture.

Katheti is the traditional fishing gear that has been used by generations of local families. Made from rectangular pieces of native cork, a weighted line, and simple hooks, it is a symbol of ingenuity

and self-sufficiency. Our name also reflects the inarguable insight of the adage: "Give a man a fish and you feed him for a day. Teach a man to fish, and you feed him for a lifetime." Katheti has deep roots in Poros. Cofounders Eva Douzinas and Fay Orfanidou were inspired by their grandmothers Lili and Froso, two remarkable sisters who spent their entire lives on Poros island. The name honors their legacy of self-sufficiency and lifelong love of fishing and the cultural traditions of the island.

Katheti's offices had been in Galatas for several years. Now it is in a renovated old taverna on the Poros waterfront, in the old Kerras building that housed the Sotiris taverna, a site of many good memories for locals and known for its collection of navy uniforms, antiques, coat of arms, and artworks.

Katheti's move from Galatas represents another important effort to restore and strengthen Poros culture and legacy against the contemporary influx of negative transforming influences. Tasos's return to Poros and Katheti's move are like strong new shoots on ancient trees.

After all his wanderings and return, Tasos declares, "In life, it's okay to find yourself lost sometimes. That might lead you to find what you were missing." Tassos's story replicates the famous lesson of "The Wizard of Oz"—"there is no place like home"—and demonstrates that the meaning of nostalgia is the pain we feel when our souls, not only our bodies, are not in their true and fitting homes. The *Odyssey* is the ultimate story of *nostos* and our longing and return helps restore us to who we truly are.

What Foreigners Find

Asylia is not only for the politically or historically oppressed. It is for people seeking sanctuary from the hyperrational, technological, consumeristic, alienating, violent and stress-filled modern world. It is for people seeking soul. From ancient times to today, pilgrims find their way to Poros for just these reasons. The soul is thirsty. It needs what truly quenches. As Jung said, the archetypes have dried up and must be watered.

108 ∽ A History of Asylia (Sanctuary)

Poros and Galatas, 1969

In 1969 American sisters Polly and Jane Petersen enrolled in the Aegean Institute summer program. They traveled through Spain with a Eurail Pass, then made their way to Brindisi, Italy, where in late June they boarded a boat bound for Athens. Polly relates,

I have little recollection about how our communications worked then, with no cell phones, computers, or email. Telephone calls were few to none, though we did sometimes send cables. We received mail at American Express offices. The first sights I remember were the steep high cliffs of the Corinth Canal shining in the sun and the astonishing turquoise blue of the Aegean Sea. Even the memory of it forty-five years later takes my breath away.

From Piraeus we headed for Poros in the cool gray of a light rain. We disembarked and immediately took our luggage to a small boat that ferried us across the channel. We were soon in Galatas to spend the next five to six weeks. Our lodging was a modern hotel along the waterfront. We ate our meals outdoors at tables that were separated from the channel by a wide walkway with a view of rustic small-town life. Round loaves of bread, each with a hole in the center, were strung on poles and delivered to hotels and cafes by men who carried the wooden pole between them. There were no motorized vehicles that I can recall, though there were donkeys. Travel was by boat or on foot.

Our classes were held on the grounds of a villa in a shady pine grove on a hill above the village. The walk to classes was a narrow dirt path that wound past goats and olive trees. The language teacher was a small Greek woman who arrived each day by boat at a landing that must have been a private dock for the villa. She was a cheerful presence and a wonderful teacher.

Strangely, we never climbed the hill to the temple of Poseidon. Poros was important because it was our view. I was busy with studies, letter writing, napping, or swimming in the hot afternoons, and never took that hike.

I remember watching the Apollo moon landing on July 20, 1969. Our hotel had no TVs, so our small group stood in a dark, narrow

*street in Galatas, starry sky overhead, staring at a small black-and-
white TV in the window of a hardware store, watching U.S. astronauts
leap about in their bulky spacesuits on the surface of the moon.*

*One take-away from that summer is Cavafy's poem "Ithaca." I
memorized it in Greek and have called on it endlessly since to get me
through tough times.*

*My mother saved the postcards I wrote home. The first postcard
I sent had a photo of Poros on the front and read, "Dear Family,
Here's the view from the window of my room, but photography can't
catch the beauty. I love it here so much! I've never in my life been so
happy just to be someplace."*

British Surgeons Find Refuge and Direction

Nick and Sue are two surgeons from the United Kingdom who moved
to Poros part-time in the 2010s to escape "the madness in our country"
with Boris Johnson as prime minister and the struggles over leaving the
European Union. For years they lived on Poros and only flew home to
vote. "We do not want to live in the social instability and right-wing
politics that is a severe danger to us all."

Nick and Sue are both neurosurgeons. They are not keen to operate,
but study medicine and health issues as deeply as did the ancients. After
decades of advanced medical experience, they affirmed together, "We
no longer know how to differentiate actual physical conditions from
psychosomatic or spiritual conditions. Doctors should often tell their
patients to wait and allow a process to slowly unfold. Instead, they love
their new discoveries and technology and jump onto symptoms that
would resolve over time."

What does Poros offer them? Rest, safety, friendship, distance
from the politics now dominating their country and our planet. Time
to think, ponder, study their patients and the human condition with
respect, reverence, and patience. Time to study the ancient wisdom that
once guided humanity and its healing but has now largely been for-
saken. Sue and Nick as modern surgeons find professional and personal
asylia on Poros and in it return to their roots as medical healers.

110 &ro; A HISTORY OF ASYLIA (SANCTUARY)

A Lost Daughter of Greece Comes Home

Andie I. is a fifty-two-year-old Greek American psychotherapist. Her parents were both born in Greece, and both sides of the family come from Tsamanta, a village in Epirus on the Albanian border where her paternal great-great-grandfather was a doctor. Her father was born there and her mother in Korinthos. They left the village after the civil war, and no one is left there. Family history has been lost because records were destroyed through both World War II and the Greek Civil War.

Andie is bicultural but, like many children of immigrants, she only speaks a little conversational Greek and when young had resistance and denial about being Greek because of wanting to fit into American culture. She explains, "My interest in Greece began to grow as I emerged into adulthood. In recent years I have been led back to connect with my heritage, identity, and restore my connection with my roots." She has traveled around Greece many times, once passing though the family's home village of Tsamanta on a dusty afternoon. It appeared to be a ghost town.

Andie returned to Greece in 2021, feeling like "I was called home in a way different than before. Like an imperative to reclaim this identity, I felt like a 'lost daughter' to Greece who discovered a thread, grabbed onto it, and have been following it back to remember my origins. I feel Greek in my blood, bones, and marrow. This all emerged spontaneously."

In recent years, after many wanderings on many occasions since she was sixteen, Andie became interested in the god and goddess myths and archetypes. She reflects,

> *It started with an awakening I experienced in 2019, where I met or was reunited with the goddess within me, my divine feminine. It was a kind of "womb awakening." I realized the necessary healing around both my feminine and masculine aspects and the hard work of unifying these within. I've been following this thread ever since, knowing that I must follow my intuition and continue seeking my path to home, my nostos!*

After several years away, Andie returned to Greece for five months in 2021 and serendipitously ended up on Poros.

Spending a few days in Hydra, I felt stirred with a lot of emotions. It was nearing a full moon. I wandered up the town's hillside one night trying to deal with this turbulence, restlessness, loneliness. I encountered a musician and a poet who invited me into their home for a tsipouro. It was a momentary salve for my loneliness. That night I knew it was time to move on to another place, less full of tourists, where I could feel the true Greece again. The next day, with no plan to go and no knowledge of Poros's history or mythology. I simply got on a ferry and booked a room. Who knows why I chose to go there?

I rented an e-bike and explored the wilder eastern part of the island. It held a magic for me. Late afternoons I glided down hills on the bike, inspired to hum and sing aloud—and I am not a singer. I felt carried by winds that felt alive, like guides. Then one evening, with a near full moon, I stared at the sea transfixed, and felt some sense of the gods nearby, as if a veil between worlds was thin.

Poros was modest, authentic, and exactly what I needed.

Accidental Travelers from Germany

Dominique Muller, a young technical writer from Germany, arrived on Poros accidentally, as many do, simply seeking a quick, accessible, relaxing vacation in the warmth and beauty of Greece.

I wanted to visit Greece and knew that there are numerous different small and big islands. I had never heard of Poros and finding it seemed coincidental. A lucky combination of Airbnb search filters and the wine I drank that evening made my companion and I book Poros. Arrival and departure alone were highlights. We arrived on the last ferry due to a turbulent taxi ride. The ocean was restless, and on docking it was pouring rain. We fought our way through narrow streets with countless stairs. Exhausted and soaked to the bone, we were warmly welcomed at our rooms.

We visited Poseidon's sanctuary twice. Ignorant of its history on our first visit, in the scattered ruins where there is not much left to see, we left cold and confused. But we were lucky again. We met people in the village who taught us the sanctuary's ancient history. We

112   A HISTORY OF ASYLIA (SANCTUARY)

had to return. During the second visit our perceptions changed, and I was full of curiosity. I erected the sanctuary in my imagination and could feel the presence of ancient worshippers and its special energy. The rain started again while we were walking back.

Departure was a challenge as well. The winds and rains were so bad that the ferries did not run. Forced to take the bus to Athens, I gained new perspectives and views of the island, the countryside, and the stunning sea. It was a happy mixture of enjoyment and annoyance at the same time. My arrival and departure, combined with the rain, the stormy sea, and the newly gained knowledge of Poseidon and the island's history somehow became magical. We felt Poseidon's presence. It was just like the god had spoken.

When travelers like these arrive on Poros thinking it is just another small and beautiful island, they are often stricken by its spiritual energy and presence and by the overwhelming welcome by its people. In this they experience the love, support, and welcome of the divine.

With Poseidon, Demosthenes, and Lord Byron on Poros

Steven B. "Cicero" Katz and I traveled together to Krete and Santorini in 1997. We climbed the Santorini caldera, stared into the lava-stained depths of the volcanic cones, and contemplated the overwhelming powers of fire and quake ruled by the god-powers called Hephaistos and Poseidon. Then we journeyed to Poros, where on the island and nearby volcano, these god-powers are well known. Professor Katz declares, "The ancient sacred places not only exist geographically and physically, but in our hearts. Decades later, my spirit is still on Poros. It has never left the ruins in the hilltop grove. I can still smell and taste the ground and see the placement of every pinecone."

"Cicero" is drenched in literature, the classics, and rhetorical scholarship. He roams far and wide in intellectual investigations and imagination. He affirms Cicero's teaching that those who do not know the past are as children. He explores the origins and purposes of our vari-

A History of Asylia (Sanctuary) ∽ 113

ous forms of linguistic expression, affirms that we need both analysis and poetics, and believes, as did the first Cicero, that "the Pythagorean unity of all things in the universe is embodied *in the music of speech*."[10] How we express our inner lives poetically and how we persuade others discursively are intricately related.

> Originally there may have been little if any distinction between the forms and functions of poetry and rhetoric. In ancient societies, lyrical poems may have been used to deliberate and investigate as well as to condemn and eulogize. Plato was a poet in his younger years and, ironically, poetry may have helped originate his philosophy of Ideal Forms; it certainly did his dramatic style.[11]

Living experience combined with thoughtful analysis—Katz returned to ancient sites to investigate these dimensions of language and culture and breathe and stand where they had first developed.

The British Romantic poet Lord Byron also excelled in both oratory and poetry. He traveled in Greece from 1809 to 1811, explored remote territories by boat and horseback, visited Sounion and Marathon, lodged at the foot of the Akropolis on the old Street of the Tripods. He declared that Greece made him a poet. He returned to support and fight in the revolution and died while with the rebel troops in Missolonghi in 1824.

Though on the Peloponnesos and not far from Poros, there is no evidence that Byron was on the island. Still, Katz imagines that the passionate Romantic had carved his initials into the sanctuary's ancient stones. "I have seen it," he muses, "paid homage to it. I have heard his spirit there in the soft breeze like the ghost of a winter wind that easy blows."

Poet, orator, lover of Greece, and pilgrim, like the old poet he honors, Steven reflects on what did happen in the sanctuary.

> *Demosthenes had been here, seeking safety from the troops of Philip of Makedonia who pursued him because he stood up for truth, and because of the clarity and persuasive power of his pebble-filled mouth. Fleeing into the outstretched arms of this small island and seeking refuge in Poseidon's cove, he ultimately found that the escape offered*

by the sometimes fickle but always deep and profound god was through death—as gods usually do with the lucky ones. Perhaps death is better than being turned into a tree, a bird, a rock, or a hunted animal fleeing through the morning woods. Demosthenes's oratory could not save him this time. Suicide is a chosen door to freedom. But on clear days you can still hear the orator's stone-mumbled words ringing and roaring and articulate against the Saronic Gulf sky.

From the sanctuary that year, Steven, our companions, and I descended the snaking roads down a steep hillside to the beach and cove of Vagionia, now a sheltered and cave-strewn bay. In ancient times it was the sanctuary's harbor where Demosthenes and other asylum-seekers originally landed. Swimmers today can see the old harbor ruins under the crystalline waters. In those waters and on his mountain slope, Steven encountered the god-powers.

My relationship with Poseidon is one of ambiguity and wisdom. Poseidon knew before I did the guilt and sorrow that hovered over pleasantries of flowers and the heavy depth of the stones like darkening storm clouds, unseen. Thinking I escaped by finding my way through the maze of jellyfish Poseidon sent to "greet me" in his snoring cave of shallow water, he marked me with a searing wound to the calf as I tried to make my way up the hill winding from the ruined temple. It has become my Odyssean scar, a sacred wound that I happily carry until this day.

Steven describes the event in his poem,

I Swear by All the Gods
We were on motorbikes that day,
our modern versions of steeds
once nobly reined by the sea god
but now mechanized, loud, impersonal.
Our offerings in the churches, his prayers in the temple,
did not help me when, unable to climb
the twisted hill bent around the cliffs

A History of Asylia (Sanctuary)   115

below the temple . . .
where the grotto grumbles with the waves . . .
where in the grotto the god still snores . . .
But then Poseidon
abruptly gurgled, woke up, slowed me down
as my motorbike tried to climb the steep hill
and turn, and I began to spiral, I say:
he tipped me over and seared my leg against
the hot exhaust pipe—prayers did not help me . . .

Steven reflects,

I immediately understood why this had happened. While we circled
the island, the flesh of my leg flapped and burned in the breeze, as if
in joyful reverence of some unknown ritual. Poseidon had hurt me out
of warning based on love. I was at once in pain and happy, humbled,
and exalted.

In another poem, Steven affirms this mystical connection between
the human and the invisible and how we understand the physical events
of our world to derive from archetypal sources:

Poseidon is still here in his grotto,
his face in every tree and rock;
his trident split this little temple
of stone apart, broke it open.
Two thousand years later . . .
the archeologists
still came to sing the praises of
the ruins and the god. We come
to separate, depart, and pray
for safe passage. And below
Poseidon still
loudly snores
in his grotto,

> *a coastal grove,*
> *the island shaking—*
> *where I drove, swam, dove*
> *into the Styx, and almost*
> *drowned, but didn't[12]*

We hear, in these unsought, accidental, synchronistic occurrences, how we can experience and interpret them mythically. We seek the invisible behind the visible. Steven embraced his "accident" on the physical plane as a visit, teaching, and wound from the invisible energies we call Poseidon. We can do this with important and challenging life events by following synchronicities, interpreting events both literally and symbolically, using our imaginations and associations, realizing that suprapersonal powers are visiting us and discovering what they meant to the ancients. Thus, we learn to live mythically.

7

THE SUN OF POROS
Writers and Artists on Poros

> *It is never the floating mask we seek to capture, but the everlasting something beneath the mask, the kernel hidden in the husk.*
>
> HENRY MILLER, *GREECE*

Plato taught that beauty is food for the soul. For centuries, writers and artists have sought that soul food on Poros. Seferis rhapsodized, Ritsos contemplated. European landscape painters have been traveling and painting here for centuries. During the twentieth century, Marc Chagall and Lucien Freud both spent long artistic retreats on Poros with significant influence on their painting styles. Poros, though small and little known, is a haven that has exerted a subtle influence on Western art over the last several centuries. When Zorba's heart filled beyond what words could express, he danced. In the light of Poros and how it fills us, some of us write, some of us paint, and all of us can dance.

American Writers Find Poros

It was a beautiful and mild autumn. I sat at a small table under the Rota canopy, along the promenade and close to the water. I was in brilliant late sunlight, before gentle blue waters, under a huge sky stretching from the eastern end of the strait to the dark green mountains of Sleeping Lady.

As I ate, Christos Drougas put his hands on my shoulders, then pulled out a vacant chair and sat down. "I have a story to tell you," said my waiter and friend, smiling. "It is about another writer who came to our island." He then narrated a tale as if he had personally seen it and it had just happened yesterday. It was as Henry Miller had found during his travels here: "The poet would say 'there *was* . . . they *were* . . .' But the shepherd says *he lives, he is, he does* . . . The poet is always a thousand years too late. The shepherd is eternal."[1] And so are the waitstaff, postal clerks, laundry, and fisherfolk. Greeks live at once in the temporal and eternal and demonstrate that there is really no difference between these worlds.

Christos narrated,

In the 1930s, an American writer came and loved our island. He won a big lottery ticket, so he lived here until World War II. He returned after the war to see friends who had survived. He loved the island then. There were no cars, no internet, only small wooden boats. He felt our galini.

Along with some friends he rented a wooden boat to sail to Tinos island for the August 18 holy day. Floating through the islands he noticed many white spots. Inquiring, he was told they were small wooden churches. They were visible because there were no trees to block the high winds. "Why are there few churches on Poros?" he asked. Because at that time Dionysos ruled. Here where the rows of tavernas serve our tourists now, there were also endless rows of tavernas, but these had no food, no cooking. Instead, countless barrels of local wine were piled to the ceilings. Local men came to drink, talk, sing, and party, sometimes nonstop for two or three days.

THE SUN OF POROS ⟡ 119

Hydra, our southern neighbor island, was discovered decades later because in 1968 the movie Girls in the Sun was made there. Following that, artists and writers built it up and the regional development slowly spread to Poros. In the mid-1980s British companies arrived. They built up Askeli Beach with thousands of new modern rooms along the bay. From that time on, Poros has been steadily transforming into the tourist island it is now. The long rows of wine barrels disappeared. Tavernas added kitchens and transformed into eating establishments.

Christos sat back and smiled.

"Do you know who the writer was?" I asked.

"No." He shrugged, rose, and walked off to tend others.

Was Christos referring to Henry Miller, who rhapsodizes over his time on Poros and other islands and his friendship with George Seferis in his book *The Colossus of Maroussi*? I asked later if he thought so.

"Maybe," he said. He pointed to Galini, Seferis's villa across the bay. "Seferis was a gentle and sensitive man. We know they had a friendship."

It could not have been Miller because Seferis was in residence on Poros after World War II. It had to have been Peter Gray, the American journalist and novelist. He lived here during two, two-year periods at the beginning and the end of the 1930s, recorded in his *People of Poros*, published during World War II. Library director Yannis explains that Gray's book was influential in both the United States and Great Britain in evoking support and sympathy for the Greek cause during the war.

During Gray's first stay there had been no cars, water taxis, or radios, and he had joyously joined the local men in those wine emporiums. By the time he arrived for his second visit in 1937, twenty radios had arrived. Then, instead of carousing, drinking, storytelling, and singing together, many locals gathered in front of their radios to listen to the tinny music broadcast for mass consumption on those early machines.

Peter Gray's sojourns here were in the 1930s, Henry Miller's time with Seferis and in the region was at that decade's end as World War II was first igniting. The literary history of Poros continued to unfold during the twentieth century. The Greek American poet and translator

120   *THE SUN OF POROS*

Kimon Friar retreated to Poros in 1950 to work on his monumental translation of Kazantzakis's *The Odyssey: A Modern Sequel*. During this time, James Merrill, the young American poet and Friar's lover, first visited. Friar and Merrill had met as English instructor and gifted undergraduate at Amherst College in Massachusetts and entered an erotic literary mentoring relationship modelled on ancient Greek practices. Friar had been enticing Merrill to come to his "spiritual home" of Poros for years.[2]

After their affair ended and beginning in the 1950s, Merrill spent much time in Greece. He lived on Poros from 1956 to 1957 and dubbed it "Diblos" in his writing. It was from this literary dubbing, Yannis Maniatis declares, that Poros became known as a double island.

Merrill traveled, visited, and lived on the island, composing *The (Diblos) Notebook* about this time. He wrote experimentally, at once working on a novel, demonstrating its composition through an unusual incomplete manuscript-like structure, recording ordinary people and events to squeeze human passions and follies from them, and documenting the "brotherhood" he had shared with Friar.

Merrill described the art of conversation in the tavernas that keep people long beyond mealtimes and that we share to this day:

> Time for people, time to talk and show interest, to make . . . listeners feel that their minds were rare and flexible, time to welcome a stranger into the circle with some deft bit of nonsense from the speaker's well of inexhaustible friendliness. This kind of conversation finds its happiest expression in the dialogues of Plato. . . . The system worked like a charm at the waterfront café where half a dozen idle citizens would be spellbound for hours on end.[3]

Merrill, like Seferis, was captivated by the island's nights. "What one *can* use is the poetry of the night, the lights running across the black water toward us . . . the music dwarfed . . . by the immense starry silences around it. To swim then . . . the genie conjured up out of oneself."[4]

And like Peter Gray decades before, Merrill decried the impact of "America . . . buying Europe, country by country." He saw Greece being

Fig. 7.1. Fishermen on the waters in the early morning off the northern point of the island and into the wide sea.
PHOTOGRAPH BY TASOS RODIS

spoiled, its traditional charm along with its tavernas disappearing. "The next victim was clearly Greece."[5]

Kimon Friar was born in Turkey in 1911. His family moved to the United States in 1915, and he became a naturalized citizen. He spent many years on Poros, living in a cottage on the secluded Love Bay as he worked on his translation of Kazantzakis's massive epic, which was published in 1958. He married and spent his elder years on Poros and in Greece. His wife was considered an oracle and an expert tarot card reader.

John Lennon visited them on Poros in 1980 during a time of personal confusion. He sought guidance from Friar's wife. Her tarot reading for Lennon revealed this oracle: "Take care of your life." Half a year later, Lennon was assassinated.[6] Friar died in Athens in 1993.

Gray, Miller, Friar, Merrill—and Hemingway?*

I was on my early morning walk, a mile along the harbor front, past old houses and small shops, fisherfolk and lines of yachts and fishing vessels still moored in the dawn light. I reached the northern tip of

---

*See Giannis Soudiotis, *O Poros Einai*, for a Greek literary history of Poros from ancient to modern times that includes the American writers considered herein.

122   THE SUN OF POROS

the road where it ends at a small church and half-crumbled lighthouse. There I met my friend Evangelos Papaioannou walking back toward the village. Evangelos is a recreational fisherman, itinerant philosopher and artist, and the father and helper of Mary, the owner of a small laundromat down Ermou St., the stone-paved alley from my hotel.

Evangelos is tall, strong, and loquacious. His expressions range vividly from joyous to thoughtful to concerned to resigned and back again. Whenever we meet, we dive into at least a few minutes of philosophical and cultural reflections ranging from the intimate to the cosmic. Strutting up to me this day, Evangelos spread his arms wide to embrace the early spring summerlike day. "What are our little human problems," he declared by way of greeting, "when we live in paradise?" Evangelos then launched into his morning story.

"I awoke this morning at 5 a.m.," he began in his full, enthusiastic voice. "I usually go fishing in the afternoon. But I was wide awake at dawn. So, I turned to my wife fast asleep by my side. I thought to myself, 'Fishing is better.' I quietly climbed out of bed and left."

"I understand your choice," I chuckled.

"We men need our adventures," he affirmed.

"So how was fishing this morning?"

Evangelos spread his long arms wide again. "I hooked a big one." He smiled. "But not only did he get away. Not only did he take my bait and its small hook. He took my big hook imported from England. I cannot replace it here." He shrugged. "Oh well. It's the eternal struggle between man and beast, man and the sea."

"Yes," I agreed. "Do you know the American writer, Ernest Hemingway?"

"Of course," Evangelos declared. "He stayed and fished here," he pointed to the wharf. "And there." He pointed across the bay to the Villa Galini.

Was this yet another confusion of American writers? As a young journalist Hemingway had spent 1920–1922 in Constantinople reporting on the violent expulsion of the Greek population for the *Toronto Star*. This was portrayed in his short story "On the Quay at Smyrna" and mentioned in *Death in the Afternoon* and "The Snows of Kilimanjaro."

THE SUN OF POROS ᕲ 123

But, no less than Lord Byron, Hemingway had never been to the island. The spirit of Poros spins out literary myths beyond the history that occurred here.

I clapped Evangelos on the shoulder. "Do you know his book *The Old Man and the Sea*?" I asked.

"Of course!" he smiled. "The heroic and tragic contest between man and beast, man and man, man and himself."

"Yes," I said. "You lost your great fish today. You had your version of that tale. It is your story too."

"*Alitheia*!" Evangelos declared. "True! Thank you," he smiled. "You are a good man." Then he strode on.

At the end of Christos's tale narrated as if it were his memory, his gentle eyes looked into mine. He said, "I tell you this story because you are the next American writer coming here to understand and love our island. Tell the story. Share it."

I felt an election, a charge of responsibility. Living myth and memory, not literary artifact. Everything is story. Story here is history. Mythic history. Mythistorema. Tell the story. Join our small, short lives to the living myth. Be the next chapter in the endless story.

Modern Artists Seeing Anew

I sit on the small balcony of my room at 7 Brothers Hotel, on the quay next to Rota on one side and the post office where Dmitri worked for decades on the other. I look northward down the quaint alley lined with the Ipapanti Church, a sweetshop, optician's office, herbalist, used book exchange, and newly opened traditional taverna Sokaki. The other direction reveals the tables and chairs of Rota and Clock Tower coffeehouse. Straight ahead and over the red-tiled roof in front of me is the blue strait and across the waters the small smiling row of houses and stores that is Galatas. I sit here in the quiet, soft first light of dawn when the early garbage collector clangs by on foot, pushing his heavy can. The lights go off in the morning or on in the evening, small and soft yellow circles against the blue-black night. I gaze into the eye-squinting light of midday and the sinking colors of twilight. The black

124 ∽ *THE SUN OF POROS*

mountains of night become gray, then green, then fade to black again. I feel as though I could sit here as if beside Heraklitos's eternally changeless yet ever-changing river, content to watch the centuries flow by as if each of us were souls of flickering light that endlessly arrive and quickly leave the ever-living earth.

These changing lights and colors, this shifting yet eternal vision that Poros gifts, has attracted artists for centuries. In the 1800s many seers wandering Europe seeking the most arresting lights and vistas found their way to Poros. They were enthralled with the landscapes. They climbed the heights, painted the bays, the town from a distance, the monastery among green trees, close-ups of the volcanic outcroppings, even portraits of rocks. They painted the women in traditional and colorful dress, the low buildings in all the changing lights, small groups in festive gatherings before the waters. They contemplated and tried to capture the ever-shifting colors and shapes to freeze them on canvas so that for moments, as art can do for us, we feel rooted and can contemplate our place in the ceaseless cosmos.

On this island, artists and writers seeking inspiration find much more—a sense of belonging. They are embraced as critical, necessary, and beloved participants in the life of community, humanity, nature. If we have an art form, we are taught to see anew. We are restored, reunited, and celebrated by the locals for whom life on Poros even with its modern challenges is paradise.

The eighteenth and nineteenth centuries brought artists from various European nations who left realistically rendered canvases of the landscapes, boats, faces, and dress they saw here.* The twentieth century brought names of renown with radical styles challenging how we see.

Apollonian Light

The Russian Jewish artist Marc Chagall painted his canvas *The Sun of Poros* in 1968. We see rectangles and squares of vibrant colors: blue with

---

*For a history (in Greek) of nineteenth-century European painters who worked on Poros, see Giorgos Athanasiou, *O Poros Stous Zografous Tou 19th Aiona*.

THE SUN OF POROS ∽ 125

lovers embracing; a vase of bursting yellow, red, and white flowers on a lively green field; a red sky with a hot orange sun; and an island floating in the background seen through a vaguely open window. This was painted when the artist was in his eighties, fourteen years after his last visit to Poros. Approaching the end of his days he displayed his recollection of his joyous Poros months with bright sun and lively colors that had penetrated his imagination and remained with him during his long life and creative career.

In 1952 and middle age, while researching for illustrations to the Paris production of Ravel's opera *Daphne and Chloe*, Mark Chagall spent time in Greece. He lived in the Villa Galini for three months. He returned in 1954 and also traveled to Lesbos.

Before these sojourns his canvases were characterized by dark and somber scenes and tones expressing his Eastern European heritage. His time on Poros transformed his art. One of his paintings entitled *Poros 1954* shows a blue boat next to a flower vase with greenery, and red and white blooms against a blue sea with the harbor town across the bay. Another canvas by the same name shows a happy man on a green hillside holding the hand of his beloved as in her purple dress she floats in the cloud-billowing sky above him. The floating couple and scattered animals and faces are familiar from his Russian-inspired canvases. But these are full of vibrant rather than somber colors and people. We have the sense that the floating people are celebrating island life rather than elevating above it to escape earthly hardships. In his late-1980 painting *The Island of Poros* a young man with his artist tools is held aloft in a soothing blue sky flying over a fish-thick sea with a small island in the distance. The artist is supported in flight by an angel. Both are surrounded by nude figures and animals along with fresh greenery, all in a grand circle of life.

About his sojourn on Poros, Chagall said, "That summer I learned the Apollonian light." New shapes, colors, and images paraded on his canvases. His art had previously been sunken deeply into the Jewish European experience and that root of Western civilization. On Poros the second root, the Greek, penetrated Chagall and suffused his canvases with "the sun of Poros." From this time on and into old age, his art portrayed both explosive colors and mythological as well as

126   THE SUN OF POROS

Russian peasant and Jewish themes. On Poros he and his art achieved an awakening that captures and transmits the irresistible penetration of Mediterranean sunlight.

Chagall lived in Villa Galini where Seferis had, but he often painted on the highest pinnacle of Poros town. Today a modest, incense-thick and icon-rich church crowns his height. A high street with his artist's-eye view bears his name. From this height we too are penetrated by the light and view that helped evolve Chagall's art into a twin-rooted and vibrant celebration of life. We observe how even as great of an artist as Chagall had his "doors of perception" blasted open and remade by the natural sensual qualities of humble Poros. He literally saw light more vibrantly, more brilliantly than before being on Poros; and his canvases enable the same for their viewers.

In the Houses of Art

Climb steep white stairs. Saunter between picturesque old houses with citrus fruit trees, grapevines, colored shutters. Pass the library. Pass a doctor's office. Arrive at a traditional old house on the street above and parallel to the water. It looks down on the quaint, winding street that continues to climb steeply up the village hill toward the clock tower. This old house with a modest historical marker was where the British artists Lucien Freud and John Craxton lived and painted from 1946 to 1947.

Lucien Freud, the British grandson of Sigmund, is recognized as one of the great portraitists of the modern era. He spent months on Poros with his friend and early painting experimentalist, John Craxton. Craxton received less distinction in his lifetime than Freud but has gradually been recognized as a leading artist of Greek portraiture, landscapes, and village scenes. He spent years on Poros and decades in Greece, finally making his home on Krete.

Early in their careers Freud and Craxton were both influenced by the expressionism and surrealism of their era. Later each veered back to a realism with unique styles. Freud's portraits are intimate and intense and seem to reveal the psychology of the subject through their mul-tilayered faces and torsos. Craxton was a hedonist who delighted in drenching himself in the many lights, landscapes, meetings, and experiences available through his love affair with Greece that he eventually portrayed across hundreds of canvases.

Freud and Craxton shared a short but intense friendship that deeply influenced their lives and art. They met in college, cavorted around London in wild bohemian fashion, and finally Freud followed Craxton to Poros. They lived together for months that were spent drawing and painting each other in a passionate and consuming way. Later they fell out and developed bitterness and rivalry, Freud returning to England and Craxton making his home on Krete. Their time on Poros was pregnant and transformational for each. The intensely private and personal Freud delved into his unique portrait style. The hedonist Craxton fell deeply and passionately in love with Greece such that he would live and work there until his death. Months and a few years on Poros led each artist to his own true style and path through life.

Pamela Jane Rogers is an American artist who has been devoted to a decades-long study of the island's grand and minute revelations. "On Poros," she wrote, "I'm able to bask in the immediate and translucent quality of life." Pamela, from North Carolina, moved to Poros in 1990. She not only basks. She captures and records this translucency in her countless paintings of the island rendered in oils, pens, or especially in watercolors, with styles that range from realistic to impressionistic to abstract. "The fluid process of watercolor," she explains, "seems to best capture the colorful and impulsive spirit of island life"[7]—not only in her art, but in her focus on the minutiae of island life and how it shapes her creative process, translucency beams.

One evening I was inspired to use watercolor for a trio of colorfully decorated and delectable slices of cake from the sweet shop after I'd tasted one of them. Another afternoon I was motivated to open my gouache tubes to capture bright fruits and vegetables fresh from the farmer's market, spilling from their brown paper bags. . . . Yesterday morning I watched fish being pulled from their nets, with seaweed still attached, and that rang my chimes to paint in oil.[8]

128 ∞ *THE SUN OF POROS*

On Poros, lemons and tomatoes, boats and clouds in the glaring light, ripples of the sea and steaming cups of tea inspire Pamela. It is as if artist and island have entered a permanent and reciprocal exchange of beauty, sensuality, and serenity.

Pamela and I first met over our mutual love of Poros. Traveling here since 1987, I published an article on the island in *The New York Times* in 1995. Pamela, here since 1990, attests that the article brought many people to Poros seeking the authentic and traditional Greece. It fed her work and enlarged the community. She saved and referenced the article as over decades she worked as director of an educational program, bringing around eight thousand U.S. and Canadian university alumni to Poros over sixteen years in spring and fall.

Debra Brown is an African American navy veteran and artist who has visited Poros with me twice. On our journey before the pandemic, she had arranged to connect as artist-to-artist with Pamela. They were to meet at the clock tower. At the appointed hour Debra climbed the steep stairs and waited on the tower heights while Pamela waited at a coffee shop called Clock Tower on the street in front of our hotel.

I walked up. The pert, polite woman with blond hair asked, "Do you by any chance know . . . ?"

We figured out the mix-up and I called Debra. Then Pamela asked, "Well then, do you by any chance know Edward Tick?" Proof of our small world! We were friends from that moment, and she completed another story.

The *Times* article featured a photo of a slender smiling fisherman dangling his catch of octopus. "Your article was published when the man was quite ill," she told me. "His family brought the paper to him on his sickbed. 'I am famous,' he said. 'They know me in New York.' He died with a smile on his face."

Pamela paints Poros. And then she paints Poros. And more Poros. She is primarily a landscape painter, not a portraitist. She declares, "I have been on and painted more than thirty Greek islands. Poros is the best."

Pamela's paintings display colorful soothing or striking landscapes— hills, beaches, rocks, trees, multicolored shimmering waters, coves, old buildings in variegated lights, fishing boats, close-up and distant views, schoolchildren, a decorated donkey, placid gardens, sun-sleeping balconies, thick and gnarly olive trees. In her home, some of these works are neatly but thickly spread between strong and handsome old furniture belonging to a bygone age. Garden, furnishings, artwork all create a Poriot* ecology of—what else?—*orea kai galini*, or beauty and serenity.

Pamela's dwelling itself is in the artistic tradition of the island, across the bay from Seferis's Villa Galini. It is a strong older home, built in 1892, that towers over the stone-paved street below and is in the village's protected historical area with a view over the main harbor. Pamela moved there in 2005, when church bells seemed to shake the walls and donkeys clomped in the street below to collect the trash. Now, Pamela explains, "The quay has been expanded and is much busier than in years past, with sailing and other yachts filling it with holidaymakers throughout the summer. I cherish painting time during the quieter late autumn, winter, and early spring months when the island is less crowded."

Pamela has lived on Poros more than thirty-three years and has painted more than one thousand images of it. This makes Pamela Jane Rogers of North Carolina the longest in residence and most prolific in output of any artist that has lived or worked on Poros.

Pamela's work has been extensively shown throughout Greece and in the United States where she is represented by City Art Gallery in Greenville, North Carolina and is shown around the southern states where she has won numerous awards. Her work is included in numerous collections, including the British Royal Collection. A few of her blue-green landscapes hang on the walls of Taverna Sti Rota. Yet she never runs out of inspiration. "All my paintings of Poros are from life and experience," she explains. "Here I am drenched in the lives, languages, sounds, music. This island is forty-five thousand years old. It is volcanic rock on a seabed of crystals. The island feels like it floats, but layers and layers of brilliance show through. That is what I endlessly seek to show in my paintings." She testifies to what we need now more than ever— "The beauty and serendipity of Poros continues to encourage the arts and literature through these difficult times."[9]

---

*"of Poros"

130 ～ *THE SUN OF POROS*

I have wandered in silence, awe, and sensual joy before her canvases. Her work displays Poros in every aspect—bright sun, cloudy skies, dawn, dusk, countless colors vibrating in the waters, green and purple mountains in repose. Of all Pamela's paintings, my personal favorite is *Poros Twilight*. The writers Seferis and Merrill both wrote of the magical evening lights. I am rendered drunk every twilight as the blue sky fades and darkens and small yellow and white lights click on along both the Poros and Galatas coasts and among the houses that climb their hills. Pamela's painting reveals the myriad shades of blues, grays, purples, and blacks that are never still but, like Heraklitos's river, in constant motion and change. Her paintings draw the curtain aside to reveal eternal beauty manifesting in every small Poros moment.

"How do you let your paintings go?" I asked her.

"Letting a painting go is like raising a child," she said. "You birth it. You wean it. You let it go into the world."

After one of our discussions on the complexity of life and art, I ask simply, "How do you choose what you paint?"

Pamela smiles. Her eyes shine. Her hands open to indicate the world. "I don't paint by assignment," she says in her slight southern lilt. "Not by style or conscious choice. I paint what I fall in love with. I must fall in love. Long ago I fell in love with Poros."

Symbolism on the Strait

I walked along the sun-drenched blue strait to one of the many old buildings fronting the waters past the museum. I climbed the stairs to a second-floor apartment. The slender smiling artist welcomed me into her flat. As I crossed the threshold my eyes and brain flooded. It seemed I was not in a Poros harbor apartment, but in some archetypal terrain bursting with giant sea turtles and sea horses, priestesses and goddesses, hummingbirds and volcanoes, flowers flowing out of women's heads or cascades of colorful hair sprouting with their breasts, waters in a ceaseless movement of bright superreal and unreal reds, greens, blues, purples. The walls of every room were thick with these images. They danced in my subconscious so that I felt propelled into a dream world even as I could see the calm blue waters of the strait through the living room windows.

Ivi Gabrielides qualifies for Diogenes's word *cosmopolitan*. Her heritage, ancestors, family, educational, and personal histories have roots and passages over much of the eastern world. Her grandparents were from Izmir, Turkey. Politics forced them to move to Anatolia, then forced another move after World War II. Grandfather grew up among vineyards and so opened the first wine production business in Syria. Ivi was born and raised in Aleppo.

Ivi attended French School in Syria, then moved to Italy to continue her education and development as an artist. From schooling through practicing and exhibiting as a fine artist, Ivi spent twenty-four years in Rome. She moved to Greece and has been active in exhibitions and teaching since 2010. Continuing the family world citizenship tradition, her son lives in Portugal, where she visits and paints.

I roam her apartment. I stand before a painting called *Double Idol* in which numerous masculine and feminine symbols erupt from a volcano. A mandala of swirling red energy erupts from another volcano that seems liquified. Yet another is made of colored energy lines flowing into the sea below and sky above. Poros is a volcanic island, and Ivi's colorful and movement-swirling canvases evoke the invisible emanations of energy from its unique ecology. I study an icon of St. George she painted for her brother and another that looks like Apollo with his own volcano that seems to sprout a question mark in billowing fumes. A colorful inverted pyramid also radiates intense energy. Ivi says it is the same energy she felt at a volcanic lake in Italy. And perhaps the energy radiating beneath this house on Poseidon's island?

"I feel like I am in another world," I say. "It is magical, mystical, full of invisible realities, vibrating with cosmic energy and movement."

"Yes," Ivi explains. "My life experiences have taught me to travel between realities and worlds. I seek to move slowly and with clarity between them."

"How do you describe your style?"

132 ∾ THE SUN OF POROS

"I don't have a style or dwell in a box," Ivi answered. "I studied iconography and antique techniques. Now I use them in my own way. I meditate and receive images. I make the images real in my art."

Ivi is an open spigot of archetypal imagery. Magical hummingbirds of every hue sail across many canvases. Female heads, busts, torsos of goddesses, priestesses, kores—some echo archaic statuary but with renewed energies, colors, movements, fauna. I imagine standing in front of a kore with a frozen stone visage while seeing scores of faces with different markings and colors cascade out, as if Ivi is showing us how images sprout in a mystic's visions.

Ivi's website proclaims, without explanation and below every image, the one word, *Symbolism*. A symbol is an image used to represent something else, something deeper, older, larger, more abstract, something ineffable that can only be grasped when grounded in its material manifestation. In Ivi's imaginal world, we are awash in archetypal symbolism—the unseen energies and invisible realities behind appearances made tangible and visible through art and dreams.

"Why Poros?" I ask.

"Like everyone I had periods of hardship in life, so my dream became to live on an island. I had come to Poros in summers for holiday when I was young. So, I knew that here was where I could find serendipity. It seems impossible and a great blessing to me to have accomplished my dream. I have lived serenely in this house for eleven years."

I wander her dense and vibrant collection. Dear to my heart, Ivi has painted many turtles—mating, sunning on each other's backs, swimming under water, heads breaking the surface, sprouting flowers, carousing alone and together, emerging beside a volcano, swirling in yin-yang fashion around each other.

When I leave Ivi's apartment the blues of the strait and sky, reds and whites of the buildings, undulations in the mountains and waters seem stronger, more pronounced, more fluid. Ivi's art shows that what we see before and around us is the invisible and eternal embodied in the material. Her art takes us on travels between worlds.

Voice and Vision

Not a native Poriotis, Demosthenes Koumaridis is known as Demos. Of average height but broad and with a huge warm smile, he can be found swimming off Askeli Beach "at least eleven months of the year."

Demos was born in northern Thessaloniki and has lived around Greece and abroad, especially in London. Though he returns to the UK to visit friends and family, he always aches to return to the island where he settled permanently fourteen years ago. As a musician he has become known as "the Voice of Poros." With a huge inventory of traditional, folk, dance, and modern Greek and international songs, he sings and accompanies himself on the bouzouki and guitar at different tavernas and cultural events.

I have known Demos for years. I attend his performances whenever possible and he plays for my pilgrimage groups, infecting them with joy and vitality. I sit near him to watch his fingers fly, discuss songs, translate, or ask for meanings, sway, and clap along. Whether with locals or visitors, in cold weather or warm, Demos enlivens the atmosphere so that strangers become friends and dance partners. Dionysos the dancing god seems to dwell in his voice and instrument.

Many evenings another regular guest, a good friend of Demos, has perched at a nearby table. We often sang "Sto Periali" together. It is Seferis's poem "Denial." Though previously unacquainted, in the song our eyes met, and we smiled as we both squeezed "Orea . . . Beauty blew the breeze . . ." out of our voice boxes and into the atmosphere.

This singing companion is Christos Papadopoulos. He is trim, fit, slender, strong. His eyes are intense, and his face seems sculpted. As a young man he was a national champion in gymnastics and diving and continues to keep himself in top condition. At eighty-two years old he seems going on sixty. Shaking hands, he could have crushed mine. "I expect to live to be more than a century old and remain in good, strong health," he declares. "Why die when there is so much to live for? And why live if we can't enjoy it?" As both athlete and artist Christos would agree with Hippokrates that "the human body is the greatest work of art."

134 ✺ THE SUN OF POROS

Christos is world famous in painting, mosaics, tapestry, macrame, bronze and copper sculptures. Born on Poros in 1941, he grew up in a poor family so as a young man took charge of his own life. Disliking traditional school, he entered the Naval Academy at age sixteen, at the same time teaching himself art. "I realized I was not a soldier," so Christos arranged to spend his naval time copying the works of great artists. His commander allowed this at the cost of taking Christos's paintings for himself. "It was no loss," Christos reflects. "They were only copies, and it allowed me to train myself as an artist."

Christos left the academy at age eighteen, lived in Philadelphia and Athens, all the while teaching himself art while he met teachers and helpers. Over the years he met sponsors and gained significant recognition that has grown into an international reputation. His art is now housed in many museums, and he has decorated corporate headquarters, hotels, cruise ships, and royal palaces in Iran, Jordan, and Morocco. After a quarter century abroad, Christos returned to Poros to contribute his skills to beautifying his home and island and teaching children to honor and use the arts. He has contributed to the island's evolving beauty by painting some of the striking municipal and shop signs around the waterfront and village. His painting style has great range, from colorful, striking, and exquisitely rendered landscapes to folk-art style depictions of Greek social life in tavernas and kafenia, from archetypal imagery of red devils to surreal depictions of human figures in fantastical colors and settings. He seems Platonic in declaring that beauty is a spiritual property and the best thing we can do is teach children to create, respect, and worship it. Christos is a world-recognized artist of many forms and styles whose parenthood is this humble island. He could rightly be considered a renaissance artist of Poros.

We sat together at a table at Rota as Demos played.

"Artists reveal truth that others cannot discern," Christos said as Demos plucked. "The artists discover it, and the generals take it and use it. It has always been this way."

Christos, as so many Greeks, is enthusiastic about Greek contributions to world culture. "It all descends from Homer," he says. *"Musiki, harmonia, tragodia, comedia, poesis,* the sciences," he says. "We cannot talk about truth without the Greek."

"You have lived all over the world and brought your art to powerful people. How do you communicate this to others who do not know?" I asked.

"A scholar once told me that Greece was a small and unimportant country," he answered with a sly smile. "I kept instructing him on our contributions until he broke down and cried. Small does not mean unimportant. It can be even more so."

"How does your philosophy shape your strategy for living in our troubled world?"

"It is the general's task to control," he answered. "It is the artist's task to see. My goal as an artist is simple—help people see."

Demos's music got stronger and louder. Diners swayed in their seats, then pushed their chairs away and surrendered to the dance. The small floor at Rota became a stage of exuberance and joy. Dionysos was arriving.

"Do you want to join them?" I asked.

"I can dance," Christos smiled. "But I'd rather paint."

We chuckled. Demos saw us. Knowing we both loved it, he played "Sto Periali." Our eyes locked, we stretched our necks, and together we clumsily but passionately sang in Greek, "with what heart, with what ache / what passion and what strife . . . Orea." Beauty.

8

IN THE AGORA
Meandering the Streets

He whom I sought I am.
ODYSSEUS ELYTIS, "LACONIC"

Poros is indeed a village in the old-fashioned sense. Among the permanent residents and those who become part of the community, everybody seems to know everybody. Many people are related. Extended families stretch throughout the town and over many generations. Giorgos, Christos, and others affirm that they have grown decades-long friendships with many visitors who return again and again and invite them to their homes overseas.

After decades of visits, and though I value and have used several, always on the old harbor, I have settled into my own favorite hotel, 7 Brothers, in the village center and on the strait. I often visit and dine next door at Taverna Sti Rota. Indeed, 7 Brothers feels like my living room and bedroom, with a narrow balcony from which I contemplate the strait, Galatas across the way, and Sleeping Woman to the southwest in every variegated light and weather. Rota feels like my dining room and strait-side veranda where I meet friends, have lively and deep conversations, and am told, "You are not a visitor, you are a local." Giorgos and Nikki, my hotel hosts, have become friends and I attended their son's baptism in the Church of St. George. One of their cousins is my barber. Giorgos of Rota was a close friend, confidante, mentor, wise elder, community rock, and sincere follower of Orthodoxy. His sister Marina is my dentist with an office down the street. Sitting in her dental chair as we chat and she works on me, I gaze out her eastern window and enjoy the view of the sparkling blue strait and gleaming village across the way. Dental work has never been so pleasant, responsive, and reasonable.

Here is my typical Sunday morning on Poros. The sun is high and bright, the sky and waters gleaming blue. The low white buildings of Galatas across the waters sparkle. People stroll. Elders teach grandchildren how to fish. Tavernas and coffee shops fill with families, friends, and neighbors visiting as they sip their coffees and share life's mysteries and trivialities.

I walk down my hotel staircase and meet another guest. Stathis, from the mainland, is visiting his son in the Naval Academy. We have a twenty-minute conversation about ancient versus modern Greek languages and cultures. I proceed down. Nikki and I greet each other and discuss the night or the local conditions. I walk to a nearby coffee shop and meet with Babis, the journalist. We discuss twentieth-century history on Poros, service in the military in our two countries, the ethics built into Greek culture, how to live a life of honor. We force our conversation to end because he has other responsibilities. I take a long stroll along the water's edge. From the island's only book and stationary store a half mile down the street, I buy the *International Sunday Times* and a children's mythology book in Greek to practice my language skills. Gregorios the proprietor smiles and suggests that I watch Greek television news to hone my language skills. "We speak very fast," he explains. "You will not understand much but it will accustom you to our way of talking." Continuing my stroll, I meet Menios in front of his house with an ornate 1800s iron gate and a tall and scraggly orange tree full of dangling fruit. It has been in his family for three generations. We compare living and housing, populations, and weather conditions in our two countries. I continue and greet my dentist Marina at Sunday feast

138   IN THE AGORA

with her family. I find Christina from Sweden, living here much of the year now for her health and fair weather. I greet artist Pamela Rogers, having coffee with another friend. Arriving back at 7 Brothers, Giorgos the host and I discuss the educational system, how it is changing, and the challenges and negative consequences of shortened attention span and lack of respect for tradition and elders that even Poros children are experiencing due to the influence of the internet. Giorgos is a high school science teacher during the week. He feels compassion, not judgment, for his students as they are growing up in such challenging times. "It is not their fault," he says. "It is ours." As we talk, Fay Orfanidou, director of Katheti cultural center, finds me and we plan a coffee and meeting in a few days. Katheti is building a new center right on the Poros waterfront and Tasos, now home on Poros to stay, works with them. Finally, I step inside my hotel and Nikki delivers the message that Yanni called to make an appointment for our library meeting tomorrow when we will continue to plumb the complexities of Poros history and culture. My sense of isolation, alienation, and anomie, carried from the United States, dissolves as I become an active and engaged part of the village life of Poros.

This, on Sunday when the entire village turns out, characterizes daily life as well.

In the agora, businesspeople conduct their work for survival, of course, for what the ancients called instrumental values. But business here seems often to be "the bottom line," which should not signify the ultimate, as the phrase is used in America, but the matter of least importance. I step into a small traditional gift shop. My discussion with Manolis, the owner, is so rich and complex that when I am ready to leave, he says, "Wait. I'll close my shop and we can continue our discussion over coffee."

"Mustn't you work? You will lose business," I protest as he hangs a closed sign in his door.

Manolis counters, "Work is not important. Friendship is."

There are times other than for friendship that shops might close and business ceases. National and religious holidays bring out the entire island as priests, officials, families, schoolchildren, and cadets

Fig. 8.1. The agora facing the strait, for centuries the island's traditional marketplace.
PHOTOGRAPH FROM THE HATZOPOULEIOS PUBLIC LIBRARY ARCHIVES

gather in the squares and at their monuments in communal pride and celebrations.

The agora thins annually during November. This is olive harvest time and involves nearly everyone. Many Poriotes own small plots of land on the island or on the Peloponnese side that are thick with old and hearty olive trees. Many others hire out as workers. During harvest, several weeks of intense labor bring the many barrels of olives off the trees to be trucked to the mill and processed into fine oil that will feed a family for the entire year and, perhaps, give them some to gift or sell. It is also a time to gather wild herbs and teas and harvest honey. These practices are healthy and maintain old traditions. They are also a necessity as some families are partially dependent on self-sufficiency. They must gather wild greens and, struggling to afford electricity, do their own laundry.

In both ancient and modern Greek, the word *agora* is used for an open marketplace, a place to buy and sell food and goods and exchange monies. But the ancient agora in Athens and other places was not only for shopping. It was full of altars, temples, official buildings, shops, open stalls, money changers' tables, artisan and craft shops. Sokrates,

140   IN THE AGORA

the Stoics, and the Sophists taught and preached there for all to hear. Warriors and athletes drilled on its central common.

The English word *agoraphobia* traces to this: *agora*, or open marketplace; *fobos*, or phobia, terror, worshipped in archaic times as a godpower. Agoraphobia is literally terror of the open marketplace. But the word *agora* derives from the ancient verb *agoreuin*, which meant "to talk." "The market aspect of the agora was but a by-product of any gathering's chief function: talk."[1] Agora originally referred to talking together, and in ancient Greek it also meant a place for meeting, public assembly, congregation, council. When people meet to talk together, a passionate Greek love, they create their civic center. And wherever they gather, farmers, jewelers, potters, sandal makers will market their wares. A gathering place naturally but not exclusively becomes a marketplace. American malls do not qualify; they are places to shop, have coffee or food, see movies. But they do not have philosophers roaming and teaching, athletes and warriors training, civic business being conducted, philosophies being taught and debated. Strangers do not gather. Malls do not host public gatherings or even allow political freedom of speech.

Greek and Poriot tavernas and kafenia are not restaurants and coffee shops in the American sense. We do not go there to be alone or with a few family members or friends to be served for a short time while others do the work. And we do not rush away after finishing our meals. On Poros and throughout Greece, these establishments, and the agora itself, is a place where people congregate to pass and enrich time together. There, Peter Gray wrote in the 1930s, and we still do today,

> You told myths . . . watching the street. . . . You fingered conversation beads, swapped lies, read newspapers, talked politics, played backgammon, sauntered, drank, bragged, intrigued, bargained, peered, quarreled, dozed, knitted, embroidered, argued, swaggered, and flirted.[2]

Such gathering places evolve into cultural and civic centers and naturally attract those with goods to sell. Marketplace, of course—but that is the bottom line, the instrumental not the ultimate purpose, in

IN THE AGORA ∞ 141

Plato's terms the consequence and not the cause. The higher purpose, the cause, is gathering. So it was here in Greece and on Poros. So it is now. On Poros I gather with friends and neighbors whose lives are entwined, with philosophers trying to understand life's mysteries and complexities, with a public passionate about their history and politics. Ancient or modern become irrelevant; we are in an agora.

Psychotherapist and poet Kate Dahlstedt has traveled to Greece numerous times. She describes her first visit and encounter with the old city and agora of Athens.

> My first memory of Greece was in 1984 with my new husband walking through the winding streets of Plaka, the oldest part of Athens, just outside our hotel. The narrow streets had little shops each selling statuary, sweet-smelling olive oil soaps, unique jewelry, colorful clothing, and all manner of handmade crafts.
>
> We were on streets where the ancients walked, and we were thrilled. Sokrates and Plato, Sophokles and Euripides had all been right here! This was the agora, the political, cultural, and economic center of ancient Greece, where news was passed from shop to shop, philosophy and politics discussed on street corners, and artisans produced their goods.

On Poros, as everywhere today, prices are higher, salaries strained, benefits disappearing. People have less and so they eat out and travel less often. Taverna and small business owners are more worried than they have ever been. Many have closed and others do not know if or how they will survive.

Nonetheless, Poros is a village; people live in and as community; and Sunday afternoon is time for extended family, friendship, feasting, talking, and visiting. A collective roar of gossip rises from the village. Children run, play, laugh, climb the memorials, squeeze between tables, chase cats. Every taverna is full, every seat taken, the aisles tight packed. The waitstaff bustles. Platters of meats, fish, vegetables are piled high and disappear. Wine and beer bottles, coffee cups, empty dishes crowd the tables. At some tables older men lean over their *tavli*, the national

142 ⟋ IN THE AGORA

board game, a version of backgammon, as opponents slam their chips on the points while their friends crowd around to argue or cheer. No matter the daily life challenges or difficulties caused by climate change or politics, as Evangelos says, stretching his arms wide to embrace the day, "How can we complain when we live in paradise?"

After her earlier visits to Athens and elsewhere, Kate Dahlstedt, also captivated by its spirit, finally landed on Poros.

I had no idea that I would return again and again to this endlessly interesting place and the vast and beautiful country that surrounds it. My life has unfolded with the blessing of being able to do just that. I have been to sacred sites on windy mountain tops and deep in the bellies of caves. I have stayed in remote villages and on distant islands. I have been intrigued, inspired, and delighted. But nowhere have I felt the serenity, freedom, and sacred joy as I have on the island of Poros.

It was only a few years ago that I was able to extend a trip and stay for a few weeks on the island. Like most of the islands, Poros has a small port across from the many shops and cafes for tourists, the modern iteration of the agora. In the morning, I liked to walk along the old back streets above the village where I was greeted by old women hanging laundry or pulling weeds, wanting to know where I'm from, and young women who wanted to know about life in the U.S. and practice their English. Along the shore I watched strong men, young and old, haul in their catch of the day as their fathers and grandfathers had before them. In the evening, I would meet some of them at a taverna drinking wine or playing their bouzoukis for the rest of us.

As the days passed, I felt a wonderful sense of being taken in. The Rota taverna was staffed by immigrants that Giorgos, the owner, had helped gain citizenship. They all knew my name. They all greeted me in the morning at breakfast. A walk along the shore drew more conversation from shopkeepers I'd met and resident shoppers alike. One would tell me where to get the best bread, another would advise me about computer repair. And later or the next day we'd smile and greet each other in passing.

After my first week, there it came—the deep, warm connection, the sense of belonging I'd never felt so strongly. Community, right there, day in, day out. No need to check my calendar or set up a time to meet. I was in the agora. Like the ancients, I could walk through town and meet people and talk and laugh and complain together. I could get advice, or a recipe, or a suggestion for an ailment. Even with the language barrier I could communicate with gestures and pointing and be understood.

One favorite activity was walking up the hill at dusk to perch by the clock tower and watch the vast ocean flowing below as the sun set over the mountains. There I felt taken in, like one of the refugees in asylum. Life felt simple. It was not about achieving, or having, but about being with others in community. The poets and philosophers and playwrights we admire once walked the streets of the Athens agora. But it's the Poros agora, the timeless center of

Fig. 8.2. Mornings and evenings, fishermen, and now women, line the wharf seeking the day's fresh catch. See also plate 12.

PHOTOGRAPH BY BABIS KANATSIDIS

community on that small island, that endures and pulls at me from wherever else I am.

This spirit of Poros is both ancient and created by the living and infects all visitors. It includes the permanent residents of the island and everyone allowing themselves immersion and penetration. Alicia Halverson is a nurse-practitioner and midwife living on her own small island off the Pacific Northwest coast. She visited Poros for the first time in November 2023. She reports:

I walked past large, clearly expensive yachts and sailboats on the water side, the majority empty of human life; mostly closed shops and empty tavernas on the other. The busy tourist season has ended. Traveling southwest, toward the Mediterranean Ocean, the boats become smaller, many well used and worn, some broken, some sinking. Then there are fishing boats, some not much bigger than a dinghy, others larger, with decks full of fishing nets and buoys. I catch the attention of a young, feral cat; one of the plethora roaming the island. As I squat down, stroking the young cat's soft fur, I hear a voice, speaking in heavily accented English, "She's a sweet one, take her home with you?"

I look up and see a man standing on the deck of a small boat, fishing nets spread out, his hair dark and graying, his warm and smiling face clean shaven, years of exposure to sunshine and salty air evident in his tanned and roughened skin, dressed in fisherman's overalls and rubber boots. I reply that I would love to take as many of the young cats I have come across in Greece home with me as possible but can't imagine they would make it in my suitcase. He smiles as he tells me he offers bits of fish to many cats each morning after bringing in his daily catch.

Jumping easily from his boat onto the portside pavement, strong and flexible, he introduces himself as "Stelios, like Steve in U.S.," and asks me where I am from and what brings me to Poros. I introduce myself, tell him I like "Stelios" better. He laughs. I say I am on Poros to learn from and connect with the people, culture, history, and mythology. I share that I am also from a small island in the northwesternmost part of United States, near the Canadian border.

He offers me a seat next to him as he sits on a nearby bench. The cat accompanies us, wanting to continue the head scratches. Stelios remains warm and open. We were both raised in small communities on an island, both aware of the decline of community fishing, both aware and appreciative of the beauty surrounding us and the power in our choices to live more simply. We speak of the decline of wild fish populations and detrimental impacts of fish farming on the waters surrounding both of our homes, as well as globalization and uneducated and/or uninterested consumers.

He invites me to return the next day to see the fish he brings in. The next morning five of my traveling companions and I meet with Stelios. He sits on his boat, picking fish out of his nets, throwing them into the water once they are freed. He has kept several fish back from sale to the local markets, tavernas, and residents, to show us. He remains warm and gracious, answering our questions. He was in the navy as a youth, and spent some time in the U.S., in Norfolk, Virginia. He is proud to have lived his life in Poros and announces that he is sixty-eight years old, despite looking and carrying himself as a much younger man. We are touched by his willingness to engage with us, his humor, warmth, and openness. As we depart, we thank him, and he sends us off with blessings for safe journeys home and a hope that we will return to Poros to visit with him again.

Fishermen, laundrymen, farmers—in the living agora, philosophers and artists are everywhere and the Greek people know and value theirs. I have long conversations with Dmitri about the stoics, Babis about history, Giorgos about Orthodoxy, Christos about writers, Ivi and Pamela about artists. They do not only know them; they practice their arts. What in America are called hobbies or avocations in Greece are necessities that feed the heart and soul.

I walk down my picturesque alley. I breathe deeply as I walk by the bakery. The street air outside smells like airborne sugar; I feel like I gain pounds just breathing it. Farther down I greet Vangelis the salesman who sold me a sturdy and padded pair of walking shoes. He wants to know how I like my shoes. I play with Hermes, the baby son he is cuddling.

I walk on happily through two small plazas as raucous as the rest of the village. I cross between the crowded tables and plane trees. I need a haircut and enter the barber shop that opens on the rear of the square.

Barbershop? There are several cages with songbird occupants hopping and singing. There is old traditional artwork on the walls, pictures, and photographs of remote landscapes hanging over battered antique pieces of furniture. One customer is in the chair and the barber is floating and dancing around him as they chatter and he clips. With a warm smile he motions me to sit and wait.

My turn comes. My barber's name, like many men here, is Giorgos—if it is not Dmitri, Yiannis, or Nikos. I sit in his old rickety chair. Giorgos does not pick up his tools, but slowly circles me, studying my hair and the shape of my head and features.

Giorgos comments on the shape of my skull, where my balding hairline ends, how my eyebrows need tending, how mine compares to other heads. I learn he is more than a barber; he is an artist, philosopher, and naturalist. He does not just clip and trim my balding hair. He circles me, studies the size, shape, contours of head, face, features, the quality of the hair. Then he sculpts and shapes as if we, his patrons, were living marble.

"I wish to reveal what is most harmonious and beautiful in every face, to restore its disturbed balance." He describes the shape of my head, how the hair laying on the back of my neck should ideally be shaped, the curves it would give my entire torso from the rear. When he was young, patrons sent him to school, but not the short months-long course most barbers attend. Giorgos attended an art institute in London where, for two years, he studied and practiced figure drawing and portraiture and designed original styles for different head types.

"You aren't just a barber. You went to art school and are a practicing artist."

"Of course. How else bring out the divine beauty in each human form?"

We discuss shape, form, color, and eternal principles of proportion. We quote philosophers and reference artists and artwork. Giorgos says, "These qualities, like harmony, balance, proportion, integration, and moderation, are not only for haircuts and artistic ventures. They are necessary in art, music, and literature, and are critical in society and our institutions and relationships."

In Giorgios's shop songbirds hop and sing from several cages. Landscapes and photos crowd the walls. Furniture looks like it has been here for centuries. These treasures are Giorgos's story. He was born in the countryside of a poor family. He did not like school, so at an early age skipped his lessons to roam the mountains and study the animals. He became an expert ornithologist. The caged songbirds are his own crossbred creations. Their sizes and shapes are finchlike, but their colors, markings, and songs are striking and like none I have ever seen or heard. "Until barber school," Giorgos summarizes, "my classrooms were the woods and mountains, and my teachers were the land, the spirits, the ancients."

As I leave, Giorgos says, "Thank you for being Greek."

"I am a Philhellene," I affirm. "But I have no Greek blood or ancestry."

"That is not what matters," he counters. Then he offers wisdom like that offered by the philosopher Isokrates two millennia ago. Giorgos says, "A Greek is not a Greek because of blood. A Greek is someone who shares our mind and spirit. Most modern people, here and everywhere, are not Greeks. But you are."

As evening crawls on, I peak into the Everything Shop where one can buy church, computer, cosmetic, health, kitchen supplies. I greet the young clerk Michalis in Greek. He smiles at my stumbling tongue. "You're chuckling," I say. "How old do I sound?"

"I don't want to insult you," he says.

"I am learning," I continue in Greek. "I practice with you. I want to know."

"You talk like you are a four-year-old Greek boy," he offers.

"Opa!" I cry. "Wonderful. That means I am growing in the language. You make me happy. Thank you."

148 ∽ In the Agora

"Then I guess you are one of our children now."

Throughout the modern agora, in tavernas, shops, at meals, on walks, in endless conversations, I meet the characters of the ancient agora in modern people and events. We are each an individual mask, a persona, affixed over an eternal but invisible face and character, here long before our times and returning throughout time.

In modern Poriotes I meet Aristophanes, the comic playwright, and his characters in many people and encounters. There are comedians who taunt and tease and play tricks on each other, sometimes in dyads, sometimes in groups. I have doubled over with laughter at their teases and antics. I meet Diogenes, the beggar-philosopher, in a man treated as the traditional village scapegoat, picked on by many, yet highly intelligent with a knowledge of Greek and world history, politics, and demographics. His awkward way of relating, standoffishness in this culture of intimate contact, discourses on subjects irrelevant to others, make him a target of fun and laughter. In the United States this man might be considered "on the spectrum" with his awkward styles of communications and relating. I sometimes sit or walk with him. I respect his knowledge, relieve his loneliness, tell him the name his neighbors call him is a delightful diminutive and childhood nickname that he can be proud rather than shamed by. And Evangelos, in his tiny fishing boat, is a modern Jason for a few hours every morning as he pushes far out to sea to observe the sun's colors, temporarily escape the human din, and perhaps find the golden fleece—a new bit of wisdom. And Tasos was an Odysseus wandering far and wide over the world in search of answers to life's insecurities and questions that he finally found back on his Ithaka, Poros. And Demos wandering with his bouzouki is an Orpheus. And Giorgos, guiding and directing Taverna Sti Rota, was a philanthropist, monk, and priest of Orthodoxy, filoxenia, and right attitude and values.

Declared a four-year-old, I decide to speak only Greek for the rest of the day. That evening, I sit with Dmitri Hippos at Rota. When I talk, he looks confused, then laughs, then asks what happened and declares, "Magus. You must be a magus." I tell him of my meeting with Michalis. Dmitri says, "He was wrong. You are five!" In such ways, through open-hearted immersion in a land and people not originally our own, we become friends, locals, spiritual and cultural children experiencing a rebirth in ourselves and contributing as beloved community members to our new old homes.

Theology of the Taverna

The long row of tavernas that front the strait have names related to the island: the gods Poseidon and Dionysos; the small sailing ship, *Caravelle*; the common plane or sycamore tree, *Platanos*; the Clock Tower and Porto Café coffee shops. As everywhere in Greece, waiters stand in front of their establishments, greet passersby, make conversation, invite us in, they tell us, for the best friendship and food found anywhere.

Over the years I have eaten at most of the establishments, always finding conversation and friendship easy, offered in delicious abundance as is the food. Yet my home away from home became Taverna Sti Rota with its owner Giorgos.

Rota refers to the wake a ship leaves in the water. Taverna Sti Rota is "the tavern in the wake." We push through the waters, the passage, as we seek our life paths and the wake proceeds from our seeking. It is as if for a few moments we leave a visible path on life's ever-changing ocean. Giorgos said, "Follow the wake to arrive at the best—whether of food, philosophy, or friendship."

Taverna Sti Rota perches both indoors and out along the quay, directly opposite Galatas and the line of water taxis that cross there, on the Square of Heroes surrounding the white marble obelisk memorial to residents killed or executed in twentieth-century wars. Wide blue canopies protect the white tables spread along the street. Christos, Mimoza, and other staff shuffle around the tables when busy, or sit sipping coffee during quiet hours. Inside, another crush of tables spread out under Pamela's paintings on the walls and a French flag hanging in one corner to honor that country's visitors who regularly return. Behind the long counter, the kitchen staff bustles. Rota does not close at night until the last customer has left. It is sometimes Dmitri Hippos and me. He sips his wine, me my chamomile

150   IN THE AGORA

tea, as we watch our friends shut down, remaining until the last drop of camaraderie has been squeezed from the growing darkness. When I try to help clean up, Giorgos or Christos scold, "You are our friend. Sit down. That is our job."

Giorgos lived most of his life on Poros. He too came from a refugee family and carried the ancestral memory of displacement. His grandfather was a survivor of the Turkish expulsion and arrived on Poros in 1922. His father was a naval officer, stationed in the 1970s at the large base on Souda Bay, outside Chania, Krete. Giorgos's family lived there when he was between seven and nine years old. At one of our first meetings, when he learned of my work as a psychotherapist with veterans, he shared memories of those times that provided early life lessons he cannot forget.

"Many veterans from Viet Nam were too crazy from the war so they were sent there instead of home to the U.S.," Giorgos told me. "My father was the base club manager in a bar that catered to Americans. When they expressed their feelings, they exploded like wild animals. Then to escape their pain they drank and drank until they broke everything in sight. I remember some of those ravaged veterans to this day. My father tried to help them, but sometimes had to call the MPs. These were my first impressions of warriors, so as a young boy I learned how war makes everyone crazy. There is no escaping it."

"How did that affect your life?" I asked.

"That, and all the suffering, hardships, and lies I have seen in my time, made me determined to live a good life for others and myself. I believe in the ancient Greek values. Strive for excellence. Practice moderation. Stay humble. Love the stranger. Be accessible to all. Always choose and tell the truth. And don't just believe in Jesus. Live his teachings."

For several years Giorgos studied Orthodoxy at university in Athens. Though he loved the teachings he decided that he was not called to a monk's austere lifestyle. Theology is the study of the divine, but he did not want to withdraw from the world into quiet contemplation. "The monk's life is a calling," he said, "but I was called differently. I wanted to stay among people and serve them directly. For me, theology is not removal from the world. Theology is the reality of our action in the world. It is the devotion to help others find contentment and joy. That is my true purpose. Theology is the truth of yourself. So, I do not officiate at a church. I practice the Theology of the Taverna."

Giorgos's theology was active and practical, about how to live together well and help anyone find moments of happiness and peace. "Customers arrive at my taverna hungry. I want them to leave happy." He references Jesus's teaching in the parable of the good Samaritan. "It is faith and deeds, not theology and intellectualism, that matter," he said. "'By their fruits shall you know them.'" His theology applied Orthodox teachings and values to the ways he treated other people and ran his business and life. He attended church on holidays and some early mornings before work. But that was not his essential practice. About prayer, he said, "It is not the rote recitation of words. My prayer is work, not staying at home with hands folded. Work with honesty and sincerity, work guided by good values." All his employees—whether ill, refugee, or youth—are in asylia working at Rota. Giorgos maintained them and their salaries no matter the difficult economic conditions.

Orthodoxy encourages fasting, and Giorgos kept the weekly and long Lenten fast days for both physical and spiritual health. He said, "To fast is not abstaining from meals. It is abstaining from what you do not need. To fast is to know you have enough and to reduce what you do not need and not make waste."

In contrast to the affluence and greed infecting much of the world and reaching Poros now as well, Giorgos insisted that we should live for *agape*, or divine love. "It is simple," he declared. "Our needs are simple. Indulgence never satisfies. You want more and more until your body and belongings become obese. You accumulate until it makes you ill and your heart and soul are empty. Then you seek even more."

Giorgos affirmed that "there are miracles and they, too, do not come from theology. They can happen to anyone from any religion." He declared, "The best we humans have is reason, *logos*. This is not thinking, but the order, the meaning. It comes from the Divine. We steer our lives by it. Miracles may come as a gift from beyond. We humans cannot do better than reason."

152 ~ IN THE AGORA

In Giorgos's theology, we hear Jesus and his teachings on loving everyone; and Plato and John on *logos,* the word, and the supremacy of reason as our best human tool; and Hippocrates who taught that illness begins in the soul; and Sokrates, Diogenes, and the Stoics who sought to want and have as little as possible. All these influences from ancient Greek civilization flow like invisible rivers into Giorgos's unifying vision.

In Giorgos's understanding, Moses was a father of civilization who gave us written laws—the Torah. But the book did not transform humanity. Plato was the father of Western civilization who tried to serve the populace by creating an ideal society. But he couldn't and we can't. So Jesus came to teach us to make ourselves clean and pure so we can achieve a just world. Jesus took all the previous teachings a step further by loving everyone equally. Giorgos declared, "Jesus created and practiced 'spiritual democracy.'" He, and the sincere Orthodox monks, are on a Plato-and-Jesus path.

Giorgos saw the dangers in our contemporary bloated world—"see how empty most American lives are, empty cans."

> We cannot survive without fasting. We must be happy with what we have and live with less. Consumption is compensation for emptiness. But we must have faith. The Greeks won Oxi Day, defeating the Italian invasion during World War II, not with superior weapons and numbers, but with faith, values, and bayonets. Freedom demands sacrifice. The willingness to die for your country is the greatest fast. Our values must not just be ideas; they must be real for ourselves and others. We must give, we must know all is a circle and it will be given back, and we must seek the measure. Greek philosophy is the basis for this wisdom, and Jesus showed us how to live it.

These values shaped Giorgos's principles and practices. At Rota, his staff offers goodness to everyone and asylum to those who need it. He created sacred and safe space through his food service. He affirmed, "My happiness is not in earning money, but in seeing the happiness of my customers after dining here. That is my definition of success—people feel happy here. That is food and medicine for their hearts and souls."

Giorgos referred again and again to the teachings of Jesus. "Remember the story of a rich man who was dreaming of more wealth? The Archangel Gabriel came and took him as he slept. So the message is: Be good. Life is short. What matters is what we leave behind."

Sokrates spent his last day in his jail cell in conversation with his closest friends and disciples. Then when he fearlessly drank the hemlock, it reached his heart, and death came quickly and gently. Giorgos Dimitriadis spent his last day in his Taverna Sti Rota in joyful conversation and service to his friends and patrons. Then overnight on Friday, March 22, 2024, his heart gave out and death came quickly and gently. It is a worthy comparison. Both these good men spent their lives in the agora. Both were most concerned with ultimate matters of the heart and soul. Both lived in pursuit of the good, the true, and the beautiful. Neither wrote a word, but their teachings were recorded and spread by their friends and disciples.

Though to appearances an owner and director of a favorite Poros taverna, like Sokrates and Jesus, Giorgos lived by what is good for the soul and strove to love everyone who crossed his path or needed help or service. As Sokrates was leaving, he advised his followers, "Take care of your souls." And Jesus's ultimate lesson was that we love everybody. Giorgos lived and taught these same lessons. Sokrates said he only wished for the same challenges for the sons he was leaving behind. Giorgos's young son Gregoros has taken his place and strives to live and work by the same ideals. Like Sokrates and Jesus, Giorgos believed that our true lives were not physical or material, but spiritual, and the best of us does not die when we die.

9

THE SHADOW OF PARADISE

Struggles Facing a Rural Community

The wide world is all about you. You can fence yourselves in, but you cannot forever fence the world out.
J. R. R. Tolkien, *The Fellowship of the Ring*

On Poros it is a summer day, but it is only spring. Radiant sun with a burning blue sky and no clouds—a long, fierce drought. Farmers are already worrying that their annual olive crop is ruined; with no rain there will be little oil and nothing to market or feed the family.

Residents of Poros stretch their arms, smile, greet the day and declare again, "Welcome to Paradise." We humans have this choice; we can know that something is wrong yet embrace and enjoy the beautiful day anyway. As philosophy taught, nothing in itself is either good or bad but by the value judgments we humans impose on *what is*. And as Heraklitos taught, the way up and the way down are the same; the cosmos and mortals are inherently and eternally in strife.

Fig. 9.1. An 1800s rendition of Poros town with a view of Galatas across the strait from a high point behind the village.
PHOTOGRAPH FROM THE HATZOPOULEIOS PUBLIC LIBRARY ARCHIVES

On this summery day, I walk down the quay to the motorbike rental shop. This morning slender, dark-haired, and dark-eyed Avi is on duty. He is twenty-nine years old, was born and has lived his entire life on Poros.

"You are a lucky man to have spent your life here," I say.

He smiles broadly. "Yes! Lucky!" he echoes. "Poriotes feel that way."

"I first came here before you were born. I have seen many changes during your lifetime. What do you think and feel about all these?"

Avi scratches his head, looks confused. "I don't understand," he says.

"Tourism," I say. "Yachts, wealth, expensive houses changing the landscape, more pollution, water going bad, traditional shops closing and boutiques replacing them, locals leaving. What do you think of all this?"

"I don't know," he shrugs. "You first came in '87. I was born in '95. I grew up with all this. I never saw Poros before, so I don't know what I think. No one has ever asked me this question before."

During one visit, Vasilis, my taxi driver down the mountain from Poseidon's temple, declared, "I was born and have lived my entire life on Poros. I know I'm lucky." Back when I first visited the island, Vasilis's father owned a taverna named Zorba's. "We used to dance and dance in traditional costume," he reminisced. "I learned English not in school but by talking with customers."

"Good memories," I said. "Do you still dance for visitors? What about now?"

"Now there are too many tourists," Vasilis said, "and they are ruining our island. In 1987 everyone was a fisherman and all the houses belonged to local people. But now we are too crowded, and prices are too high for us. The landlord doubled our building rent, so my family had to close Zorba's. Now I drive this taxi while my son must live in Athens. But I don't like it there. I rush back to Poros after each visit. Oh, how we used to have fun, dance ourselves into joy, what we call making kefi!"

The psychological concept of shadow refers to what is hidden, what remains in the dark, what we are ignorant or in denial of. In Carl Jung's definition, it refers to "the negative side of the personality, the sum of all those unpleasant qualities we like to hide, together with the insufficiently developed functions and the contents of the personal unconscious."[1] Shadow contains those qualities that we cannot bear to see and so we hide, deny, or avoid them until they cause us significant difficulties or explode into consciousness in some unwanted form. It exists in both individuals and cultures. It causes endless problems and suffering unless and until we reveal and respond to it in some positive manner.

Avi, Vasilis, and other Poriotes youths raised on the island since its transition to a tourist destination are lost in shadows. Many do not know their home island's history, legacy, or culture; they do not know what has been lost.

Confronting the Shadow

Poros qualifies as a threatened traditional rural community. Inhabited for over three thousand years, it has only a small local population with a single dominant village. Its population is shrinking while tourism and sociopolitical and climactic conditions are changing its nature and culture. Recent European Union and Greek governmental decisions, the influx of the wealthy, and the growing threat of industrial fish farming in its pristine waters profoundly challenge the island.

Even small matters are transforming. The water taxi to cross the strait to Galatas had cost one euro for many years. It has gone up 30 percent, to €1.30 EUR. In Rota Giorgos declared, "The wealthy don't feel it. But even thirty Euro cents hurts the average person. All our expenses have gone up. We are all paying for the Ukraine war."

Fishermen and the local population are shrinking while the affluent, many from abroad, are building new homes to leave their troubled lands or second vacation homes to indulge in the beauty and warmth. Large houses now climb the opposite Galatas mountain to the top, sending their artificial lights into the landscape that had been dark and pristine for millennia.

The population, housing, employment, and ecological crises have been created by the influx of the affluent and policies and manipulations of the national and European Union bureaucracies, as well as the impact of the larger world beyond. Greece in general and Poros need their monies. Those who come to Poros for comfort or indulgence do not know about asylia and will rebuild and transform the environment for their own pleasure.

On one recent visit, my hotel next-door neighbor was a woman building a second home on Poros with plans to leave her endangered Middle Eastern country as soon as it was done. She had decided to invest and build on Poros within hours of first arriving. She found relaxation, safety, and comfort on the island. That was all she wanted.

"How do you spend your days here?" I asked her.

"Doing nothing," she answered.

"What did you do yesterday?"

"Nothing."

"And your plans for today?"

"I might call my brother to urge him to buy a home here as well so he too can relax and spend his days doing nothing."

158 ∾ The Shadow of Paradise

Here as elsewhere, we witness individual freedom without its necessary partner—social responsibility. Ancient philosophy warned against this imbalance and required gifting back to the society from the affluent who enjoyed its boons. Individual freedom without collective responsibility is taking without giving back and will inevitably lead to societal collapse. It is the shadow side of freedom, the shadow cast upon paradise.

Avi and the other youths, and international visitors relocating, do not know of these massive changes. Who sees the shadow creeping across Poros? How is it arriving?

I often bump into tall Evangelos around the village. We visit in Mary's Laundry where he may be helping his daughter wash the day's loads. Or we sit across the alley at the traditional Sokaki taverna and share two cups—one of coffee and one of philosophy. Or we bump into each other at the north end of the quay where he loves to fish and I love to walk.

It is summer every day in mid-November when it should be fall, cool and rainy. The sky usually remains bright and when cloudy, the rains will not let go. Poros is in drought, and it is another year of poor crops. At dinner Dmitri says it should be olive harvest time, but they are small and dry and not worth marketing.

One evening near the point, I meet Evangelos standing next to his small boat. It is being repaired by a young man scraping hard at the barnacles and peeling paint. Evangelos starts every day before sunrise fishing for barracuda and photographing. He shows me some photos on his cell phone that are half realistic but purposely unfocused and distorted by lights and shapes. When I question, he says, "I like surreal. It reminds me that life is only a brief dream."

Evangelos points to the clouds. "Look," he says. "The weather is changing. See the clouds on Sleeping Woman? There is rain in their tails. Their movement and the birds' flight show that it is coming this way. If it even comes here and releases, there still won't be enough—until there is too much. There was a climate disaster in Italy yesterday. It is coming for us all."

"What do you mean?" I ask.

THE SHADOW OF PARADISE ⁓ 159

Evangelos blurts, "There is no more *metron*." *Metron* is the ancient word for balance, moderation, the measure. "It is because of human vanity. We are only experiencing the first scratches of nature striking back to reclaim her metron. She has millions of years to do it, but we don't. The next two generations will suffer what we have done, and nature does not need us to be here at all. You and I are lucky to experience the last drops of beauty before the end."

Evangelos pats his boat and compliments his worker. "At least I have this to explore the beauty while we still have it," he smiles. Evangelos's little craft is named *Kalypso* after the sea nymph who for years kept Odysseus prisoner on her island while he was trying to return home from the Trojan War. It is an appropriate name for this philosopher's boat. He too worships beauty as he is trapped on his island home.

At another meeting, Evangelos and I sip coffees together at a small table across from his laundromat. He continues to declaim and worry about the shadowy conditions on Poros, as if he were a modern Kassandra proclaiming prophetic warnings that no one will believe.

"No one knows how much we are suffering," he declares. "It is partially financial. I constantly worry that my electricity will be shut off. I must struggle from month to month to pay my bills. But the real problems are between people. There is no more dialogue." He becomes adamant, aroused, the words spilling from his lips. "Because of cell phones, everyone is looking in a mirror and talking to themselves. People don't see or talk to each other anymore. They don't develop *nous*, the mind, the only thing that truly matters, that makes us human. The earth is becoming extinct and so is the human." With those words and prophecy, the tall man rose, squeezed my hand, and stomped off to another meeting. Evangelos affirms the natural spirituality built into both Greek and Judeo-Christian teachings that, as the Psalmist says, "the Earth is the Lord's," and we are not meant to be its rapists but its sensitive caretakers and keepers practicing metron in all things, or else.

On yet another bright hot morning, I meet Evangelos returning from his dawn fishing. He greets me with a worried look and blurts, "Poros needs help."

160 ∽ THE SHADOW OF PARADISE

"Why?" I ask. "What's happening?"

"I was a civil servant for thirty-five years," he explains. "I believed in civil service. I wanted to help my people and the island. To serve others and the common good, that is the proper calling for a man. But I watch the politicians in Athens and here become wealthy by selling our island off to the rich."

"The ancients taught that politics is of utmost importance. Plato said nothing is harder than learning to govern. Don't your politicians know this? Do you trust them?"

"Politicians become politicians," Evangelos answered, "not because they are hungry or educated or want a good job. They become politicians because they cannot do anything else. And they are not the only problem. Too many people today, even here, have become nothing but consumers. Because of all this, Poros is losing its soul."

"What about living in paradise? You declare it. Many feel lucky to live here safe from the woes of the larger world."

"Not so," Evangelos groaned. "Climate change is here too. Today is a hot summer day when it should be cool with the autumn rains beginning. But no cooling and no rain. Mother Earth herself is sick, and people don't notice. I am very afraid for the future. I will be okay; the Mother won't die in my lifetime. But I fear for our children and grandchildren and the horrors we will leave to them to survive."

"Human beings are no worse than animals," I said.

"Do not insult the animals," Evangelos chided. "They do not lie, destroy, or needlessly kill. They are natural and in the greater order. We are not. We are the beasts."

"Are you afraid for your own life, your health or well-being?"

"No," he answered. "The body is garbage," he explained, "to be thrown away, only good for fertilizer." Evangelos, like many Greeks, continues in the tradition of the ancient philosophers. Heraklitos taught that a corpse was worth less than dung, Sokrates that we are not our bodies, Epictetus that we are all souls dragging corpses. The ancients believed in the importance and powers of mind, which, as Plutarch said, is "a fire to be kindled."

As the only resolution to our eternal crises, like the ancients,

Evangelos calls out, "But nous, the mind! Nous lives on. Nous gives back to the cosmos and recycles."

Health and Refugee Shadows

Christos, kind, friendly, generous in his service at Taverna Sti Rota, is grateful for the job, friendships, and this work as the medicine keeping his multiple sclerosis at bay. Yet he works seven days a week and late into the evening. Responsible for filoxenia and others' satisfaction, he will not leave his post until every customer has left and all the cleaning completed.

Despite his health challenges, Christos does not take a siesta or a day off. Salaries are of necessity low on the island even as prices climb. Christos simply declares that he cannot afford to take time off and needs the work.

There is not enough income here to give us paid time off. Giorgos worked hard all the time to keep the business going. He maintained our salaries even during the pandemic, even in hard times without business. He took care of us all but there is little extra. We must constantly work to survive. It is not my employer's fault. It is our country. We are losing our health benefits, pensions, infrastructure, solidarity, our most cherished values. In this country as well as yours, modern politics is destroying traditional values and ways of life. Here on Poros we care about each other, but our country does not care about us.

Giorgos presented the challenges from the owner/employer's point of view:

One of my wealthy customers is the CEO of a corporation who regularly vacations on Poros. He loves to eat here. Over one dinner he challenged me. "Your restaurant is the best. So why do you employ refugees or people with special needs? Why do you help the ill and infirm? You could have better staff, give smaller salaries, charge higher prices, and make more money for yourself." I told him that I do not care about that. Service and helping others are my priority.

162 ∾ THE SHADOW OF PARADISE

He laughed and said, "With your attitude and values, you are topped out. You will not make any more money. Your business might survive, but you will never be wealthy like me." I did not say it out loud, but I thought, You are a poor soul. You will never know the wealth that I have in giving.

Mimoza, the kindly waitress, and her family, are refugees from Albania who work with a smile at Rota. Mimoza's husband Mir escaped Albania thirty years ago, seeking a safer and better life. He tried living and working in England and Germany. Both countries were too expensive and difficult. He finally moved to Poros where Mimoza joined him ten years after he left. They find Poros to be beautiful, friendly, and inexpensive. But the family cannot buy a house because, like housing markets around the world, the affluent are buying everything and renovating or building, driving prices up and causing a housing crisis. Mimoza and Mir have given up the dream of owning their own home. Mimoza worked seventeen continuous years without any days off. She holds a second job cleaning and cooking for wealthy families to help put their daughter through college. This family can never own their own house or accumulate savings. "It's okay," Mimoza says with a weary smile and the same values refugees over the ages have held, "as long as my children are safe and can have a good life."

This family and others live in the shadow of asylum. Mir and Mimoza are safe and happy, but they remain poor and oppressed by the loss of their homeland and invasion of the affluent. Rota's customers only see her friendliness. "I smile and they think I am fine and happy," she confessed. "It is our job to bring them joy. But they do not ask, and they do not see."

Suffer the Children

The 7 Brothers hotel is set back away from the Square of Heroes. The lobby is airy and spacious and opens in front to face the strait and on the side to a pert alley with stairs that climb the hill to the sokaki above. Rooms are painted in restful Greek blue and white. Balconies overlook

THE SHADOW OF PARADISE ∽ 163

the strait and Galatas. The front of the hotel has a wide covered stone porch, a comfortable and restful place to sit, read or write, meet friends, meditate.

The youths of Poros have discovered the porch. Late at night, especially on weekends and during the summer, after guests are in bed and the village is quieting down for sleep, teenagers gather on the porch. They pull chairs and tables together, open beers, cigarettes, and snacks, and sit, often for hours, talking, joking, gossiping, unaware they might be disturbing others.

Sometimes the teens are relatively quiet, and we find evidence of their parties in the morning—beer and soda cans, cigarette stubs, displaced and overturned patio chairs. But sometimes, and more so recently, they are noisy and disturb guests. Occasionally guests complain to Nikki and she must call the police, or they call themselves.

I have been on the porch when the lone island police officer has arrived. As soon as the youths see the officer, they flee down the alley, peek around corners, waiting for him to leave so they can return.

Midnight. I stood on the porch with Nikki, the officer Vasilis, and Anna, another hotel guest. The youths had fled. We straightened the furniture and collected empty bottles. Vasilis said he would remain for a while to discourage the teens' return.

"They are only young teenagers," Anna declares. "How is it they can drink? Can't you stop them?"

"Here the legal age to buy beer is fourteen," Nikki answers softly.

"What!" Anna exclaims. "They are only children."

"True," Nikki shrugs. "But it is Greece."

"Then why don't you forbid them to use your porch?" Anna asks. Nikki does not answer but her face flushes.

"She can't," I say.

"Why not?" Anna asks, then looking at Nikki, says, "It is your property. They are damaging it and hurting your customers." Still, Nikki does not answer.

"She can't forbid the teens coming here," I explain, "because it would betray the Greek value of filoxenia. We are taught to be generous, kind, welcoming, to share what we have. We are taught that what we hold or share is far more precious than what we own alone. If Nikki forbids the teens their use of the porch, she betrays filoxenia and that is a worse offense than what the teenagers do."

Anna looks shocked. She turns again to Nikki. "Is that right?"

Nikki smiles shyly, nods her head, shrugs, and says, "Yes. He is right. I cannot. It would betray our values. Besides, the kids would just move their parties somewhere else. It would solve nothing and maybe make matters worse."

"Well then," Anna blurts, "what can be done? This is a small island. These teens are bored and have nothing to do. Either restrict them or provide for them. Doing nothing accomplishes nothing."

Nikki and Anna then shuffle off to bed. I remain chatting with the police officer standing in the darkness polka-dotted with lights.

Vasilis has been on the police force for seventeen years. He is the only officer on night shift. In fact, he explains, the entire island has only three policemen, each on duty alone for eight-hour shifts. "It is against international standards for policing," Vasilis explains. "There are always supposed to be two, a team, so we have backup in any dangers or emergencies."

"Why don't you?" I ask.

"Money," he grunts. "We used to have two men on duty together, but the government has done this all over the country. They endanger us to save money."

"And the impact on you, your comrades, the entire force?"

"We are all exhausted and burned out. We feel abused and unfairly treated."

"What about these kids?" I ask. "What do you think about them? What do you do to help or change the situation?"

"There is nothing I can do," the officer says sadly. "This situation is not their fault. Greece is changing. Our traditions are weakening. In previous years families gave their children much supervision, education, attention. They taught them history. They knew where they came from. These kids are not getting it. With their computers and cell phones they know what is going on in the bigger world and are bored and angry here. They want something to do but after school

THE SHADOW OF PARADISE ❧ 165

there is nothing and families and communities no longer provide the foundation they need."

"So, what do you do?"

"I try to be friendly and scare them away when they make trouble. But parents, schools, priests, the community needs to do something for them. I cannot. They no longer know how to behave as members of our communities. Schools and families need to teach citizenship and civics again, not just the math and sciences the modern world wants."

"Are you hopeful?" I ask.

"How can I be?" Vasilis retorts. "The government has also cut our pensions and benefits. I must work at this beat until I am sixty-five. Our kids don't have the conditions they need. I don't have the employment that will take care of me through life. I feel for them. We are all being abandoned."

"You sound like a warrior," I say.

"What do you mean?"

"You serve a difficult beat alone. You constantly walk into the unknown. It may be dangerous, but you are willing. You try to protect your fellow citizens and the children. You are a protector concerned about everyone's well-being. This is being a warrior."

"Thank you," Vasilis says. "Nobody talks this way, but I think this way to sustain myself. Every day as I put on my uniform, I must always be ready for battle while hoping and praying it does not happen."

"I honor you as a warrior protecting your island, its people, its youth," I say as we shake hands and part in the wee hours.

Perhaps something could be done. Perhaps more civics, education, youth programming. Who are these youths growing up on this "lucky" place yet alienated and bored like millions around the world? A few nights later, after dark, again the porch was crowded with a chattering circle of teenage boys and girls. Returning from a late walk, instead of entering the hotel I approached the group and greeted them. "*Kalispera*, good evening. I am sorry to interrupt your circle, but may I meet you all and talk for a while?"

There were eight teens in the group, boys and girls, all around fifteen or sixteen years old. Some of them spoke English so we stumbled

166 ∩ THE SHADOW OF PARADISE

through our conversation in two languages. At first, they were confused. Who is this foreigner approaching them late at night? What did he want? I explained who I am, what I am doing on Poros, and how long I have been visiting the island.

"You've been visiting here more than twice as long as we've been alive," one said.

"Yes," I answered. "I love your island. Would you like to know why? And what it was like before you were born? Do you know your island's history?"

The youths warmed up. They became curious and talkative.

"Who here knows any island history?" I asked. "Do you know why Poros was important? Do you know what was on top of your mountain?"

The teens knew nothing about Poseidon, the sanctuary, the island's history. They knew the names Theseus and Demosthenes, but no details, nothing about their places in local or Greek myth, history, or legacy. One says, "We thought the mountaintop ruins were just a cool place to have a picnic."

"Would you like to hear some good stories about your home?" I asked. They were enthusiastic, so I told them of Demosthenes's retreat to and suicide on this island promontory—vividly, like an adventure story.

"That happened here?" one grunted. Another blurted, "That's an amazing story. Why didn't we know?"

"Don't you learn this history in school?" I asked. They did not. As in the United States, their education now concentrates on the modern disciplines of the maths and sciences. "What about your family histories?" I asked. "Who here knows where your families came from before Poros?" No one did. "Or how many generations they have been here?" No one did. "Or how your families were affected by World War II or the Civil War?" Again, no one did. The entire group reported that their families did not talk about ancient, collective, cultural, or family histories. Even on such a personal and friendly island as Poros. Even in such a rich, complex, and important culture as Greece. These children, too, were being raised in the shadow, in a spiritual, cultural, intellectual vacuum.

We spoke for hours. They were fascinated by the stories I told of their island and Greek history. "Thank you for spending time with me," I said as I rose to depart. "I am sorry to have interrupted your teenage conversation and fun."

"We aren't," answered one. "We learned a lot. Please talk to us like this some more. Stop by and sit with us on other nights too."

I said I would. We separated as new friends. In the ensuing days I reported my conversation to local adults—your youths are accessible. They want to know. They want to learn. They are not bad kids making trouble. They are bored and lonely youth needing and wanting leadership, teaching, mentoring, and respect from their elders and community. Like youth everywhere, on Poros too, the shadow of world culture and technology is slowly rotting millennia-old values, traditions, and teachings. Everyone, even here, in our postmodern age, can suffer from isolation, loneliness, boredom, abandonment. Though we may try to avoid it, we cannot escape the world-wide deterioration of culture, community, and nature.

The Shadow in the Sea

The island waters are pure—or they were. I had always drank table water and felt safe and relieved to do so. One year I asked Giorgos at Rota why he served bottled water when the island waters were healthy. He apologized, had not wanted to tell me, but it was no longer true. Giorgos, then others, advised me to only drink bottled water. Even in this distant, removed, pristine location, the rainfall and ground water have become tainted, unhealthy, and insufficient.

The waters of the sea god's island are no longer safe to drink. But the strait shines in azure beauty; the sea full of fish, and the small fishing boats still go out and return with their catches daily; fishermen and women still line the quays at dawn and dusk. Poseidon's island should be replete with fish. I often eat red snapper, salmon, sea bream, cod, sardines, octopus, and other samples of the sea god's children at island tavernas. They are usually fresh-caught and expertly prepared, though now some fish are disappearing, and frozen or farmed fish are imported.

168 ∽ THE SHADOW OF PARADISE

Poros's deep, rich, clear waters, fertile for fish, have attracted corporations. As elsewhere around Greece and the wider world, commercial fish farming is coming to Poros. There are already smaller fish farms off the island's northern coast, and there have been several proposals and pressure over the last few years from New York and Dubai-based investment companies to build a fish farm conglomerate. They seek to cordon off large swaths of sea acreage for contained highly polluting fish farming. Such large commercial establishments have been proposed at the entrance to the strait and on the far side of the island in the old bay harbor of Poseidon's sanctuary.

The island residents do not want this farming. They do not want their ecology polluted, their waters dirtied and crowded, their appeal as a tourist island harmed or even ruined. For years the islanders and its local government have been protesting and resisting this development while the national government has been pushing the project. Islanders see graft and corruption, and believe bribes and favors are being exchanged and greed, corruption, and the profit motive are driving this effort rather than true economic need and the good of the island and its residents. Huge protest signs lettered on sheets hung across the central civic office building and from the clock tower heights. Their essential message is Oxi! No! Pamela Rogers says, "Taking a stand against the industrial danger to Poros is probably the greatest challenge of my life—saving the seas around Poros from mutilation! From the time I moved here and learned of the few fish farms on the north side, I was irritated, but they didn't claim much attention." As the threat has developed, Pamela has collected hundreds of signatures on a petition drive to express residents' and visitors' displeasure.

As of this writing, the project looms as a major threat to the welfare of Poros, its traditions, ecology, people, and tourist economy. As Poriotes explain, this project is driven by greed rather than good, the "bottom line" rather than the ultimate benefit. Pamela declares, "We on Poros will not give up fighting against this industrial nightmare. We are busy meeting in small groups to brainstorm; possibly the case will be taken to the European court." From this small island, she cries, "We need world support."

THE SHADOW OF PARADISE ∽ 169

Ancient philosophy differentiates between ultimate and instrumental values. Ultimate values are goals, ends, highest aspirations. Instrumental values help us achieve them. Moneymaking is an instrumental value that provides resources to find our way—Poros, passage—to our ultimate ends. With the fish farm, we see the instrumental, the bottom line, the profit motive, replacing ultimate humanistic, environmental, and spiritual values meant to guide and enrich our lives. Here, perhaps, the spirit may be strong enough to resist the pollution and protect Poseidon's waters and children.

Shadow and Spirit in the Chapel

This day I had rented a quad to carry me around the curving roads, under the pines, through the orchards, to my two favorite meditation sites. I began at the Monastery of Zoodogos Pigi, only open for visitors in the morning. I drove through the sunlight and gentle breeze, seeking another immersion in the heart of the Divine.

It was a mild and bright day, and I was buoyant. With every visit I hope for an infusion of good energy and feelings. I parked my mechanical steed and walked up the slanting path toward the entry arch. Beside the long set of stairs, a youngish man dressed in black was digging in a ditch among the church's scattered trees.

"Kalimera," I greeted him. "*Ti kanette? Pos sas lene?*" (Good day. How are you? What is your name?)

The man's eyes were dark and piercing. He put down his shovel and stared into me. "Manolis," he grunted. "Why are you here?"

"To pay my respects. To meditate and pray," I answered.

"Where are you from?"

"America."

"Ah," he immediately retorted in a refrain I have heard countless times. "Here we work to rest and play. But in America you rest to work and work."

"True about many people," I said. "But I am here for spiritual reasons."

"What? You are American," Manolis inquired, his eyes sharpening as if to pierce me.

170 ❧ THE SHADOW OF PARADISE

"How is that possible? What is your religion?"

"I am Jewish."

"Oh! You killed God."

Careful not to be defensive, I remained calm and said, "We all have the same God."

"We do not," he challenged. "You killed him. We do not have the same Father."

Hoping for a chance at reconciliation of this ancient prejudice, I answered, "I did not kill him. I was not there and not born. And Jews did not kill him. The Romans along with frightened collaborating Jewish officials did. Like the people who killed Sokrates."

"*Entaxi*, okay," he grunted. "Jesus is God. What do you Jews think?"

"We think he was a great prophet sent by God, like Moses, like Buddha. We all have the same one God."

"No, we don't! There are different gods. Only we have the real one."

"Then why do you think I am here to pray?"

"Because you are lost and searching."

"Perhaps I am here because we all worship the same God, and I honor him in you and everyone."

Manolis picked up his shovel, climbed back into his ditch, grunted, "Okay!" and turned away from me. I was disturbed. Of course, I knew of this ancient prejudice blaming the Jewish people for the death of Christ. I entered the church. I tried to feel a universal presence, to return to my small heart as a droplet of God's great heart. But I could not. I exited the chapel and climbed down the hill.

Manolis was hard at work in his ditch as I walked down the slope. I stopped again. He looked up. "What are you digging?" I asked.

His eyes darkened and pierced more fiercely than before. "My grave!" he called and cackled like the devil.

I breathed deeply of the sweet air. "I wish you a good rest, both in this lifetime and in your grave."

His expression softened and his gaze became quizzical. Finally, he gently said, "*Euxaristo*. Thank you," and returned to his digging.

Troubled, I returned a few days later to seek the heart. Again, I sat in the ornate chapel. Again, I drenched in the incense smells and

THE SHADOW OF PARADISE ∽ 171

iconography. I was not alone. A local woman, stooped and dressed in traditional black, was noisily dusting the candelabrum and altars. I greeted her but she did not even look at me or interrupt her work. Then a black-robed priest entered, pushing a groaning vacuum cleaner. He, also, would not return my greeting, The two gossiped and continued their raucous cleaning, just a few feet from me, as if I did not exist. I sat in the now-noisy chapel and drew deep, calming, solemn breaths, trying to connect to the beyond.

Some Orthodox practitioners feel that their sacred sites and rituals are only for them. I have had troubled travelers who asked for priestly blessings and been refused because they were not Orthodox. This is not common, and I am often welcomed with love and respect. But this trouble is embedded in our collective human history of endless religious conflicts and wars. These were my first visits to the monastery in thirty-three years during which I experienced trouble, rejection, and judgment rather than serenity.

Giorgos Kanabos expressed this sad condition in his poem "Décor."

> *In the garden of God*
> *the ancient priest hints*
> *at a sacrilegious roaring*
> *but me—I breathe!*[2]

The talk and vacuum in the chapel were roaring that day. All I could do was breathe and remember how my heart had come to life during previous visits. I returned to Rota. I wanted immersion in Giorgos's theology of the taverna.

"Don't let this bother you," he said gently. "What happened to you is a betrayal of Jesus. Jesus loved everyone. He forgave the thief and the prostitute." Giorgos affirmed, "The church was supposed to follow Christ's love. But it has in too many ways become the same institution that killed Jesus. The hierarchy of today are the Pharisees of the past. Some people are uneducated and ignorant. Stay on the ground. Forget about it." I remembered Plato's words, "Wand bearers are many. Inspired mystics are few."

172 ∽ THE SHADOW OF PARADISE

A few days later Giorgos approached me again. In his thoughtful, calm voice he said, "Jesus demonstrated universal love. He tended the woman at the well. When others rejected the Samaritans, he told the good story, demonstrating that we must live and be judged not by our theological beliefs but by our deeds. 'By their fruits shall you know them.' All our great teachers brought this message: Jesus, Sokrates, Gandhi, Martin Luther King, John Lennon. And they were all killed for it."

Giorgos the unrecognized monk, in his taverna chapel, healed the invisible spear thrust to my heart that the appointed servants had caused.

Apocalypse on the Island

We live in an age of apocalypse. *Apocalypse* is an old Greek word that literally meant "to uncover or reveal," to take the lid off. Not originally a negative word, the biblical Book of Revelation has the literal Greek title, "The Apocalypse of John." That book of the New Testament recorded John's divine vision acquired during his solitude in a cave on the island of Patmos. John warned of "the four horsemen"—plague, famine, war, conquest—galloping down on humanity, destroying everything in their path. But the end of the world is not its point or goal. Apocalypse tears the cover off the shadow—all that humanity has hidden—to release or reveal it and give us the opportunity to recreate our world order before it destroys us. The signs of apocalypse that are sweeping over the world are also on Poros: the changing weather, drought, waters going bad, alienated youth, division of wealth and development by the affluent no matter the consequences. It is everywhere and we cannot escape. We have heard of the upscale development on this island, the yachts, homes, disappearance of traditional tavernas and shops, in their place boutique shops opening to cater to the affluent and further transform the island into a playground for tourists and the wealthy.

Every fact is also a symbol. A lion is a wild animal that is also a symbol used for courage, strength, and ferocity. Actual and metaphorical, physical reality and dream, the personal and the mythic—all one.

Walk the Poros quay around the curving bay, past the tavernas and shops, the banks and municipal center, the Mermaid statue. A shop

THE SHADOW OF PARADISE ❧ 173

stands at the end of the long line of businesses before the road crosses the canal. It is a women's clothing store. Its marque is a symbol for the changes happening to our world that are also infecting Poros. The name of this shop at the end of the street is "Apocalypse."

In my earlier years and visits to Poros, I experienced and imagined the island to be pure, pristine, idyllic, an escape from the crises and deterioration infecting our world. Now I know better. I know Poros's shadow. The forces of decay and despair, alienation and impoverishment, class divisions and ecological deterioration have reached the island.

I used to retreat to Poros to escape the world rot. In recent years I have asked myself if I want to seek another more remote, undiscovered, less accessible island for my journeys. But Poros also taught me this: To love something or someone is to know them fully, light and shadow, good and bad, blessed and challenged, strengths and weaknesses. To know fully is also to know and embrace the other's shadow and to devote oneself, as much as possible, to help transform it back to its origins, its ideals, to help it be its best and heal its wounds. Poros also teaches this: to love fully we must embrace the shadow. On Poros I do.

10

A Healing Island
Physical, Emotional, and Spiritual Transformations

If you don't want the truth, don't come to Poros. Poros makes you see yourself.

PAMELA JANE ROGERS

In asylia, or sanctuary, we seek safety, rest, refuge, respite, accepting and supportive community, and divine presence. In ancient times and in Poseidon's sanctuary, Poros offered these. Throughout history, as a place of refuge, displaced, oppressed, and dispossessed people found these here. These are qualities people are desperate for today in our challenging and endangered world and times. Though the physical sanctuary is long gone, Poros still offers them in abundance.

What is the nature of Poros as a millennia-old sanctuary for healing? How does the island function as a healing sanctuary today? How can it help us achieve psycho-spiritual and holistic healing? How and why do modern seekers travel to Poros for healing? How do I conduct modern incubations and healings in the ancient Asklepian and other traditions? What are our dream interpretations and the long-term impact of incubation therapy for patients? How do we achieve a synthesis of sanctuary and healing through evoking the original powers represented by Poseidon and Asklepios? And what efforts are being made by other healers to restore the ancient ways and redevelop Poros as a modern sanctuary for refuge, safety, and holistic healing?

"I'm Going to Poros"

Kristina Gustafsson is a former activist and artist in her late sixties. She lives in cold Lapland, in the far north of Sweden. At home she had a severely broken leg, was on crutches and in a wheelchair, and was told she might never walk again. She refused to accept the prognosis. Against doctors' and friends' recommendations, and with limited income, she first traveled to Poros in 2001 to seek healing.

Kristina found Poros accidentally. She was in Athens and simply wanted to find a small, quiet, inexpensive, and peaceful island that was, to make travel easier, not far away. She stayed in 7 Brothers and met the brothers, the original owners, who, she says, were very friendly. She remembers Poros twenty years ago. The post office, now on the same stone porch as the hotel, was a taverna. There were no modern shops with expensive goods for the affluent, but only small family-run trinket and souvenir shops. Though doctors said it would not happen and she was in danger traveling, she stayed into 2002 and healed her leg.

Kristina returned later that year with her seven-year-old daughter. The precocious child dressed herself up, went out to dinner alone, was treated as a princess by those she met, and returned to her mother radiant with joy.

I met Kristina in 2022 on the village streets. At the time she was struggling to walk with the aid of two canes. This time she had a severe staph infection in her toes. Again, she was told she would never walk again and should not travel. But she declared, "I'll be okay because I'm going to Poros." On arrival, struggling to disembark the ferry, she broke into tears as both crew and residents tenderly helped her onto shore.

Over months of slow walking, she healed and now can walk distances without canes. She declares that the healing ingredients on

176 ⌒ A HEALING ISLAND

Poros are sun, warmth, exercise, healthy foods, and affordable and accessible living situations. She uses Louise Hay's teachings to work on self-healing, agreeing that her diabetes is not just a physical illness but her soul's hunger for sweetness.[1] She finds it on Poros. She affirms Hippokrates's teaching that illnesses begin in the soul. She says, "Fifty percent of healing is the mind, 50 percent the body. We must ask ourselves what the soul is saying through the body."

The most important healing ingredient Kristina has found on Poros is filoxenia—the encouragement, support, and belief she receives from local people. "Come home with me and have a coffee," she is invited, or "I'll cook your dinner." Now she strolls, sits, shares. She declares, "Everybody cares. They are so kind. Everybody becomes family." She feels this so deeply that she bought Christmas gifts for all the locals she knows.

Now Kristina often walks without canes and proudly dresses in bright Scandinavian-design clothing that affirms life. "Now Poros is my only Greek destination. This is my island too. I belong here."

The first time we met she smiled, lifted her arms to the sky, and declared, "This is a healing island."

With the God of the Forge

Not only Poros island, but the surrounding region is suffused with opportunities and sites through which we can enter the archaic world that lives behind appearances. Torrence Chrisman is a thirty-four-year-old man born with Apert syndrome, a rare and severe genetic mutation that effects the bones in the skull, hands, and feet. Since birth he has had more than twenty surgeries to correct his deformities. He has worked long and hard not only on his physical functioning but also on recovering from the medical and social traumas in his difficult history while shaping a positive identity to carry him through life. In this effort Torrence adopted Hephaistos, the disabled god of the forge, as his personal mythic deity and traveled with me to Greece to encounter him.

We drove a short distance from Galatas up the eastern coast of the Peloponnesos, then crossed the narrow road stretching between boulders and over the sea to arrive on the Methana peninsula.

Plate 1. Still waters in the bay perfectly mirror Poros town with its iconic clocktower.
PHOTOGRAPH FROM THE HATZOPOULEIOS PUBLIC LIBRARY ARCHIVES

Plate 2. *House of Serenity.* Across the bay from town is where writers and artists have retreated for two centuries.
OIL PAINTING BY PAMELA JANE ROGERS

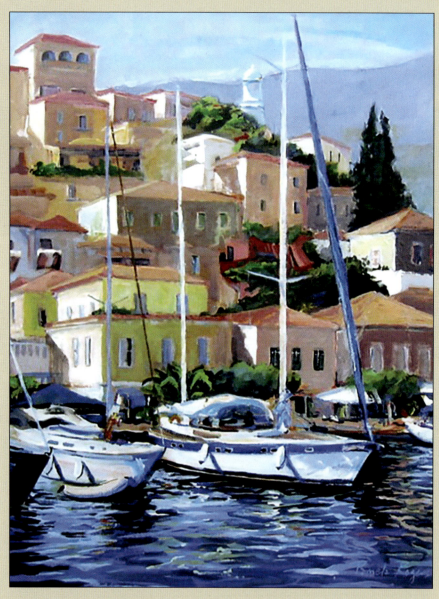

Plate 3. *Poros Harbour.* Built on volcanic rock, picturesque buildings climb from the water up the steep hills of Poros.
ACRYLIC PAINTING BY PAMELA JANE ROGERS

Plate 4. The century-old clock tower on the town's highest point has become the island's celebrated symbol.

PHOTOGRAPH BY BABIS KANATSIDIS

Plate 5. *Return from Hydra*. Entering the strait from Hydra island at its eastern end, the waters show endless flows and shades of blue.

ACRYLIC PAINTING BY PAMELA JANE ROGERS

Plate 6. Sleeping Lady Mountain dressed in magnificent sunset colors and displaying her goddess form.
PHOTOGRAPH FROM THE HATZOPOULEIOS PUBLIC LIBRARY ARCHIVES

Plate 7. *Olive Harvest*. The island's interior and Grecian mainland across the strait are replete with olive groves providing villagers with food, oil, and commerce.
WATERCOLOR BY PAMELA JANE ROGERS

Plate 8. *Dvořák Quartet*. Traveling and local musicians bring Dionysian revelry to the island.
OIL PAINTING BY PAMELA JANE ROGERS

Plate 9. *Sleeping Woman Mountain at Sunset*.
For centuries Sleeping Lady Mountain has attracted artists and poets to contemplate and render its sun-stricken beauty.
WATERCOLOR BY PAMELA JANE ROGERS

Plate 10. *Punda, Poros*. The high, back streets of Punda town district where past and contemporary artists live, work, and find new vision.

WATERCOLOR BY PAMELA JANE ROGERS

Plate 11. The blazing sun chariot eternally settles at dusk over the goddess-form in the mountain.

PHOTOGRAPH BY THE AUTHOR

Plate 12. Mornings and evenings, fishermen, and now women, line the wharf seeking the day's fresh catch.

PHOTOGRAPH BY BABIS KANATSIDIS

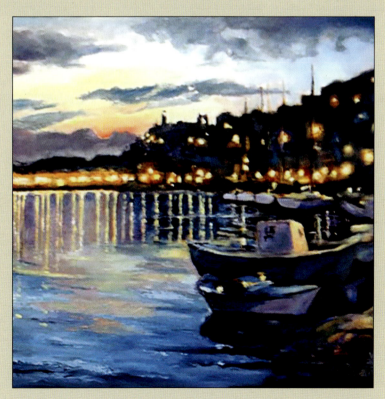

Plate 13. *Poros Twilight.* When the lights of the Poros and Galatas villages create a universe of beauty.

OIL PAINTING BY PAMELA JANE ROGERS

Plate 14. *Trizina Landscape*. On the island of Poros and on Peloponnese across the strait, the land is fertile.

OIL PAINTING BY PAMELA JANE ROGERS

Plate 15. The full moon glows over Poros island and sea, creating endlessly changing visions.

PHOTOGRAPH FROM THE HATZOPOULEIOS PUBLIC LIBRARY ARCHIVES

Torrence reports,

At first approach, the Methana volcano looks like an average mountain, but once we started the climb, I realized its sheer vastness and steepness. Unknown to the average hiker, volcanoes house the forge of Hephaistos. Deep in the bowels of the volcano was where the god of blacksmiths fashioned the armor of the gods and goddesses. Methana is not just a great hiking spot but a fiery protrusion for pilgrims to seek something like I did. Our group clambered over lava boulders as we scaled the volcano. Once at the top, with our pilgrims as witnesses, I asked for the god's blessing. Who better to ask than the one god on Mt. Olympus who has a similar disability as me? Standing on the mountain's crest, I felt as if the ground was vibrating beneath my feet. I closed my eyes and listened. I seemed to hear the distant muffled strikes of a hammer on the anvil. As we hiked back down, I felt as light as a feather dancing on the wind. Reaching the trailhead again, our group celebrated. We had earned something rare and precious. From my encounter with this disabled artisan god-power and in the company of veteran and civilian pilgrims, I achieved an awakening and identity transformation. I realized what I was born for and that I have a profound purpose. I am a warrior for disability justice. Now I can say that I love and embrace my disability.

Restoring an Ancient Practice

An ancient practice is being resuscitated, and a local native healer is bringing it to the island. Konstantina Vlachou is a native of Trizina, the modern village attached to ancient Troizen a few miles north of Galatas. It was the home of Theseus, the site of an Asklepieion and a Temple of Hippolytos. There was a sanctuary of Poseidon beyond the city walls, where he was called *Poseidon Phytalmios*. This name was given because the god was once angry with the Trizinians and flooded their fields with salty sea water. The curse was lifted after many prayers and sacrifices.[2] It was the place of sanctuary for Athenians during the Persian invasions.

178   A HEALING ISLAND

On Poros today Konstantina practices massage in the ancient style as taught by Hippokrates, as well as using other international and holistic modalities. Ancient Troizen was an important and sacred city that thrived for a long period and into recent times. Konstantina's love of Greek civilization set her on her lifelong path as a healer. "I studied the philosophers' records and especially Hippokrates, the great master of medicine. These many influences helped me evolve as a person and channel their philosophies through my work."

Konstantina's Ancient Healing Center is named Amaltheia. It is on one of the many old, quaint, and stony side streets that radiate off the waterfront, a few blocks beyond the Museum. Clients step through the wooden door and climb the stairs lined with wooden plaques with quotes from Hippokrates, including the one that declares that all illness begins in the soul. As in the ancient Asklepieia, these attune arriving patients to the body-soul healing they will receive. Upstairs, her offices are a sanctuary of serenity, calm, safety, and peace. Her massage room hosts a ceiling-high mural of Hippokrates giving massage, energy healing, or therapeutic touch to a patient lying on a couch, a *klinikos*, before him. When patients lie under this painting, they feel not only Konstantina but the master healer himself offering treatment.

Konstantina practices many different styles of massage. She was educated in and offers Ancient Greek massage, spa therapies, and sound, crystal, aroma, shiatsu, Taiwan, Siyanda, lymph, pregnancy, hot volcanic stones, and hot wax massages. Of all the techniques she says, "Massage is one of the oldest therapies for someone's physiological and psychological conditions. I have been working with ancient Greek massage for years and consider it to be the greatest of all the massages."

The name of Konstantina's healing center is Amaltheia because,

Zeus's nursemaid, Amaltheia, a significant presence in mythology, is described alternately as a nymph or a goat. The word itself describes a condition of nondeprivation. Her horn is a symbol of abundance and prosperity.

As a boy, Zeus was at risk of being devoured by his father, Chronos, who ate his offspring to keep from being displaced. To save

her son, his mother Rhea secretly hid him in a cave on Mount Ida on Krete, known as the Idaean Cave. She assigned his care to Amaltheia, who tended him with love and fed him milk and honey so he would grow up strong and take over his father's position as supreme god.

One day Zeus accidentally broke Amaltheia's horn as he was playing with it and, sad about hurting the nursemaid's feelings and wanting to express his gratitude, used his divine powers to ensure the horn was always abundantly filled with all of earth's seeds. This is the source of the cornucopia.

Our wellness center is inspired by the tender, loving care Amaltheia gave to young Zeus. We seek to be a wellspring of all good things, like the source of life itself, a space where harmony meets Hippokratic knowledge.

Konstantina affirms that there are only a few centers and practitioners of ancient massage today. A few special schools teach it, especially from the records left by Hippokrates. Why do Konstantina and others revive, study, and practice it now? What are its powers and benefits?

Ancient Greek Massage is based on techniques supported by Hippokrates. These were applied in wrestling schools, in gyms by coaches, and to patients in Asklepieia. As a healing process it releases stress, offers deep relaxation and wellness, and brings us closer to ancient philosophy. It combines "dry massage" with pressure and movement, following with a brush that reinforces blood circulation to the back. Afterward hot oil is applied with essential oils, followed by a special massage using a unique suction method. The oil is removed by a wooden scraper, the "curry comb." The treatment is completed with a "sadness rubbing," essentially a head massage during which the emission of serotonin is increased, and cortisol decreased, thus leaving a person relaxed and feeling like they have experienced ancient Greece. For the hand massage, virgin olive oil is used that has been processed in the traditional way of combining cold pressing with essential oils from the Earth. The therapeutic properties of ancient music and the Olympian gods' nectar take us back in time.

180 ∾ A HEALING ISLAND

This process has been in Greece for three thousand years. It is based on Hippokrates's principles and later doctors' philosophies. It is personalized, based on knowledge and insight into an analyzed historical background. It gives special emphasis to observation, palpation, and the cautious physical examination of the patient. Moreover, Hippokrates's meridians are used. Also, the target of healing is cure, elimination, symptom relief, and physical and mental recovery. Our holistic therapy helps guests relax their bodies, souls, and spirits because sadness is released, as sadness is the source of all illnesses.

Konstantina affirms Platonic and Hippokratic teachings that illness begins in the soul where our life's sorrows and losses lodge, and over time manifest through the body. Hippokrates taught, "Illnesses do not come upon us out of the blue. They are developed from small daily sins against Nature. When enough sins have accumulated, illnesses will suddenly appear." We must release their original sorrows and restore vital balance. Konstantina's work does this.

"Ancient Massage," says Canadian veteran advocate Susan Raby-Dunne, who has traveled here several times, "is aptly named." She relates,

Between Konstantina's skill and tools and the ambience she has created, I felt as though I stepped through a portal into antiquity. I showered, donned a full-length, light cotton tunic in the ancient style, and laid on her table under the larger-than-life, realistic depiction of Hippokrates treating a patient. Gentle hints of timeless essential oils such as frankincense wafted in the air. Relaxing acoustic music played in the background. Konstantina seemed to intuitively know which areas of my body needed work and discreetly worked on me from head to toe. One of my favorite parts was her use of a not-quite-soft brush. Konstantina's ancient massage was the best massage I've ever had. I still dream of it.

One year I arrived on Poros in intense pain, hobbling on two canes from a back injury and severe spinal stenosis. No conventional or alternative treatments stateside had helped. I was told dangerous back surgery was medicine's only response, and there was a good chance I could be worsened from it. I refused and traveled to Poros. After one month of biweekly sessions with Konstantina, and the warmth and filoxenia from community and climate, I threw away my canes and pranced in the streets.

Yet again, in my own and other's healing experiences, we see that holistic services based on spiritual wisdom applied with love in a supportive and healthy community can give us what we need for transformational healing, even to those conditions judged intractable by modern medical standards. Hippokrates's practices in ancient and modern times bring friendship and harmony back to the troubled body and through the physical restore the soul. Konstantina's practices do. The essential healing formula: spirituality in community.

A Peaceful Warrior[3]

The sun is strong and bright, the waters gleaming, even in early morning. I sit on my balcony sipping tea and watching the ripples glimmer, boats ferrying passengers or returning with their morning catch. Strollers and a few joggers are out on the walkway along the strait. The island is crowded this weekend for the Naval Academy graduation. Families have arrived from all over Greece to witness and celebrate.

A strong and slender middle-aged man emerges from his room onto the balcony next to mine. We each sit close to our railings and send greetings across the narrow abyss between our perches.

Jason is from Thessaloniki, Greece's second-largest city up north. Like many, he is on Poros for his son's graduation. He, too, graduated from this naval academy more than three decades ago. He served for thirty-two years, rising to the rank of commander; in the Greek navy this is equivalent to brigadier general.

Of all the actions during his service, Jason declares his most important to be one against the Somali pirates ravaging international shipping lines during the first decade of the millennium. Many attacks were successful, some ended in deaths of pirates or captives, some in

Fig. 10.1. Early morning sun and fishing off the northern point of Poros island.
PHOTOGRAPH BY TASOS RODIS

huge ransom payments. Jason's was different. Commanding a ship that intercepted a stolen vessel, he related to me across our balconies that,

> Our strategy was not to fight but to help. Most of these men were pirates because their country is very poor and at war and they are desperate people without food or money, with no way to support their families. We could either help or harm them. If we help them, they will not be pirates anymore. As commander, my mission was to protect ships and at the same time to help the pirates. If I must shoot, I have failed.

From my balcony seat I turn fully to Jason. His words are a true warrior's creed. The incident of a captive ship being rescued with no violence and no shots fired was reported on world news sources. It was Jason. On the Akropolis in Athens, as supplicants went through the sacred gates, they were first greeted by a statue of *Athena Promachos*, the goddess of war who stands in the forefront to protect and defend.

I meet Jason's gaze and say, "Promachos."

"Yes," he declares, "To Protect. To stop violence. That is the true calling."

"In my work, I call you a spiritual warrior."

Jason pauses, reflects, then smiles. "Yes. Exactly!"

We discuss the value of mandatory service that can mature the young. "No war," Jason says. "That is not why we create warriors. Only peace and love. Warriors are meant not to incite or rely on violence, but to stop it."

"How do you feel about your son entering service now?"

"Now my son follows in my footsteps," Jason says. "Now he understands me from the inside."

"And you both follow the great Greek tradition of seamen."

"Yes," he answers, "from ancient times until today."

"*Poly timi*," I respond. "Much honor."

Jason smiles and says again, "Yes. Exactly."

Warriors on Poros

I was lecturing to a large gathering in Athens on how I use the Greek tradition for war trauma healing. The American veterans I brought were in the front rows. A few uneasily whispered to each other. They were used to being an alienated minority in any gathering. One asked, "Does this audience understand why this is important to us? Are there any veterans present?"

I invited my veterans to stand, turn around, look at our audience. Then I asked the gathering, "Will all veterans present please stand up."

In the crowded room, every man stood. The American veterans gasped.

"Oh," one said. "Universal service. They're all vets."

"The Greek warrior tradition is still alive and well," another said.

"I've never been in a room full of veterans before," a third said. "I always feel alone and misunderstood. Not here."

I sat in a kafenion with tall, strong Kostas. He was interested in my forty-year career of working with soldiers and veterans suffering the wound that today is called post-traumatic stress disorder but was known and tended in ancient Greece and other warrior cultures around the world.

"Of course, we know of this wound." Kostas said. "It is in the epics and tragedies. It goes with war. When we have done violence, the Furies will have their ways with us."

"Yes," I said. "The ancient world had community ways to heal it. The tragedies were communal healing rituals. Warriors were honored no matter the outcome of the conflict."

Kostas looked pained and confused. "That is what I don't understand," he said. "No matter whether they were for or against the conflict, how can Americans dishonor their warriors when they return and not give them whatever they need to be restored?"

"Yes," I agreed. "As Perikles said, 'it is honor, not gain . . .'"

"No honor," Kostas groaned. "That is betrayal. That causes trauma." He stood up, agitated, as if in the assembly addressing a nation. "Win or lose does not matter. Politics don't matter. How can you abandon them?" he asked aloud. "They are your warriors!"

Though America has endless parades and political speeches extolling the service and sacrifice of warriors, very many American veterans, in contrast to Jason's report or Kostas's demand, do not feel like they fulfilled the warrior's calling and did not become spiritual warriors. Veterans from American wars since World War II generally feel that their conflicts were politically and economically motivated and not a necessary last resort purely for defense. They had wanted to serve as promachos but were used as pawns and aggressors. They served as servants of Ares, "the god who delights in slaughter," as Homer called him, not Athena, "hope of soldiers." Healing the trauma to their souls means transforming their devotion from the god who slaughters to the bright-eyed protectress.

I bring veterans to Poros to tend this special healing. My entire Spring 2023 group were warriors. They had served in Viet Nam, Iraq, Afghanistan, and at nuclear weapons facilities. We were sitting in the Hatzopouleios Library listening to director Yannis's lecture on the mythology, history, and ecology of the island. My group was polite but restrained. When they discovered he was a retired navy commander, the veterans exploded with curiosity, interest, and questions. Where and when did you serve? What was your ship? What missions were you on? Did you encounter the American navy? How were your ships, weapons, equipment compared to ours? The lecture morphed into an energetic sharing of experiences, attitudes, values fostered by military training and experience.

Susan Raby-Dunne is the Canadian veteran advocate with our group. Of our meeting with navy veteran and library director Yannis, she says,

> It was a privilege to meet retired Commander Yannis. Not only is he an accomplished military man, but he also gave us a fascinating history lesson on Poros and its area. We also got an intimate look at the island's natural history in the extensive "Seashells and the Sea" collection, which Yannis colored in for us, beyond the informational plates.

As I have seen countless times around the world, when veterans from any time and place meet each other, they launch into an immediate sense of brother- and sisterhood, affirm the similarities of their histories and sacrifices, and feel themselves to be in a close-knit group, highly compatible, easy to understand each other, and in a world separate from the civilian populations that do not share the legacy. Formal handshakes upon meeting transform to smiles, hugs, gratitude, teasing, and solidarity. This is common when warriors meet, more intimate for being on Poros. It is as Plato said, "He who has suffered . . . is willing to tell his fellow sufferers only, as they alone will be likely to understand him, and will not be extreme in judging of the sayings or doings which have been wrung from his agony."[4]

Babis Kanatsidis and I meet for coffee and talk, often in Porto Café, with cappuccinos for him, *tsai vounou* (wild mountain tea), for me, over our shared interests. As a journalist, he devours history, politics, and social movements and transformations. He is as interested in my work, especially with warriors, as I am in his and Poros. We met with my group. We sat together in a tight rectangle around a table under the

186 ∽ A HEALING ISLAND

Rota awning. American veterans wanted to know his military experiences and history as much as he did theirs.

Like all Greek men, Babis served in the military. He was in the army in the 1990s during a time of high tensions with Turkey. He was stationed on the border with Turkey. Though everyone was fearing and expecting the outbreak of war, from his foxhole he could see Turkish soldiers opposite him. Even under those conditions, the Greek and Turkish soldiers were friendly to each other.

Even on the front lines, Babis did not fully realize that his purpose was to kill. He was shocked to learn that the United States military teaches all its young recruits that killing is, indeed, their job. How, he wondered, does it shape a young person's character to be trained and encouraged to kill rather than to protect and preserve? He reports that he retains warm feelings toward the ordinary Turkish troops he met; he is glad war never erupted and he did not have to use his weapons. His most shocking service experience was the discovery of sixty immigrants fleeing the Middle East trying to arrive to safety and freedom in the West.

American veterans learned that in Greece military service is universal. It is very poorly paid so families must support their child in service. Recruits are trained to fight if necessary but not encouraged or reprogrammed to kill. People in Greek military service think of themselves as defenders. They live up to Athena's creed, promachos, be in front to protect and defend, but do not become Ares, the berserker and aggressor.

Babis learned that the moral injury to American warriors is extensive and inevitable. They, not he, were used as aggressors. They, not he, were given missions they did not believe in that were politically and economically motivated and not purely for defense. The younger American veterans, not he, were in a small minority of people who enlisted voluntarily while most Americans don't serve. Some of the Americans had enlisted for other than patriotic reasons—needing a job, help for college, escape from abusive families and inner-city violence. The Americans, but not the Greeks, were decently paid. And no American vets felt that the government had been honest with them or that civilians appreciated and understood their sacrifices.

After listening to the American warrior stories and how it affected them, Babis declared, "In Greece we don't think about veteran status. I am not a veteran because here everybody serves. I was never in combat, so I did not earn that honor. Here military service is civil service. As in ancient times, everybody serves, and every family supports that service as their way to give back to the country. The Greek military is the only model of socialism that we practice. Ancient or modern, we strive to live up to the ideal to give back to the country that has given so much to us."

"I understand," I said. "That is why Sokrates accepted his execution. Give back instead of taking all you can get. I wish all Americans felt that way about our country."

Warrior is an archetype, a universally recurring motif in human experience. Warriors stretch in an unbroken lineage from Spartans and Athenians to modern soldiers, from the ancient to the contemporary. Uniforms and weapons change; the archetype is eternal. The more deeply a warrior feels part of that lineage, the more strength, guidance, and resilience they have against the horrors they must encounter. Warriors not only honor all who served. They also honor and wish to protect and mentor the warriors who will come after them. It is part of their ancient tradition.

Major Nate Graeser, in my group, is an active-duty American Army Chaplain about to be deployed to the Middle East for the third time. He will be in command of the chaplains and spiritual care of warriors for an entire division—eight or more chaplains in charge of the well-being of more than ten thousand troops for a year in the desert on the borders of active and brutal warfare. Nate is on our journey as spiritual preparation for this time and task. Quaker peace activist Andrew Grant and Chaplain Nate were roommates. Andrew says, "We found common ground in a need to heal war trauma and a curiosity about the makings of peace. Our reflections about Ares and Athena, the aggressor and defender characteristics of war, continue to unsettle my Quaker notions of peace. When must a community defend itself from aggression and by what means?"

Chaplain Nate and Quaker Andrew swam together across the strait. In mythic times, in Mary Renault's retelling, Aegeus, the king of Athens, swam the strait for his secret rendezvous with Aithra, and "she did not doubt that Lord Poseidon himself had come to claim her." Theseus swam it too, as well as spending one month out of every four on Sfairia for three years, in service to Poseidon. Nate and Andrew replicated this story. Andrew says, "The swim kept pitching into the mythic realm: the invigoration of the cold, clear channel, the quest to cross over and back, our elder friend and guide waiting for us as if by divine appointment to return." Army-strong Nate led the way as well as kept track of his new peacemaker brother. When they emerged on Poros again, panting and dripping, a retired octopus fisherman scolded them, "That was dangerous. Passing boats could not see you and you might have been harmed. You might have been arrested." Andrew agreed, "We were arrested by the forces of beauty and wonder." As the mythic heroes did, so did they. *Moira* means both "fate" and "destiny." "It is when we stretch out our hands to our moira that we receive the sign of the god."[5]

My group of veterans and I are dining together at Rota where food

Fig. 10.2. Swimming off the northernmost tip of Poros village.
Photograph by Tasos Rodis

A HEALING ISLAND ⁓ 189

and conversation flow easily and deliciously. Andrew, the only non-veteran in our group, is working to heal white–Indigenous relations in America. Across the way under the same canopy, a group about as big as ours also dines. They are all young men with close-cropped hair, strong builds, determined eyes. Beer bottles crowd their table along with heaps of food. While the older people at our table eat fish, vegetables, and salads, the other group asks for meat and more meat, and their conversation is raucous.

Nate reports, "I was struck by the noisy table of young men. They felt to me like young warriors. Just like those I serve with in the military." Nate looks at the table and asks Christos, "Naval Academy?"

"Yes," Christos smiles. "They are here to defeat the American navy." We laugh.

"Let's buy them a round," Nate suggests. We all agree and ask Christos to serve fresh beers to each cadet. The cadets receive the bottles and lift them high. We lift our bottles or glasses, and all shout toasts across the room. Nate nods toward them. "Should we?" "Let's go," we call in unison and rise to join the cadets. Chaplain Nate loves young warriors and leaps from his chair. He says,

I ask them why they are here, and they explain they are naval cadets. I ask lots of questions about their service, and they share how much they want to learn. I am struck by how devoted and excited they are to serve in their military and how much meaning Poros has that they are unaware of.

Though the cadets had been up the mountain, they do not know it had been Poseidon's sanctuary or the history or importance of the island. I share stories of sacrifices and old ways to honor the gods. The cadets light up.

Everyone exchanges names. Most of the Greek men have common names—Nikos and Michalis and Dmitri. There is also Ajax, the only one in this group with a mythic name for the second-fiercest warrior among the Greek army at Troy. We launch into storytelling and comparison of military values, experiences, and history.

190 ᔓ A HEALING ISLAND

These young men will graduate the Naval Academy at the end of the week. As advanced trainees they will become officers and lifers in the Greek Navy. The American veterans want to know how they feel about serving.

These officers-to-be feel honored and proud. "Service is necessary and honorable," one says. "We truly believe that we are protecting our country and its values," adds another.

"Then how do you like your government?"

The cadets laugh. "We don't! How do you like yours?" We all laugh. "Our government is betraying Greece and all of us," one says.

"Then is service still honorable?"

"Yes. Service is for the country and its values, traditions, and security. It is not about supporting the government or any political party or position. It is about protecting and preserving our freedom."

"Eleftheri i thanatos," one chimes. The others smile and echo it aloud.

"Don't you American warriors feel this same way?" another asks.

The Americans express their loneliness, isolation, sense of betrayal, alienation from the public, lack of healing know-how and resources, depth of pain from serving the wrong causes for the wrong reasons. "We wish we did feel as you do," air force veteran Charlie says. "Each of us did at the beginning of our service, but we were disillusioned and betrayed. We could not believe the causes we were told to serve. Our idealism and belief burned away. We've come to Greece to heal because we can't in America."

"How do you Greek sailors feel about the American military?" navy veteran Lawrence asks.

The cadets look at each other. Then one answers, "We envy American wealth, weaponry, and technology."

"We wish we had your ships, but not your conditions," another adds. A seriocomic comparison of ships and weapons systems in both navies follows. Conditions for the American and Greek warriors are reversed. The Greeks simply wish they had the firepower and resources of the American navy, but not its conditions or missions. The Americans honor the Greeks, their values and sacrifices, and their ancient traditions. We affirm they are continuous with it. The Americans envy their moral purpose, that their service is purely for defense, they are proud and feel no moral injury.

"You still believe. We do not," says Lawrence.

"That," I say, "is the worst wound. Not combat itself but the loss of belief. It leaves a hole in the soul."

We wish them safety and bid each one goodbye by name.

"Be especially careful, Ajax," I say to him. That ancient fierce warrior committed suicide upon being dishonored by the army. "Your name carries utmost warrior power," I say. "But you do not want his fate."

Ajax chuckles and thanks me. "I know," he says. "My name is both a gift and a warning. I listen!"

"As we should have long ago when it was our turn," Charlie adds sadly.

A few days later, Nate wanders to the lighthouse to watch the sunset. There he meets the cadets again. Together they contemplate the Sleeping Lady in her yellow, orange, and scarlet dusk colors. He tells them the best version of the history of Poseidon's sanctuary and island that he can conjure. Their faces show wonder and awe. Their smiles become radiant. They thank the American chaplain profusely. "Learning that they were becoming Greek naval officers on their sea god's island transformed their experience." Nate says, "Our meeting felt like a way to help young warriors find a deeper meaning in their service—one tied to the gods."

A Green Island

The only constant is change, Heraklitos taught. Along with climate change and the shake-up of the world economic and political orders, Poros is inevitably changing. We witness the negative impact on the environment—little rainfall, high temperatures out of season, thirsty and thin crops, changing patterns of fish migrations. We hear the impact of tourism and affluence and the increasing hardships of residents. In response to these changes and if a sustainable future is its goal, Poros must change as well.

As of this writing and in contrast to the dangers from fish farming,

Poros has become the third island in a "GR-eco" sustainability program. Goals include electrifying the water taxis that cross between the island and Galatas, installing a photoelectric park to provide most of the island's power needs, electrifying public and private transportation and delivery services and adding charging stations, and introducing significant recycling and waste reduction.

It is easier to achieve these changes on a small island than in a major population center. In the same way that tiny Poros has led as an example of asylia, safety, and refuge for millennia, so it may also help lead the way toward the greening of all Greek islands and the restoration of the metron, a healthy and sustainable balance between Mother Earth and our human needs that can take care of us all.

11

Asklepios on Poros
Dream Incubation and Therapeutics

> *But I tell you: Sleep, my baby, and let the sea sleep, let*
> *Our trouble sleep; let some change appear.*
> Simonides, "Danaë and Perseus"

Though I have visited and used numerous ancient sites all over Greece, I have been guiding pilgrims to Poros, using it as a modern healing sanctuary and conducting incubations and rituals on Poros and in surrounding sites for three decades.[1]

I conducted my first Asklepian dream healing incubation on Poros in 1995 and have led about two dozen since. In earlier years, I used to guide pilgrims to many different sites, two or three nights in a place, see as many Asklepieia as we could, and incubate in an appropriate and selected peaceful site along the way. In recent years I have changed this practice. It has proven to be far more effective, restful, nourishing to body and soul, welcoming to the heart, and embraced by the community, to bring my groups to the healing island of Poros for most of their stay in Greece. We root on the island, use its sites and good people for our healing work, make day trips to nearby sites relevant to the issues

194　ᴄᴏ　ASKLEPIOS ON POROS

we seek to heal, and do our incubations on Poros. From Poros, we easily visit Epidauros and Troizen, both with Asklepieia, or nearby Methana peninsula to climb the volcano and contemplate ultimate power and universal change. Or for warriors, we visit Mycenae and Tiryns, the Bronze Age sites of Agamemnon and his warlike people.

In Asklepios's Hospital

Torrence Chrisman joined our group on Methana where we climbed Hephaistos's volcano to appeal to his god-power, "the only imperfect deity among the Olympians." Before proceeding there, we drove from Poros to the ruins of ancient Troizen, ally of Athens and birthplace of Theseus. We explored Troizen's relationship with both Asklepian and Hippolytan sanctuaries, as refuges for their people. Then our group dispersed around the low, brown, and green ruin site nestled in the mountains, each pilgrim meditating and praying on their own. Torrence relates:

The sanctuary of Asklepios is a remote site nestled deep in the countryside. I walked upon these impressive ruins that once were an epicenter of healing in ancient Greece. Our modern hospitals have nothing on the healing powers of a place like this. Walking amongst the unrestored ruins, I realized how critical this sanctuary must have been to those seeking healing. I knew what they must have felt. I came to an outline of a rectangular room that seemed to have been a prominent place. I stepped inside and walked around the center of the room. As I walked, I felt a breeze arise out of the still hot air. The breeze carried the strong smell of a sterile hospital, a smell that I am all too familiar with, along with a recognizable tinge of anesthesia I had been given decades before. An olfactory flashback! How was this possible? How did my body seem to know I was walking through an ancient hospital? My old medical memories and traumas were still in my body. Immersing in the ancient healing site enabled their release.

For those who have strong medical experiences, the bond between the ancient and modern world is still very much alive. The ancient Greeks traveled many miles to seek the healing powers of this sanctuary. Thousands of years later in the twenty-first century I felt those same healing vibrations walking amongst the ruins.

Warrior Healing on Poros

Lawrence Markworth is a tall, gaunt eighty-year-old man with a warm smile and piercing eyes. He is a navy combat veteran of the Vietnam War. He was exposed to Agent Orange and has had post-traumatic stress disorder and cancers. Rather than relying on traditional talk therapy, Lawrence has mastered dreamwork and practices pilgrimage and cultural immersion for healing. He takes himself salmon fishing in Alaska. And we have traveled together twice to Viet Nam and twice to Greece.

During our first journey together, as we entered the ancient agora in Athens, Lawrence "felt immediately and spontaneously transported back to my life as a Greek warrior." He affirmed his belief in past lives and that he had been here before. He meditated at the Temple of Ares to reconcile with this fierce destructive power and there realized that Ares's rage was not his. He prayed to be released from the rage and guilt he carried over his Viet Nam service.[2]

Our second pilgrimage to Greece together was for warriors. We first went to Athens and from there to Marathon and Thermopylae to honor and connect with the ancient warrior tradition. Then we proceeded with our warrior dream pilgrimage on Poros. Poseidon is a power that is both fierce and gentle, destructive and protective, explosive and soothing. Poros is of the sea and Lawrence is a sailor. Together we twice visited the ruins of Poseidon's temple.

On the evening of our first visit, Lawrence had this dream.

I'm with my Greek pilgrimage warrior and dream group on the shore of a cove on Poros. In the distance we see a man in a red life jacket floating in the Aegean Sea. The wind appears to be rapidly blowing him away from us. He obviously needs to be rescued. I think no one in the group is capable of swimming that fast. I see a silver inflatable raft about four feet by ten feet, with a pointed bow and stern and two flimsy oars, on the shoreline. It is partially inflated. Then Arnold

196 ～ Asklepios on Poros

Schwarzenegger suddenly appears. "I vill get him," he says. I reach down to feel the raft. I think it does not have enough air in it and I tell that to Arnie. "Don't vorry, I vill get him." I don't think so, I say to myself. We all turn around to leave the beach. There we see Arnie and the rescued man in the red life jacket standing before us. Arnie says to me, "Vhat did I tell you?"

Lawrence shared the dream with the group the following morning. He reflected, "I was blessed to have my own personal visit from Poseidon, doing the work he does best, rescuing sailors from the sea." Air force veteran Aishi suggested the title of the dream should be "ASAP: Arnold Schwarzenegger as Poseidon." Lawrence said, "That only adds to the humor. The humor in this dream made me laugh when I awoke."

I pointed out the dream's importance. "You had a visit from the Poseidon archetype in the guise of big, strong, confident Arnold. It is an honor and confirms the rescue we experience here. You didn't think the sailor in the life jacket could be saved, but he was, not by human but divine intervention. Were you that sailor? Arnie was Poseidon's messenger."

Lawrence is no stranger to Poseidon. Rather, his visits on Poros strengthen his lifelong connection, rooting it deeper in his psyche. Poseidon has been with him for a long time. He reports:

From 1963 to 1965, while deployed on the USS Castor offshore Viet Nam, during a typhoon in the South China Sea, several other sailors and I feared we would capsize and sink. We felt Poseidon's power. Fortunately, he bestowed upon us his lifesaving abilities, as we survived that horrific storm. Gods and goddesses do watch over me. I've experienced too many life-threatening events, worse than a typhoon, and I have survived.

Dr. Charlie "Aishi" Blocher is an air force veteran who served on American Intercontinental Ballistic Missile Systems. He was one of a group of six specialists on his base, Missile Communications and

Instrumentation Branch. This small group had immense influence in that, as Charlie explains, "We had power over whether the missile left the ground or not." Charlie was metaphorically in the Underworld working with weapons that could destroy the planet, and sometimes literally underground serving in deeply sunken missile silos. He contemplated missiles as world destructive as the fiercest creatures of mythology.

Missile system names reveal the archetypal dimensions of thought behind them. Charlie worked on several generations of missiles—Atlas, Titan, Minuteman—named for the weapons' massive powers. Atlas . . . does that signal American power upholding and staggering under the weight of the world? Titan was the largest, most destructive intercontinental ballistic missile the United States ever produced, carrying a nine-megaton warhead. It was named for the extremely powerful mythological enemies of the gods seeking to overturn the cosmic order. The Minuteman generation followed, harking to the American revolution rather than Greek mythology, giving the weaponry a protective American rather than destructive mythological name. But it was a disguise. Minuteman carried three warheads, rather than the one of the Titan. It was designed to be highly accurate rather than cause general widespread destruction. Nuclear strategy evolved from explosive to surgical strikes launched from thousands of miles away. Charlie had served during all this and seen these missiles up close and launched.

A thoughtful, sensitive man, Charlie awakened to the terrible power that could be unleashed with his team's help. He affirms that he suffers the soul wound now called moral injury. One of Charlie's ways of addressing it has been to become initiated in Buddhism, from which he received the name Aishi. *Aishi* means "compassionate service." From his world-threatening military service and wound Charlie determined to seek and offer healing for the remainder of his life. His devotion to the Buddhist and healing paths expresses why we have come to Poros together; warriors need a spiritual path to heal the depths of wounding caused by encounters with the war god.

Moral injury is the modern name for a wound to the soul as old as humanity. Sokrates taught that the soul is that which determines

198 ∽ ASKLEPIOS ON POROS

good and bad. We deepen soul when we do good and harm it when we do ill. Charlie experienced his own soul being injured during his time in the air force. He experienced himself as locked in an invisible cage required to follow orders, if issued, that would betray his soul and deepest values.

Before Poros, I guided Charlie and our other veterans from Athens to Marathon and then Thermopylae. Connecting to the ancient warrior tradition, studying its values, honoring the warriors who fought and died for Greek freedom, identifying with their version of the honorable and moral warrior archetype all contribute to healing through identity transformation.

Charlie describes the impact of our visit to Thermopylae, the "Hot Gates."

> We honored the roadside monument to Leonides, the Spartan king who fell in the battle, fulfilling the oracle that a king must die to save Greece. Then we climbed the hill to sit before the grave of the 300.
>
> At Thermopylae a tremendous energy infused us from those fallen ancient soldiers. These defenders recognized they were not going to go home; they were going to die. And yet they stayed and defended their homeland. This is the reason that I joined the military—to defend my homeland from people who wanted to destroy human rights. What I found in the American military was not a defensive system, but one that controlled, subordinated, and manipulated people for power. This is how my moral injury occurred. In the military, in the air force, I had chosen the nickname Chuck to appear tougher, one of the guys. Chuck died on this Thermopylae battlefield so Charlie could be reborn.

After prayer and ceremony at the grave site, we proceeded to the ever-flowing hot springs, stripped, and entered the waters. Charlie says,

> I felt myself walking with the spirit I had felt at the gravesite. Our group encountered profound energy running through the water molecules of the hot springs. I approached the waters with reverence and was so taken aback by their cleansing ability that I lost my glasses. I chose to

live without my glasses so that I could continue to heal and immerse myself in the energy from the springs. Their loss taught me that I needed to learn to see by myself, to live without them. During that time, someone found my glasses through what seemed like spiritual intervention. The spirits taught and reinforced my need to "walk in spirit."

Our group then traveled to Poros. Charlie continues,

Poros brought home my moral injury from being an officer in the military as part of the team tasked with evaluating the delivery vehicle for nuclear weapons. I explored healing my moral injury through a cohort of veterans in an environment that held its community with love. This started with a mystical encounter at the temple of Poseidon. There I felt infused with an energy of profound calm and accepted myself for who I am. This sanctuary gave me the safety to explore the upheavals of my past along with the traumas of the military, without being driven deeper into despair.

I first encountered the temple in silence. I felt each of my footsteps as I went to the temple to give honor and libations to the god. Walking barefoot and singing with the ancient people of this temple brought me a unique Underworld experience. I met spirits that pushed and pulled me to continue developing my own power and labor with moral injury, thus birthing a more authentic human being. During this inner battle and in Poseidon's temple, I gave up being Chuck and became Charlie.

Charlie experienced a further visitation at the little church he found at the end of the trail.

At the two-door church, I reflected on its primal energy. A spirit entered and sat down. I thought it was a person, but no one sat next to me. What showed up was the spiritual energy of Poros island, which infused me with the confirmation that I am a highly sensitive, spiritual person.

From Poros, our group visited Mycenae and Tiryns, learning about and meditating on the warrior tradition from the Bronze Age to our own. In the dank, shadowy beehive tomb of Clytemnestra each person expressed the deep anguish they carry for both their own soul wounds and our world history of endless wars. Together they cried to the ancients to release them from the old shame they carry for serving the wrong causes. We then returned to Poros to conduct an overnight Asklepian dream incubation.

Incubants spent a day fasting, praying, and meditating in preparation to imaginally meet god-powers during their dreamtime. Then we met to share dream quest intentions and ritually enter the sleeping chambers. Charlie reported, "I realized the insight 'walks in spirit' as I prepared for incubation and being in a place to have a full dream realization. I am working on soul healing step by step." Initiated in Buddhism he realized he must connect it with both warrior healing and being highly sensitive. His wife has severe multiple sclerosis, and he awakened to new ways he must live with and tend her while also caring for himself. "It is all about connections," he declared with a new holistic vision, "not one thing." He declared at our group meeting before retiring,

I am different. I am working to live in my own skin. I'll take a piece of each group member into myself to rebuild myself. I've always tried to be somebody else and shut down after being assaulted. In the air force I turned Charlie into Chuck to be a stone. Now I'm out of my cage. I'm chucking Chuck. During the incubation, I entered a strange consciousness in which I was dreaming while being fully aware of my environment. It started with the first dream tender—the supporter from our group who visited while the incubants slept. She sat in the chair, and I felt her peaceful presence. She spread her hands and spoke calming words. I felt settled. This happened with all the dream tenders all night long. I was asleep, yet able to feel and be with them as I dreamt. They each told me the next day that I had slept and was not agitated in any way. I learned that I am very aware of the environment, and this enables me to help others rebirth into their *authentic selves. I recognized that each of the dream tenders were there for me to discover this power. At the time I was unaware of what was going on. It took two months to let the incubation settle into both my body and mind.*

During incubations, I always choose "the graveyard shift," 2 to 4 a.m., to tend the dreamers. I use active imagination. I pray, meditate, recite the Hymn to Asklepios, and surrender my conscious and rational self to envision the presence and healing that the god and his totems offer. Sitting by Charlie's bedside at 2 a.m., with everything still around us and the dark waters still outside, I see,

The snake of Asklepios appears coiled with its head rising. It is huge. It opens its mouth and Asklepios is inside, small and upright. A voice says, "People think Asklepios is the great one and I am small. Not so. Look. I am great, of the cosmos. I open my mouth and the god appears inside. He enters me. He leaves me. I am always here. Contemplate this mystery. It will rebalance yours." Asklepios goes in and out, in and out of the great serpent's mouth.

"You see," the snake says, "In and out. Up and down. Appearing and disappearing. Always. You wish to chuck Chuck. Then upchuck. Then swallow. You wish to un-gunk. Then vomit or swallow. You have done neither. Big things have been stuck in your gullet."

He closes his mouth. Asklepios disappears. A large lump moves down his length. "See," he says. "Like this." The lump moves and grows smaller. "Swallow. Digest. Let it pass. Your Buddhism teaches you. Swallow that too." The lump grows smaller. "Digest everything. Eat your shit. Even the undigestible. Be Aishi, the Buddhist name you were given, be him knowing you are not." The lump dissolves. From its tail a tiny Asklepios appears. "There," he says, "now you are baby Aishi. Swallow him too. Shit him out too."

The snake rises on its coils. It is huge. It towers over Aishi. "Now it is your turn," it says. Its jaws open wide and hover over him. It lowers its neck and takes him inside. "Now your turn," it says. "All that is left for you is to say Yes, and finish dying." The snake closes

its mouth over him. He disappears. The head and neck relax on its
coils. "Swallow until you are not even a lump." It lays its head on
its coils and sleeps. "You are my dream," it says. "Time to dream
another dream. Go and practice the art of disappearing." It sleeps.
"Not even impermanence," it says. "Believe in nothing and you will
have everything." Silence. The coil breathes.

Poros morning, clear and bright. Charlie and the other incubants awaken and recover at their own pace, then gather around a large table at Rota. We feed them well to celebrate and break their fast, then receive their dream reports.

Charlie Aishi declares, "I am no longer 'Less-than Man.'"

"Opa," the group calls.

Aishi reads a letter he has written to himself. It says that Chuck is gone. The name and identity were a rejection of who he really is, and it hid his high sensitivity. It was a false persona so he could fake it in the military. That led to alcohol abuse, depression, anxiety. The shadow of Chuck is disconnecting from Charlie/Aishi who can be in this beautiful world. "I choose my lifeline with flow," he declares. After writing his letter to himself, Aishi sees Sokrates enter and say, "I am resilient. When they come to take me away, it will be my pleasure." Aishi summarizes our retreat to Poros and what it did for him.

My retreat to Poros was fueled by my desire to heal my moral injury
and to "walk with spirit" with those around me. Poros's ancient energy
became my catalyst for being reborn into my authentic self through my
spiritual path. The spirits showed me that it was possible to heal and
help others to heal through my work as a spiritual companion.

What of Chaplain Nate Graeser? Did Poros help strengthen and prepare him for his Middle East deployment, which would follow our journey by only a few months? Can time on the island do this?

Nate's mission in the Middle East is named "Spartan Shield." He sat before the Spartan grave at Thermopylae in utmost reverence. A small turtle crawled to him, and he gently held it in his lap, echoing my turtle on Poseidon's mountain and presaging more turtle encounters several of our group would have on Poros. As ranking officer among us, he led an honor guard ceremony before the tomb. Back in the States after our journey, preparing his chaplains and troops for their year in the danger zone, he says, "I'm using the Spartan name and my visit to their site as an excuse to talk about Spartan warrior principles and how they can apply to our work as soldiers—accepting our destinies, lives, and discipline. And asking ourselves this question: what are you willing to die for?" Nate summarizes the impact Poros had on him.

Upon arrival, I immediately felt the depth of story, the smallness of the island, and its profound connection to the ocean. The sleeping lady in the mountain beckoned us to lay down our troubles.

Over the course of our week there, I walked, ran, and swam daily across the island. I listened for its healing touch. It was as though Poros was beckoning me to be, to see, and to open. I was filled with wonder as the churches and temples asked the same of me. Each time we prayed, left alms, or made ceremony, I opened a bit more. In Poseidon's temple, I felt it call me back. A few days later I returned, made alms, and felt a deep sense of being held, that all the forty-one years of my life had led to this place, in this time, with these precious fellow travelers. Poros was both a spiritual destination and a place to prepare me for my next journey. It was the place where I felt my spirit pull me into a new life.

On our final day together on Poros, we ascend to Poseidon's sanctuary a second time. We gather on the old temple grounds in what Andrew calls "the grove of dancing pine trees." We share all that this visit has meant, how we have changed, what wisdom we will carry home. We celebrate our meeting with the naval cadets, who until our time together did not know that they were becoming naval officers in this sacred way—on the sea god's island beneath his ancient sanctuary.

As is my custom, I bestow Greek names on incubants. This is a replication of the practice in many traditional cultures of receiving new names in new life stages or after initiations or other significant transformational experiences. We are different with different identities and our names can express that.

Nate is a beekeeper, communing with and protecting them. He and others had significant encounters with bee swarms climbing Poros's mountain. Nate receives the name Aristeos who was a son of Apollo raised on nectar and ambrosia. He was an ancient rustic god of shepherds, beekeeping, and honey. His roommate Andrew, who had been given the name Seeker of Truth by his Native American mentor, receives the Greek name Apollodoros, the gift of the god of truth.

We draw runes in Poseidon's temple. Runes are an old Viking way of receiving oracles. This final ritual gives each group member a guiding oracle to carry forward. Nate receives Self, instructing him to focus on what abides as he tills the field of his new endeavors. Andrew receives Hail, indicating elemental power that rips away his old reality. And Aishi receives Opening Reversed, indicating that he is in a time of crisis with a difficult passage at hand. Indeed, at home he is devotedly nursing his wife who is slowly deteriorating and dying of multiple sclerosis.

We recite Poseidon's hymn together and descend his mountain, supplied with new names, identities, dream visions, and guiding oracles to carry forward on our mythic life journeys.

A Greek Doctor Encounters the Mysteries

Maria, a small, dark-complexioned woman, is a medical doctor from Athens, working half of her time in a hospital and clinic and half in private practice. She is an adult internist committed to natural and holistic healing. She uses homeopathy and sound healing, seeking a complete and noninvasive treatment regimen for her patients. Her personal and professional goal is "to move beyond medicine and psychology to help my patients heal their essence."

Maria and I met years ago. We have walked the Athens streets, prayed, and studied in the agora, shared with mutual friends. In our private conversations Maria confided some of her history with family and love relationships. She is a loving, caring, gentle person and her patients experience this from her doctoring, but she has not often been treated in kind in personal relationships. Notably, Maria's traumas began in the womb. As a fetus she almost died, and she had a very difficult birth.

Maria is an avid dreamer. She often has archetypal material in her nighttime adventures. As a Greek woman, they are full of mythological imagery. But they are busy and chaotic, and she did not understand what they were telling her. She decided to join my 2022 Asklepian journey. She had never been to Poros and had never practiced a formal incubation.

Our group of American and Greek pilgrims first met in Athens. At our first meeting, Maria shared two dreams:

> I am helping a friend who is in the hospital. I cannot find a doctor and feel much anxiety. Surgery is ordered for my friend.

Indeed, Maria's older friend and mentor has cancer; Maria, her primary support, is quite worried about her, and will miss some time with our group to be with her in the hospital. Another dream:

> I see a small dog biting the full moon and a lake. The full moon is in my left palm and the sun in my right.

"Balance," a group member calls out. "See it. Do it," another says. "Moon and lake," I say, "Earth and Sky. And a dog, Asklepios's messenger. Let's discover what he brings you."

As our group meetings proceed, it becomes clear that almost everyone on this year's journey, including Maria, has severe intimacy wounds; each one has experienced abandonment, betrayal, domination; none are in satisfying intimate relationships. Each has suffered from the archetypal pattern of patriarchal dominance and abuse built into Western civilization that, tragically, has deep roots in ancient Greece and is well-portrayed in mythology and history. Greek women in particular replicate this ancient pattern; often older men marry younger women for sex, family, and home, but not intimacy or equality, and women feel lonely, frustrated, and dominated. This has been Maria's and the other women's experiences. From Athens, to confront and work to heal this old wound, I decide to lead this group to Eleusis, the sanctuary of Demeter and Persephone where their ancient mystery rituals were practiced.

At Eleusis, Maria meditated in front of the Cave of Hades where Persephone was brought to the Underworld and Demeter grieved.

In the meditation I felt myself going down into the cave. It was like returning to the uterus. I didn't want to leave that place as I felt safety that I usually do not feel. But I decided to continue. Descending further, I could see many shadows: my own, all the people I know, and one who had hurt me in the past. I could feel his pain as mine. I cried from compassion, love, and forgiveness. I felt I could die there and didn't care at that moment because I was in a field of love. Then another traveler touched my hand, and I started to come out into the light. I saw the image of Jesus in front of me, full of light and emerging from the tomb. I felt that the essence of Eleusis was about the dying of my small ego for my true self to emerge through the power of love and forgiving myself and the others.

One of our group members brought Greek oracle cards. Like the runes or the I Ching, the images of mythological figures portrayed on each card help a seeker attune their present life circumstances with the archetypal movement of their psyches and the cosmos. What myth am I living? What myth is living me?

We gathered in the great theater at Eleusis, sitting together on the long stone seats that line the hillside where in ancient times the officiates revealed the mysteries to supplicants. With the group witnessing, Maria drew a card representing Harpokratis, the Egyptian son of Horus. He was a god of innocence and silence. His greatest treasure was to travel silently deep inside himself to affirm that what we know inside is true. This represents Buddhist beginner's mind, the invitation to start again. As a deep and quiet person who dreams, meditates, and prays much, Maria felt affirmed to continue her path and encouraged to continue with inner work.

In Athens, Maria had to miss some of our group time to tend her hospital-bound friend. Finally smiling and relieved, she reported that she had indeed found a doctor and her friend had undergone successful surgery. Her earlier dream, which she feared was predictive, instead proved to be a warning she heeded to a danger she successfully averted.

On Poros our group meets and shares the impact of our time at Eleusis. Maria says that she felt our group connection and that everyone was traveling deep inside. That gave her support. She connected with her shadow, realizing that the abusers of her past were also hurt and ignorant. She achieved a compassion for them she had not known and affirmed that her death will be okay because she will live through others.

We travel to Epidauros for the day. We roam the ruins, receive teachings, and each traveler incubates for a time in the ruins of the *abaton* (the sleeping chamber).

Maria has this dream after visiting Epidauros and praying in front of the tholos.

> I was in front of the tholos. It was already built, and I was knocking on the door to go in. Priests asked my name and parentage. When I replied, they told me, "You are a daughter of the earth and sky, and your name is Dorothea." With that name they opened the door and gave me a pomegranate. I went into a labyrinth and met people from my life. I would stop in front of them and say, "I am Dorothea, and this is my gift to you," and give the pomegranate. Some accepted it and some were not able to see me. Inside the labyrinth I felt tired and couldn't go on. I stopped. They told me, "It doesn't matter if you go to the end. There is no end and no beginning, only the movement in between." I continue and arrive at a white circular marble, like the one in the Epidaurus theater. I sit on the marble and the whole place lights up. I am looking for the source of the light and realize that I am the only one holding a torch. I remain there, peaceful in the white light.

208 ∽ ASKLEPIOS ON POROS

Maria is in a holy place and receives the pomegranate of Persephone. She offers it to others so they too can make the Underworld descent to heal. "A daughter of earth and sky" mirrors the dream of sun and moon in her palms and she realizes goddesses were portrayed that way; she is connecting with the divine feminine. Her archetypal dreams gift her a new name and are transforming her identity. In the Asklepian tradition, we watch for the dreams and signs that come before incubation as well as during the ritual. "Beckoning dreams" tell us it is the right time to incubate and approach the healing god. Maria/Dorothea seems powerfully and continually beckoned. She continues to dream up until incubation.

Maria/Dorothea has another dream before incubation that again confirms she is changing, healing, and is called to incubate. Again, it connects with an earlier dream showing that she is achieving a new inner balance.

> I was in front of a lake, I open my left palm, and the full moon was there. After I opened my right hand, the sun was there. The lake opened in the middle and a temple appeared.

On Poros, we have a long group gathering to prepare for incubation. Maria says that at Eleusis she experienced her heart opening to compassion and forgiveness. After Eleusis she had the dream telling her that her name is no longer Maria, it is Dorothea. And at the temple of Poseidon, she became accustomed to her new name. She spontaneously had visions of deities and gave thanks. She met a writer in the ruins taking notes for a book on identity changes and shared her story. Arriving back at our hotel, she felt flooded with a newfound joy.

It is time, for Dorothea and the other pilgrims, to enter the dream temple. During her incubation she has this dream:

> I started to rotate and scanned my body to relax. But I found that the first chakra was on the top where the seventh would be. I thought I was doing something wrong, but the priests told me that you find the lower chakra above because you are below the earth, you are in the tomb. Then they told me that they took me to the

Underworld and now it is time to take me to the astral plane. I felt that I should leave my body but was afraid. Then I was in Eleusis again where the temple was. I started going up a staircase in the temple that led to the sky.

First, I made a stop by Selene, goddess of the moon, where the other women of the group were. I made a prayer for all of us so Selene would heal our traumas and help restore our feminine energy. Then Selene gave me her blessings. I continued going up until I arrived at a place full of light. There were other people with light bodies. I felt them to be like my family. At the same time, I felt strong energy like electricity that ran down and up through my entire body. After a while it stopped. Then I was in Poseidon's temple. I sat on a stone and another woman, who felt like my twin self, also sat back-to-back with me. We both got up and went to the sea where we dove in. I felt totally relaxed and went into a deep sleep.

When Dorothea awoke in the morning, she felt tired and at the same totally renewed, "not only in my physical body but also in my mind and emotions."

As in all incubations, I sat by Dorothea as she slept in the darkest hours and channeled an Asklepian vision. To Dorothea:

Panageia stands by your side, looking down with utmost love and compassion. "You were named for me," she says, "because your birth and life were a difficult gift from me. You have carried my name with honor until now." Tears for you dribble down the Virgin's cheeks. "I grieve that I gave you a difficult birth, but it was so that you could lead a blessed life."

Panageia stands tall and becomes Hygeia. "Now you are my servant. You died and were reborn. You descended and returned. Your heart and soul never left, only floundered. Now they are returned. Through your love, devotion, and courage you have gathered them back into your heart, which is my heart, which is the loving heart of the world."

Hygeia becomes Quan Yin, the Asian goddess of compassion. "See. We are all the same, all one. You are one with us. You are truly

*Dorothea, the gift of the goddess and the goddess's gift to all who
serve to our suffering world. Go forth as Dorothea Maria, from me to
all, from your difficult birth to your will to live. You are my gift to the
bleeding heart of the world. Please light candles for me in our little
church and behold my loving face loving you."*

*The divine mother leaves, goes into the church, and enters her
icon awaiting your blessing and consent.*

Dorothea reports that after returning home, she felt that she was
no longer alone, that a divine presence was with her, "like my higher
self to guide and support me." She felt grateful for the incubation, the
Asklepian energy, the support of the group, and the Greek archetypes
that "I felt are alive, connecting, and communicating with me." As
we have seen, and as was practiced in the Asklepieia, supplicants are
drenched in the imagery of the archetypes and previous healings so
that their own unconscious responds with dreams and visions using the
same pictures and stories and showing us how our individual lives are
connected to the cosmos and replicate the eternal stories.

Months after our journey, Dorothea continued to dream vividly and
mythologically. Since her incubation and rebirth, she reported feeling
her double spirit close to her. She continued to dream avidly, many with
Dionysos. In one dream she was in a lake at night with stars blazing
overhead. A voice said, "You cannot fix the cosmic order." Another time
the "eternal Dionysos," male and female, appeared. She felt wise and revitalizing male energy returning. In yet another, Athena appeared, expressing gratitude to Dorothea for working for her for so many years. Athena
presented her with a golden spear and the instructions to "rise above."

The impact on Dorothea's medical practice? "The female patients
in my practice heal very quickly. They talk more easily to me. I am
becoming a soul doctor."

The Statue and the Dream

*I am on the second floor of the archeological museum. I have walked
past the urns encrusted with sea creatures and shells, the cases of*

jewelry, and many small terra-cotta votive offerings of Poseidon's totem animals, bulls and horses, a few figurines showing horseback riding, bull leaping, and driven oxen. I am surrounded by antiquities as I stand in front of the fourth-century BCE statue of Asklepios.

The god is standing upright, left knee slightly cocked, left arm draped with his robe that hangs across his muscled stomach. He is larger than life-size. As I contemplate the statue, I recite the Homeric "Hymn to Asklepios," "doctor of our ailing. . . . By my song I beckon you." Suddenly, gently, silently, I see not the statue but the god emerging from the stone and standing before me. He is both formed and formless, seeming to be both mist and solid, real and ethereal. He towers over me, a head taller, more upright. I see his curly hair and beard, his deep and shining eyes. His right arm holds his caduceus. He does not move, yet I feel his vitality and an energy radiating from him that penetrates me with wonder and awe.

I awaken and stare into the darkness. I look around and am surprised. I'm not in the museum but in my hotel bedroom. I look for the god but neither he nor the antiquities are visible. Then I remember, the museum statue is headless and about half life-size, not bigger than mortals, and mounted in a protective case. The statue is only a torso from shins to neck; I saw the god's face, arms, feet. I saw the larger-than-life, humanlike figure of the god emerge from the statue in a dream-vision. I felt whatever we mean by the spirit of Asklepios come alive, emerge, radiate from the stone, and penetrate me. I lie still and absorb.

Heraklitos declared that most people pray to images as if they were houses—things in themselves—rather than discerning the nature of gods. The divine, he complained, escapes men's notice.[3] The ancients did not believe that statues were deities. Rather, as was said, they created representations of the cosmic powers in human form to attract those powers into their statuary and temples. Art, humble, beautiful, created with sincerity and devotion, attracts the god-power into it. Then the work, the representation in paint, clay, or stone, serves as a daimon—an intermediary between the mortal and divine that channels images and energies into us. Reason is our best tool, Plato reminded us; the only better is divine revelation. We need reason to interpret the messages we receive and guide us with wisdom through the mysteries and storms of life.

In the Poros archeological museum of my dream, Asklepios the god emerged from his statue to bless and teach me the reality of these powers and our relationship to them beyond anything we can understand or explain. I still see the dream god and feel him trembling inside my chest. Far beyond my reason, profession, or human education, I strive to respond to this calling.

12

Restoring Poseidon's Sanctuary

Living in Agape

Nothing the gods accomplish passes belief.
BACCHYLIDES, "THESEUS AND THE RING"

Our world is challenged and threatened to the utmost. We are all frightened, traumatized daily by climate change and political and economic upheaval and violence, unsure if individually or collectively we will survive. We all suffer what Professor Randy Morris calls "extinction anxiety." In such apocalyptic times, we all need the sanctuary that Poros can provide.

Sanctuary has been practiced on Poros for millennia. Great and ordinary people, in the near and distant past, and now in the present, practice it. We see how through travel, study, practice of ancient ways, and deep cultural immersion and dreamwork, we can recreate the sacred dimensions of sanctuary.

Poros with its ancient sanctuary, and Poros today with its filoxenia suffused with generosity, welcome, warmth, and wisdom, teaches and

214 ∾ RESTORING POSEIDON'S SANCTUARY

offers safety, inviolability, and hospitality to the oppressed, lost, and homeless, whether their conditions be physical and historical or invisible and psycho-spiritual.

Life on Poros today recreates some of the most beautiful and supportive ancient Greek values and practices. We gather the gifts, lessons, and legacy of Poros as a refuge for achieving spiritual presence, healing, and connection to ancient and eternal forces, values, and practices, and to each other. We practice pilgrimage and immersion in this sacred place for soul renewal today.

It has been almost four decades since my first visit to Poros and encounter with Sea Turtle on Poseidon's mountain where I received what can best be imaginally conceived of as a gift from the sea god. I met a research archeologist and naturalist in the sanctuary one day about a quarter century after my meeting with Sea Turtle. I asked his opinion of my story. "A sea turtle on a mountaintop? Impossible! Never in my decades of work and study here. Only in the sea and near other islands. But our sea turtles don't even favor Poros." Further research revealed that loggerheads favor Zakynthos, Kyparissia, Lakonikos, Messenia, Koroni, and Rethymno and Chania on Krete where I have also seen them. These are their seven biggest egg-laying destinations. But Eva Douzinas, a founder of Katheti, saw one in Poros Bay while protesting the fish farms, and I met one on its mountaintop.

It happened, whether by chance, happenstance, or intervention. As recorded in the Bible, ancient Greek philosophy, and modern archetypal psychology, there are ways that the transpersonal, the divine, the numinous breaks through our barriers of reason and conditioning and communicates with us. The divine can speak to us through dreams, oracles, visions, and unusual events, synchronicities that seem impossible. Miracles are experiences that seem to break the laws of nature. They can't happen, but they do. A sea turtle on a mountaintop? It happened.

And there was a third meeting with turtle—in case I still doubted. Sitting in my seat on my Olympic Airways flight back to the United States, I was thumbing restlessly through the in-flight magazine while wondering what had happened on the mountain. The centerfold of the magazine opened to reveal a full two-page photo of the sea turtle accompanying a story of conservation efforts in Greek waters. As is said in several traditions, "the third time is the charm."

The meetings with the turtle touched and changed me in profound ways. Since it was so unusual and both turtle and I had to travel long and far for this mountain encounter, it seemed to be personally for me. The universe shaped this meeting. The meeting reshaped my life and pointed me toward new dimensions of healing work that still unfold today. Turtle provided me with an archetypal model into which to steer my character, work, and evolving life journey.

Others know, sense, or feel the unique energy of Poseidon's sanctuary. On one recent visit, sitting alone by my traditional altar stone I met Eleni, a small, stooped, older local woman who lived nearby. She was wandering the ruin site, cutting fresh greens with a rusty old knife, and stuffing them into a blue plastic bag. She was of a sweet and happy disposition. I asked if it had to do with living on Poros. "Oh yes!" she exclaimed. "I am very lucky!"

Eleni asked why I come to Poros. I briefly explained why I bring travelers and how I work in the Asklepian dream healing tradition.

"Oh!" Eleni blurted out. "You teach people about *psyche*, the soul. I know. It was the beginning of therapy. People need to learn. I live part-time in Athens. I go to lectures and read modern psychologists as well as ancient teachers. I like much. We must bring back psyche or we are lost."

Poros and Poseidon's sanctuary long ago offered asylia, inviolable protection from violence and life's many dangers. In ancient times and in sacred places throughout the ages, to be granted asylum was not to be locked away as a danger to self and others, as the word has come to connote, but rather to be given safety that could not be violated because one was wrongly endangered and receiving divine protection. "Sanctuary," the cry of Quasimodo in Victor Hugo's *Hunchback of Notre Dame*, was a traditional call to religious authorities to provide protection for the sensitive and unjustly oppressed against the violent mob. Demosthenes's Makedonian pursuers violated sanctuary when they surrounded the Poros sanctuary to take him prisoner, yet even they would not profane the sea god's temple.

216   RESTORING POSEIDON'S SANCTUARY

In modern times, El Salvador's Archbishop Oscar Romero had represented ancient sanctuary values in the Catholic Church. He crusaded against the torture, injustice, political murder, and poverty afflicting his country. In 1980 his sanctuary was profanely violated when death squads stormed his church and assassinated him while he celebrated mass.

Providing sanctuary to the oppressed and needy is a sacred task, and invading or denying it is sinful. In the United States, the bombing of Afro-American churches, murders in synagogues and mosques, and killing of innocent worshippers are instances of such violation due to racial hatred throughout American history and into our times. In recent times some politicians and the public have violated the practice of sanctuary represented by the Statue of Liberty, denying the right of asylia. These and other examples, including Donald Trump's removal of protections and funding from sanctuary cities in the United States, constitute a denigration of the sacred and are just a few of too many instances of the sanctity of sanctuary being violated throughout the ages and into our times by the very forces the oppressed try to flee. But after swallowing poison, Demosthenes would not profane the sea god's temple by dying in it. We must restore sanctuary to our world. Poros can guide us.

Galini

Poseidon's winds and waves can be rough and sudden. If a ship caught in his strong outbursts kept its sails unfurled and fights the wind, or if it turns sideways against the waves, it will fail. If it strikes sail, keeps to rudder and mast, and moves with the storm, it can ride it out. Reaching a safe harbor or bay, out of the storm winds, with serene waters and sky—galini.

We are all storm struck today. We are all buffeted by daily human and natural traumas, horrors, breakdowns. We are all tossed about and quaking, struggling to stay upright in the now-global economic, cultural, social, political, environmental gale.

On Poros the breeze is sweet and the god's epithet in his sanctuary was Good Wind. Here the threatening gales of living become still and quiet and we can be safe and belong. Poros is the quiet harbor, the enclosed bay. The postman pats the breeze. The soul of Poros is galini.

Poseidon-Asklepios

Before making Poros my favored base, in previous decades I led groups elsewhere in Greece and visited and used other sanctuaries and Asklepieia as well. I have guided groups to Krete and used the Asklepieia at Lendas and Sougia.[1]

The modest Asklepian ruin site at Lendas on the southern coast of Krete is attached to a small traditional village. We drive through stark mountains, then descend to the ever-warm and sun-drenched coast. We room and dine in the small village and spend days in the buff, tan, and brown ruin site. We study, meditate, pray, seek dreams and visions that commune with the past and the spirits once here. We gather in the small temple ruins that host an ancient mosaic still in excellent condition, startling in its imagery and colors.

Standing in this old site of Asklepian healing right on the edge of Poseidon's vast watery realm that is the last slice of land on Europe, we contemplate the mosaic floor of the temple ruin. It portrays a galloping white steed in front with the rear of a long, winding snake. It faces the ocean and seems to be prancing through blue and white waves. Horse in front, snake behind. Here is a vision of Poseidon-Asklepios, the sea god and the healing god, united as one.

Physical reality may not offer us such creatures. But in the inner world of myths and dreams, in my work of decades, on Poros the island of the sea god, we can achieve this unity, balance, harmony, and work with these eternal powers to bring wisdom and healing to all of us here for only a moment in the life of the cosmos.

I carry this unity in my mind, heart, and soul, and see it guiding my life and work. In the ancient world some deities were worshipped in tandem as their powers were experienced or invoked places sacred to them. On Poros I invoke the two god-powers as one.

The Heart of the Cosmos

I have stood in prayer or meditation in the quiet and contemplative atmosphere of the Monastery of Zoodogos Pigi many times. In the solemn chapel, I am surrounded above and on all sides, as in all Orthodox churches, by brightly painted or old and fading images of angels, saints, church fathers, and martyrs. The air is sweet and thick with incense. It is comfortable and mild, protected from the sun and breezes outside. I am often alone there, or with some of my pilgrims also in deep reflections. I sometimes stand directly beneath the huge, golden, ornate candelabrum hanging from the high ceiling and dangling right over the seal implanted in the floor. For the moments I stand there, like a mortal pole connecting heaven and earth, I feel like I am in the center of the cosmos.

On one visit, I stood in contemplative awe and felt energy piercing my body from the crown of my head down to my toes. Then I retired to a nearby hard wooden chair. As my bottom hit the seat, I felt the enormous strength of my own beating heart. I could feel and with my inner eye see its chambers sending tremors of energy into my lower parts. My body vibrated and shook, my heart smashed inside its ribcage, as if I had been plugged into an invisible universal battery.

In *Symposium* Plato has the wise woman Diotima instruct Sokrates, "God mingles not with mortals, but through love all the intercourse of God with the human . . . is carried on. The wisdom which understands this is spiritual. All other is mean and vulgar."[2]

Suddenly I knew. My heart is not my heart. It is the infinite heart of God beating in me. I knew that our hearts are not ours and not things, but a living drop of Divinity planted in us to give us this life and this world. If we truly know this, we can stay true to God's heart in us. If we know this, we will not malign or harm it. When we provide care and well-being for our own and others' inner beings, we take care of God's heart.

Die to Be Reborn

I am in Aris's gift shop. We have shared the story of his family's flight from Cyprus and resettlement on Poros. He has shared challenges of being a transplant, surviving the traumas of war and losing his home, as did Seferis and so many Poriotes.

Like many seekers, Aris traveled to holy Mt. Athos, devoted to Orthodoxy, covered with monasteries where monks isolate from the wounding world to focus on the soul's well-being. Many friends have recommended such pilgrimage.

Aris was in council with one of the monks. He tells his story and the pain he still carries from it. He wonders if it is possible to heal such deep wounding. The monk listens deeply. He talks of achieving nonattachment to the wounding world and devoting ourselves fully to the spiritual. Aris wonders how this is possible. The monk picks up a small pad and briefly writes. He hands Aris the note with a gentle smile and says, "Here is your prescription."

Will Aris share the wisdom? In his Poros shop, he smiles, picks up a small pad, and writes. He hands the note to me as the monk had to him. It reads, "If you die before you die, you will not die when you die."

Spiritual death and rebirth. This is not about adopting and believing in any creed. It is about difficult inner labor and experience. Letting go of the world that wounds to encounter the invisible that heals. Letting go of fears and prejudices to live in agape. Letting our ego with its wounds recede and the Self with its divine connections take prominence. Letting go of reliance on the rational and empirical, balancing them with the imaginal and intuitive, knowing that turtles and bees, dreams and visions happen and guide us. Moving, not in the material but the spiritual meaning, from *penia*, "poverty," to *poros*, "abundance." Sokrates taught that philosophy is preparation for death. If we die to that which is false and does not matter, we can be fearless and not die when we die. Carl Jung taught that what we achieve in consciousness and spirituality goes back into the universe when we pass. The best of us, the most spiritual, does not die when we die.

Aris's oracle delivered to me in the island's winding alleys sits on the altar over my desk beneath my bust of Asklepios. The two together remind me always.

The Three Loves

Dreams, visions, encounters, experiences, and teachings received on Poros project us into a community suffused with serenity, kindness, friendship, patience, and wisdom. It amounts to love.

The Greek language differentiates several kinds of love. Agape is the highest form, that which we experience from and for the divine. Poros has been infused with this since the ancient gods chose it as a sanctuary island. Poros is also infused with *filia*, defined by Professor Meagher as "the bond of fellowship and compassion, the peculiar solidarity of those condemned to mortality." Through suffering and oppression, we learn "*koiononia*, commonality, according to Aristotle the root and foundation of love."[3] And it is infused with eros, not simply sexual love, but desire, the force that attracts and connects all things through beauty, sensuality, common feeling, immersion in nature, and a sense of being drawn to completion with another, whether person or place. Through agape, eros, and filoxenia, love radiates from Poros's good people and energy.

Agape is spiritual love. It is not attained by robes, candelabrum, or incense, nor by rote prayers, rituals, or things, not even by the crucifix, Koran, or Torah. We attain agape by pure perception and awe-filled regard and connection through service and devotion, receiving the presence and touch of the divine in whatever form it arrives, giving full and devoted service to all creatures and Creation itself. This agape is the holiest of holies. Anything else is idolatry. This agape suffuses Poros and penetrates the pilgrims who find their way to modern asylia on the sea god's island.

Leaving Poros

In the whirlwind of surprise
I do not want to exist without
You

GIORGOS KANABOS, "METHEKSI,"
STON TOPO TIS ANTINIMIAS

Another *kalokeri* day, summery, very warm, very bright, too much so for early spring. A strong breeze blows. It is sweet and mild but pow-

Fig. 12.1. The full moon glows over Poros island and sea, creating endlessly changing visions. See also plate 15.
PHOTOGRAPH FROM THE HATZOPOULEIOS PUBLIC LIBRARY ARCHIVES

erful. It is a boon for sailors from Poseidon. Here the wind was his power.

The sweet yet strong breezes of Poros are its pneuma, the breath and spirit of the sea god. From the broad vista beyond my altar stone in his temple beneath the dancing pines, I see. I feel the great lungs of this invisible strong breathing in, breathing out, with each exhalation sending this powerful almost-wind across the rippling and variegated waters, across the distant mountains and islands anchored in the Mother yet looking as if floating up these verdant pine- and olive-tree-covered slopes and across this solitary but never lonely holy site. My inner eye sees the tall statue of the sea god, as in the national museum, left arm raised to hold his missing trident. I feel the shades of the ancients who fled, prayed, sacrificed, and feasted here with their god. The breeze sings in the pine boughs, plucking their needles and rattling their cones. I hear the soughing of the sea god's lungs. This music mixes with the gentle undertones of the myriad bees humming as they visit the profusion of wildflowers—daisies, poppies, so many whites, blues, yellows, purples whose names I do not know—awakening from within the earth as Persephone returns from the Underworld.

What does the wind say, the sea god's breath?

Be calm. Be still. Find your center. A sail without its mast is a sheet,
a shroud, a useless flopping rag.
    I am eternal movement—my tides, my currents, my breathing.
Be the mast. Plant yourself and stand firmly on your deck. Ride or
catch the wind and steer carefully and well. You can never stop my
movements but only use them to steer your life toward your moira,
your destiny and purpose, where not you, but I and the god-powers
want you to go.

One crow laughs. Distant roosters cackle. Their jabber floats over
these hills to remind me that Asklepios is speaking as well. I rise,
approach the stones where the sea god's altar was, stoop, and leave
gifts and offerings to the eternal invisible power. I return to my altar
stone and pour libations of wine and water, then sit. Ants labor on
the stones around my thighs. They ignore my raisin offering. A zebra-
striped spider clutches the stone and straddles between my legs. All
are heedless of me as I heed and honor them. I matter and do not
matter. Both are eternally true, and we must hold them as one. It is
the way of the human in the cosmos.

I turn to descend the sea god's mountain once again. Leaving, I can
never leave.

> *Make friends with the gods*
> *and you'll have the best magic of all*
> *abiding in your own house.*
>   EURIPIDES, *HELEN*

NOTES

Introduction

1. Cousineau, *The Art of Pilgrimage*, xxiii.
2. Ibbotson, *Coming Slowly*, 253.
3. Maniatis, *Oi Poriotes Sto Nisi Tous*.
4. Earlier versions of some material, now expanded, revised, and updated, first appeared as Edward Tick, "On an Island, Barely, in Greece," *New York Times*, Sept. 22, 1996; "The Gift of Turtle," *Pilgrimage: Psychotherapy and Personal Exploration* 17, no. 4 (Sept./Oct. 1991): 2–20; and "Counsel from the Dead: George Seferis and Poros," *Key West Review*, Fall 1988, 82–92.
5. Rogers, *Greekscapes*.
6. Miller, *The Colossus of Maroussi*, 194–95.
7. Tick, *Soul Medicine*.
8. Jung, *Civilization in Transition*, 395.
9. Roger Brooke, "Psyche and Place," virtual lecture, Western Massachusetts Jung Association website, October 1, 2021.
10. Tick, *The Practice of Dream Healing*.
11. Kanabos, "Diakosmos," *Ston topo tis antinimias*, 9.
12. Tick, *War and the Soul*; *Warrior's Return*.

Chapter 1.
Portrait of Poros

1. Yannis Maniatis, library director of Poros, provided some of the local and historical details in this and other chapters, in conversation and his lecture, "Know about Poros: The Beauties, History, Culture."
2. Miller, *The Colossus of Marousi*, 53.

223

224   NOTES

3. Kazantzakis, *Zorba the Greek*, 211.

4. Gray, *People of Poros*, 10.

5. Dahlstedt, "Soul Awakening," in *Lessons from the Garden*, 79.

6. Paraskevaidou, "Pre-Hellenic Tribes in the Area of the Argo-Saronic Gulf," 363.

7. Hagg, "Conclusions for the Prehistoric Period in the Argo-Saronic Gulf," 372.

8. Souliotis, *The Sleeping Lady*, 20.

9. Souliotis, *The Sleeping Lady*, 20.

10. The author's translation of Seferis's poem "Arnisi" ("Denial"), quoted here and referenced in chapters 4 and 8, won the Willis Barnstone Translation Award, *Evansville Journal*, University of Evansville, 2020.

11. Seferis, *A Poet's Journal*, 38.

12. Souliotis, *The Sleeping Lady*, 44.

13. See Tick, chapter 8 of *Dream Healing*, 69–76, for a full account of the history and mythology of Troizen.

14. Kiriakopoulos, *Poros / Trizinia*, 46.

15. Porou, *Holy Monastery of the Life-Giving Spring*.

16. Kyrou, "The Calureian Amphictiony," 356.

17. Seferis, *A Poet's Journal*, 51.

Chapter 2.
Counsel with the Dead

1. Seferis, *Poems*, 47.

2. Seferis, *Poems*, 79.

3. Seferis, *A Poet's Journal*, 185.

4. Seferis, "Sikelianos," 20.

5. Seferis, *A Poet's Journal*, 54.

6. Miller, *The Colossus of Maroussi*, 106.

7. Cousineau, *Who Stole the Arms of the Venus de Milo?* 15.

8. Seferis, "Stratis the Sailor Describes a Man," in *Poems*, 45.

9. Seferis, *A Poet's Journal*, 38.

10. Seferis, *Poems*, 19.

11. Seferis, *A Poet's Journal*, 36.

12. Seferis, *Poems*, 21.

13. Seferis, *A Poet's Journal*, 62–63.

14. Seferis, "Summer Solstice," in *Three Secret Poems*, 49.

NOTES ～ 225

15. Prof. Robert Emmett Meagher, in conversation with the author, January–March 2023, provided these reflections on the word and its usage.

16. Euripides, *Helen,* trans. Robert Emmett Meagher. All quotes from *Helen* are taken from this translation.

17. Seferis, *Poems,* 73.

18. Seferis, *Poems,* 121.

Chapter 3.
The Gift of the Sea Turtle

1. Gray, *People of Poros,* 209.

2. Cousineau, *Venus,* 57.

3. Seferis, "On Stage," in *Three Secret Poems,* 27.

Chapter 4.
Poseidon

1. Pausanias, *Central Greece* 2.3, 211.

2. Pausanias, *Central Greece* 5.3, 414.

3. Sophokles, *Oedipus at Colonus,* lines 54–58, 130.

4. Scott and River, *Poseidon.*

5. Pindar, "Paean for the People of Kos," in Lattimore, *Greek Lyrics,* 58.

6. Bolen, *Gods in Everyman,* 74.

7. Cary et al., *The Oxford Classical Dictionary,* 721.

8. Bolen, *Gods in Everyman,* 78.

9. Scott and Rivers, *Poseidon.*

10. Gutman and Johnson, *Mythic Astrology,* 161, 165.

11. Scott and Rivers, *Poseidon.*

12. Scott and Rivers, *Poseidon.*

13. Homer, *The Iliad* 15.194–97, 355–56.

14. Pausanias, *Central Greece* I.8.8.2, referenced by Scott and Rivers, *Poseidon.*

15. Scott and Rivers, *Poseidon.*

16. Pausanias, *Central Greece* 2.33, 211.

17. Meagher, Introduction to *Iphigenia,* in *Essential Euripides,* 309.

18. "Kalaureia," Pamphlet by the Swedish Institute at Athens, no page or date. The institute first began excavating in 1894 and has continued intermittently in recent decades. Available in the archives of the Hatzopouleios Public Library.

226 ∾ NOTES

19. Robert Emmet Meagher, personal correspondence, winter 2022–23.
20. Mahdi, *The Real St. Nicholas*, 189–90.
21. Gray, *People of Poros*, 15.
22. Bolen, *Goddesses in Every Woman*; Bolen, *Gods in Everyman*; Wolger and Wolger, *The Goddess Within*.
23. Meineck, *Theban Plays*, n137.

Chapter 5.
Greek Mythology on Poros

1. Bacchylides, "Theseus and the Ring: A Dithyramb," in Lattimore, *Greek Lyrics*, 67.
2. Pausanias, *Central Greece* 2.33, 210.
3. Pausanias, *Central Greece* 2.33, 210.
4. Renault, *The King Must Die*, 18.
5. Bacchylides, "The Coming of Theseus," in Lattimore, *Greek Lyrics*, 65.
6. Slattery, *The Fictions in Our Convictions*, 211–12.
7. Plato, *Symposium* 203c–203d, 44–45.

Chapter 6.
A History of Asylia (Sanctuary)

1. Plutarch, *Demosthenes*, in *Selected Lives and Essays*, 283.
2. Plutarch, *Demosthenes*, in *Selected Lives and Essays*, 295–96.
3. Pausanias, *Central Greece* 2.33, 211.
4. Plutarch, *Comparison of Demosthenes and Cicero*, in *Selected Lives and Essays*, 346.
5. Ritsos, "Requiem on Poros," 87.
6. Gray, *People of Poros*, 25.
7. Gray, *People of Poros*, 86.
8. Babis Katzanidis interviewed the elderly refugee and contributed the following story.
9. Hatziperos, *The Good Testament*.
10. Katz, *The Epistemic Music of Rhetoric*, 121.
11. Katz, *Plato's Nightmare*.
12. Steven B. Katz, unpublished prose and poems, used with permission.

Chapter 7.
The Sun of Poros

1. Miller, *The Colossus of Maroussi*, 92.
2. Jack L. Davis, "Euzones and Poetry: James Merrill, Greek Love, and the Making of a Pulitzer Prize Winner," From the Archivist's Notebook (website), October 15, 2015; accessed December 21, 2024.
3. Merrill, *The (Diblos) Notebook*, 5.
4. Merrill, *The (Diblos) Notebook*, 9.
5. Merrill, *The (Diblos) Notebook*, 23.
6. Yannis Maniatis, in conversation, October 21, 2023.
7. Rogers, *Greekscapes*, ix.
8. Rogers, *Greekscapes*, ix.
9. Rogers, *Greekscapes*, 237.

Chapter 8.
In the Agora

1. Lang, *Socrates in the Agora*.
2. Gray, *People of Poros*, 142.

Chapter 9.
The Shadow of Paradise

1. Jung, *On the Psychology of the Unconscious*, 66.
2. Kanabos, my translation of *Ston topo tis antinimias*, 9.

Chapter 10.
A Healing Island

1. Hay, *You Can Heal Your Life*.
2. Kiriakopoulos, *Poros / Trizinia*, 42.
3. A shorter version of the remainder of this chapter was first published as Edward Tick, "Warrior Retreats on Poros Island."
4. Plato, *Symposium* 217e, 59.
5. Renault, *The King Must Die*, 52.

228   NOTES

Chapter 11.
Asklepios on Poros

1. See my previous books, *The Practice of Dream Healing*, for my first five years of incubation practices on Poros and at other sanctuaries around Greece, and *Soul Medicine*, for my twenty years of healing work since. Each volume contains records of many modern and ancient incubations. Those included here are actual examples of scores I have facilitated over the decades, many on Poros.
2. Tick, *Soul Medicine*, 175–76.
3. *Heraclitus*, 68, fragments. 63 and 75 Wheelwright.

Chapter 12.
Restoring Poseidon's Sanctuary

1. See chapter 19 of Edward Tick, *The Practice of Dream Healing*, 205–17, for earlier journeys and incubations at this site.
2. Plato, *Symposium*, 44.
3. Meagher, *The Essential Euripides*, 213.

BIBLIOGRAPHY

Athanasiou, Giorgos. *O Poros Stous Zografous Tou 19ou Aiona*. Poros: 2019.

Bolen, Jean Shinoda. *Goddesses in Every Woman Gods*. New York: Harper and Row, 1984.

———. *Gods in Everyman*. San Francisco: Harper & Row, 1989.

Cary, M., et al., eds. *The Oxford Classical Dictionary*. London: Oxford Univ. Press, 1961.

Cousineau, Phil. *The Art of Pilgrimage*. Berkeley, CA: Conari Press, 1998.

———. *Who Stole the Arms of the Venus de Milo?* San Francisco: Sisyphus Press, 2023.

Dahlstedt, Kate. *Lessons from the Garden*. Bay Area, CA: Mandorla Books, 2020.

Euripides. *Bakkhai*. Translated by Robert Emmet Meagher with commentary. Wauconda, IL: Bolchazy-Carducci, 1995.

Euripides. *Helen*. In *The Essential Euripides: Dancing in Dark Times*, translated by Robert Emmett Meagher. Wauconda, IL: Bolchazy-Carducci, 2002.

Gray, Peter S. *People of Poros: A Portrait of a Greek Island Village*. New York: Whittlesey House, 1942.

Gutman, Arielle, and Kenneth Johnson. *Mythic Astrology: Internalizing the Planetary Powers*. Brattleboro, VT: Echo Point Books and Media, 2019.

Hagg, Robin. "Conclusions for the Prehistoric Period in the Argo-Saronic Gulf." Minutes of Argosaronikos: 1st International Conference for Argosaronikos History and Archaeology. Volume A, Poros, June 26–29, 1998. Athens, 2003.

Hatziperos, Michalis. *The Good Testament*. Kalavria, 2012. Published by the municipality and available in the Hatzopouleios Public Library.

Hay, Louise. *You Can Heal Your Life*. Carlsbad, CA: Hay House, 1984.

230 ⁓ BIBLIOGRAPHY

Heraclitus. Translated by Philip Wheelwright with commentary. New York: Atheneum, 1968.

Homer. *The Iliad*. Translated by Robert Fitzgerald. Garden City, NY: Doubleday, 1974.

Ibbotson, Anne. *Coming Slowly: A Kaleidoscope of Life on, and Around, the Greek Island of Poros*. London: Ashgrove Publishing, 2006.

Jung, C. G. *Civilization in Transition*. Vol. 10 of *The Collected Works of C.G. Jung*. New York: Pantheon Books, 1964.

———. *On the Psychology of the Unconscious*. Vol. 7 of *The Collected Works of C.G. Jung*. New York: Bollingen Foundation, 1966.

Kanabos, Giorgos. *Ston Topo Tis Antinimias*. Athens: Ekdoseis Ton Allon, 2018.

Katz, Steven B. *The Epistemic Music of Rhetoric*. Carbondale: Southern Illinois Univ. Press, 1996.

———. *Plato's Nightmare*. Anderson, SC: Parlor Press, 2025.

Kazantzakis, Nikos. *Zorba the Greek*. New York: Ballentine, 1952.

Kerenyi, Karl. *Hermes: Guide of Souls*. Woodstock, CT: Spring Publications, 1996.

Kiriakopoulos, Kostas. *Poros / Trizinia*. Athens: K. Kiriakopoulos Publications, 1994.

Kyrou, Adonis. "The Calureian Amphictiony: Origins and Development of an Ancient Tradition." Minutes of the Argosaronikos: 1st International Conference for Argosaronikos History and Archaeology. Volume A, Poros, June 26–29, 1998. Athens, 2003.

Lang, Mabel. *Socrates in the Agora*. Excavations in the Athenian Agora, vol. 17. Princeton, NJ: American School of Classical Studies, 1978.

Lattimore, Richard, ed. and trans. *Greek Lyrics*. Chicago: Univ. of Chicago Press, 1960.

Mahdi, Louise, ed. and trans. *The Real St. Nicholas: Tales of Generosity and Hope from Around the World*. Wheaton, IL: Quest Books, 2002.

Maniatis, Yannis, trans. *Oi Poriotes Sto Nisi Tous*. Athens: Ekdos Tou Dimou Porou, 2002.

———. "Know about Poros: The Beauties, History, Culture," Lecture, Poros Hatzopouleios Public Library, September 2022, March and October 2023.

Meagher, Robert Emmet. *The Essential Euripides: Dancing in Dark Times*. Wauconda, IL: Bolchazy-Carducci Publishers, 2002.

BIBLIOGRAPHY 231

Meineck, Peter, and Paul Woodruff, trans. *Theban Plays*. Indianapolis, IN: Hackett, 2003.

Merrill, James. *The (Diblos) Notebook*. New York: Atheneum, 1965.

Miller, Henry. *The Colossus of Maroussi*. New York: New Directions, 1958.

———. *Greece*. Drawings by Anne Poor. New York: Viking, 1964.

Paraskevaidou, Helen. "Pre-Hellenic Tribes in the Area of the Argo-Saronic Gulf." Minutes of Argosaronikos: 1st International Conference for Argosaronikos History and Archaeology. Volume A, Poros, June 26–29, 1998. Athens, 2003.

Pausanias. *Central Greece*. Vol. 1 of *Guide to Greece*. Translated by Peter Levi. New York: Penguin, 1979.

Plato. *Symposium*. Translated by B. Jowett. Indianapolis, IN: Bobbs-Merrill, 1980.

Plutarch. *Selected Lives and Essays*. Translated by Louise Ropes Loomis. Roslyn, NY: Classics Club, 1951.

Porou, I. M. *Holy Monastery of the Life-Giving Spring*. Edited and translated by Lawrence Damian Robinson. Poros: Independently published, 2014.

Renault, Mary. *The King Must Die*. New York: Pantheon, 1958.

Ritsos, Yannis. "Requiem on Poros." *Exile and Return: Selected Poems 1967–1974*. Translated by Edmund Keeley. New York: Ecco Press, 1985.

Rogers, Pamela Jane. *Greekscapes: Illustrated Journeys with an Artist*. 2nd ed. Edited by Bryony Sutherland. Columbia, SC: CreateSpace, 2015.

Scott, Andrew, and Charles River, eds. *Poseidon: The Origins and History of the Greek God of the Sea*. Middleton, DE: CreateSpace, 2022.

Seferis, George. *Poems*. Translated by Rex Warner. Boston: Little, Brown, 1960.

———. *A Poet's Journal: Days of 1945–1951*. Translated by Athan Anagnostopoulos. Cambridge, MA: Harvard Univ. Press, 1975.

———. "Sikelianos." In *On the Greek Style*, translated by Rex Warner and Th. Frangopoulos. Evia, Greece: Denise Harvey Publisher, 2000.

———. *Three Secret Poems*. Translated by Walter Kaiser. Cambridge, MA: Harvard University Press, 1964.

Slattery, Dennis Patrick. *The Fictions in Our Convictions: Essays on the Cultural Imagination*. Bay Area, CA: Mandorla Books, 2023.

232   BIBLIOGRAPHY

Sophokles. *Oedipus at Colonus.* In *Theban Plays,* translated by Peter Meineck and Paul Woodruff Howard Banks. Indianapolis, IN: Hackett, 2003.

Souliotis, Yannis. *O Poros Einai.* Poros: Editions Kedros, 2006.

———. *The Sleeping Lady.* Translated by Constance Tagapoulos. Athens: Solokis, 2012.

Tick, Edward. "On an Island, Barely, In Greece." Sunday Travel, *New York Times,* September 22, 1996.

———. *The Practice of Dream Healing: Bringing Ancient Greek Practices into Modern Medicine.* Wheaton, IL: Quest Books, 2001.

———. *Soul Medicine: Healing Through Dream Incubation, Oracles, Visions, and Pilgrimage.* Rochester, VT: Healing Arts Press, 2023.

———. *War and the Soul.* Wheaton, IL: Quest Books, 2001.

———. "Warrior Retreats on Poros." *Close Encounters in War Journal,* Winter 2023–2024.

———. *Warrior's Return.* Boulder, CO: Sounds True, 2014.

Wolger, Jennifer Barker, and Roger J. Wolger. *The Goddess Within.* New York: Fawcett Columbine, 1989.

INDEX

7 Brothers, 26, 123, 136, 162–63

abundance, 219
active imagination, 201
Aegeus, 53, 81, 82, 187–88
Aeneas, 40
Aeschylos, 22
Agamemnon, 9, 22, 38–39
agape, 151, 220
agora, *95*, 138–41, *139*, 149–53
Aithra, 81, 82
Albanians, 92–93, 100–101
alcohol, 8–9, 202
Alexandros, 97
Alkman (poet), 87
Amaltheia, 177–81
amphictyony, 33–34
Amphitrite, 64
anagnorisis, 54–55
Andie I. (psychotherapist), 110–11
animal sacrifice, 39, 66–67
animal soul, 61
Apaturia, 82–83
Aphaia, 41
Aphrodite, 55, 66, 86
apocalypse, 172–73
Apollo, 58, 67

Apollonian light, 124–26
archetypes, 4, 7
Ardrastus, King, 63
Ares, 184, 187
Aris (refugee), 98–100, 218–19
Aristophanes, 148
"Arnisi," 18–19
Artemis, 66
artists, 9, 123–33
Arvanites, 92
Askeli Beach, 28–29, *29*
Asklepiad, 8
Asklepios, 9, 25, 67
Asklepios's hospital, 194–95
asylon, 50, 215
asylum. *See* refugees
Athena, 9, 53, 59, 67, 82–83, 187
Atlas missiles, 197
authentic self, 3, 200–201
Averof (ship), 92–93, 96, *96*

Bacchylides, 82, 84
balance, 62, 159
beauty, 49, 117, 188
beckoning dreams, 208
beginner's mind, 206–7
Blocher, Charlie, 196–202

233

234   INDEX

Bronze Age, 200

Brooke, Roger, 8

Brown, Debra, 128

Buddhism, 197, 200

Byron, Lord George Gordon, 112–16

Candlemas, 26

capitalism, 12

catastrophes, 36–37

Cave of Hades, 206

Ceccoli, Rafaelo, 32

Center for Ancient Healing, 72

Chagall, Marc, 2, 19, 117, 124–26

change, 191–92

chapel, 169–72

Charlie. *See Blocher, Charlie*

Charon, 30

Chatzikyriakos, 94

children, 162–67

Chrisman, Torrence, 176–77

churches, 25–26

Church of the Ipapanti, 26

Cicero, 112–16

climate change, 12, 191

clocktower, *pl.1, pl.4*

Clytemnestra, 200

Cohen, Leonard, 41–42

Colossus of Maroussi, The, 5, 6

Coming Slowly, 4

connections, 200–201

Cousineau, Phil, 2, 40

Craxton, John, 6, 126–27

Cycladic culture, 17

Cyclops, 60

Dahlstedt, Kate, 16, 141–44

Dante, 41

dead, connection with living, 39–40

death, 218–19

Demeter, 63, 67

Demosthenes, 34, 48, 90–91

"Denial," 49

devotion, 220

didaskalos, 8

Dikrynna, 41

Dimitriadis, Giorgos, 1–2, 87, 161–62

Diogenes, 9, 148

Dionysos, 9, 25

Divinity, 218

Douzinas, Eva, 214

dream incubation

    in Asklepios's hospital, 194–95

    Maria encounters the mysteries,
       204–10

    statue and the dream, 210–12

    warrior healing on Poros, 195–204

Drougas, Christos, 102–4, 118–19,
    150–53

drugs, 8–9

Durrell, Lawrence, 5, 6,

Dvořák Quartet, pl. 8

Earth, 57–58

earthquakes, 12–13, 69

Elainie the Drunk, 51

Eleusis, 9, 63, 206–7

"Engomi," 49

Epidauros, 67, 206–7

eros, 220

Euripides, 46–47, 84

existence, 7

family, 3

famine, 12

INDEX ∽ 235

fasting, 200
fate, 188
feminine, 44
ferry, 19–20
filia, 220
filoxenia, 2, 163–64, 176
fisherman's chat, 5
Fisherman's Memorial, 37
fishermen, *pl.12*, 29–30, 31, 143–45, *143*, 157
Fourniades, Christos, 67
freedom, 21, 158
Freud, Lucien, 2, 6, 117, 126–27
Freud, Sigmund, 10
Friar, Kimon, 6, 120, 121
friendship, 138–39
Furies, 62

Gabriel, Saint, 32
Gabrielides, Ivi, 131
Galatas, 15
Galini, 5, 45–47, 216–17
Galini, Saint, 47
garden of God, 11–12
gathering, 141
George, Saint, 9, 20
Giorgos (barber), 145–48
God, 218
god-powers, 7, 84–85, 200
gods and goddesses, 5–6, 7
Graeser, Nate, 187–89, 202–3, 204
Grant, Andrew, 187–89
gratitude, 62
Gray, Peter S., 4–5, 16, 119–20, 140–41
greed, 12
Greek mythology

gods named Poros, 85–88
time of Theseus, 81–85
grocery stores, 94–95
guest-friendship, 2
Gustafsson, Kristina, 175–76

Hades, 39, 63, 64
Halverson, Alicia, 143–44
harbor front, 22
Harpokratis, 206–7
Hatziperos, Michalis, 93–94, 97
Hatziperos, Panagiotis, 94–95
Hatzopouleios Public Library, 5
Hay, Louise, 176
health, 161–62
heart, 8
Helen, 55
Hemingway, Ernest, 121–23
Henioche, 81
Hephaestion, 14
Hephaistos, 14
Hera, 4
Herakles, 40–41
Heraklitos, 58–65, 191, 211
heroes, 84
H Gorgoni, 26–27
Hippokrates, 8–9, 179–80
Hippolytos, 84
Hippos, Dmitri, 63, 78, 148–50
Homer, 6, 60, 184
Homeric Hymn, 13
Hot Gates, 198
House of Serenity, pl.2
Hugo, Victor, 215
human sacrifice, 39
Hydra Island, *pl.5*
Hygeia, 25

236   INDEX

Hymn to Asklepios, 201
hypocrisy, 12

Ibbotson, Anne, 4
icons, 72–73
Iliad, 60
illness, 8–9, 180
intimacy wounds, 204–5
invasions, 69
Iphigenia, 39
"I Swear by All the Gods," 114–15

James II, 31–32
Jason (peaceful warrior), 181–83
Jesus, 151, 153, 171–72
Joyce, James, 41
Jung, Carl, 7, 22, 71, 156, 219

kala aura, 44–45
Kalaureia, 15, 27, 57–58
Kalaureian League, 17, 33–34
Kanabos, Giorgos, 11–12, 171
Kanali Beach, 27
Kanatsidis, Babis, *pl.12*, 95–96, 97, 185–87
Katheti (organization), 106–7, 138
Katsambalis, George, 5
Katz, Steven B., 70–71, 112–16
Kazantzakis, Eleni, 41
Kazantzakis, Nikos, 15–16, 41–42
King Must Die, The, 83
"King of Asine, The," 49
Koimomeni, 21–22, *22*
koiononia, 220
Kollias, Nikos, 102
Kontos, Giorgos, 24
Kordomenidis, Makis, 21

Koryzis, Alexander, 23–24
Kostas (warrior), 183–84
Koumaridis, Demosthenes, 133–35

Lennon, John, 121
Leto, 50, 57
logos, 151–52, 211–12
love, 220
lust, 63–64

magic, 12
Makedonia, 90
Maniatis, Yannis, 5, 24, 34, 68, 119, 120
Manolios, 21
Maria (doctor), 204–10
markets. *See* agora
Markworth, Lawrence, 195–96
Mary (Mother), 9, 31
massage, 177–81
Mathana volcano, 176–77
Meagher, Robert Emmet, 46, 66, 69–70, 220
medications, 8–9
meditation, 200
Menelaos, 55
Mercouri, Melina, 27
Mermaid, the, 26–27
Merrill, James, 120–21
Methana, 14
metron, 159
Michael, Saint, 32
Middle East, 97
military service, 183–91
Miller, Henry, 5, 6, 7, 18, 40, 118–19
Milonakis, Panagiotis, 71–72
Mimoza (refugee), 100–101, 162

INDEX ∽ 237

mind, 8
Minotaur, 24, 53, 63, 81
Minuteman missiles, 197
miracles, 151, 214
missile systems, 197
modern world, 8–9, 10–13, 46
Modi, 33
moira, 188
moirarchos, 8
moirologia, 39
Monastery of Zoodogos Pigi, 10, 31–32, 218
moral injury, 186–87, 197–98, 199, 202
Morris, Randy, 213
Mother Mary, 9, 31
Mount Athos, 99–100
Mount Olympus, 9
Muller, Dominique, 111–12
Muses, 9
Mycenae, 200
mystery, 12
"Mythistorema VIII," 42
"Mythistorema X," 43
mythology, immersion in, 7–8

names, 203–4
Navel Academy, 27–28, *28*, 72, 190
Nazis, 24
Neptune, 60, 62. *See also* Poseidon
Nereid Galateia, 46–47
Nicholas, Saint, 72–73
Nick (surgeon), 109

Odysseus, 36, 39, 40
Odyssey, 6
Odyssey: A Modern Sequel, 41
Oedipus, 58

Oli (refugee), 100
Olive Harvest, pl.7
Olympians, 61
oracle cards, 206–7
Orpheus, 9, 40–41
Orthodox Christianity, 12–13

Palati Plateau, 33
Panagia, 9, 31
Pandora's box, 12
Papadopoulos, Christos, 133–35, 161–62
Papaioannou, Evangelos, 122, 158–61
passage, 10–11, 14, 17
patriarchy, 204–5
Pausanias, 57, 58, 65–66, 68, 82, 90–91
Pelops, 81
Penia, 86–87
People of Poros, 4–5, 119
Persephone, 9, 40–41, 67
personal responsibility, 158
personal suffering, 12
personification, 86
Petersen, Jane, 108–9
Petersen, Polly, 108–9
Phaedra, 84
pilgrimage, 1–4
Pindar, 60–61
pirates, 181–83
Pittheus, 81
Plakas, Dmitri, 46, 77–78
Plato, 7, 8–9, 22, 86–87, 117, 171, 185, 218
Plutarch, 68, 90
pneuma, 44
Poet's Journal, A, 19, 38–39

238   INDEX

Pollux, 40–41
Polyphemus, 46
Poros. *See also specific topics*
  confronting the shadow, 156–61
  descriptions of, 10–13, 14–16, 20–23
  as green island, 191–92
  harbor front of, 22
  inhabitants of, 17–19
  introduction to, 1–6
  issues with children of, 162–67
  meaning of, 10–11
  pictured, *2*, *11*, *16*, *18*, *155*
  shadow in the sea, 167–69
Poros (gods), 85–88
Poros Harbour, *pl.3*
Poros Twilight, *pl. 13*
Poseidon, 8, 9, 12–13, 25, 34, 53
  archetype of, 70–77
  gifts of, 77–79
  identity of, 58–65
Poseidon's Sanctuary, 51–56, 65–70
post-traumatic stress disorder, 184
Poulakis, Theodoros, 32
poverty, 219
prayer, 200, 211–12
Priam, King, 60
Prospero's Cell, 6
Proteus, 55
Psykhe, 40–41
psyche, 215
Punda, Poros, *pl. 10*

Raby-Dunne, Susan, 180, 185
reason, 151–52, 211–12
rebirth, 218–19
refugees, 88
  Demosthenes, 90–91

for foreigners seeking soul, 107–12
history through the ages, 91–98
in modern times, 98–101
return of Poriotes, 101–7
Renault, Mary, 83, 187–88
"Requiem on Poros," 91
Resolution of 480 BCE, 25
resource, 10–11
Return from Hydra, *pl.5*
Revelations, Book of, 172
Rhea, 65
Ritsos, Yiannis, 88, 91, 93
ritual sacrifice, 66–67
rock music, 44, 45
Rodis, Tasos, 104–7
Rogers, Pamela Jane, *pl.2*, *pl.3*, 6,
    pl.7, *pl.8*, *pl.9*, *pl.10*, *pl.13*, *pl.14*,
    127–30, 168
Romero, Oscar, 216
Rota (restaurant), 103–4, 136
runes, 204

sacred sites, 4, 97–98
sanctuary, 68, 97–98, 107, 174–75,
    213–14, 215–16
Sanctuary of Poseidon, 10, 17, 25, 48
Santorini, 112
Saronic Gulf, 2, 48–49
Schwarzenegger, Arnold, 196
sea turtles, 52–56, 214–15
Seferis, George, 2, 5, 8, 15, 17–18,
    36–37, 39–40
service, 220
Sfairia, 17, 27, 81–82
Sfairos, 17, 81–82
Shirley Valentine, 2–3
Sikelianos, Angelos, 39–40

INDEX 239

simplicity, 45

Sinis, 84

Slattery, Dennis Patrick, 85

Sleeping Woman Mountain, *pl.6, pl.9,* 21–22, *22,* 158–59

snakes, 201–2

Sobel, Irving, 73–74

Sokaris, Fay, 2

Sokrates, 5, 8, 90, 104, 153, 187, 197–98, 218, 219

Sophokles, 58–59

soul, 5–6, 7–8, 44, 197–98, 215

Sounion, Cape, 53–54

Spartans, 21

Spartan Shield, 202–3

spirit of place, 8

spiritual death, 218–19

spiritual pilgrimage, 2

Square of Heroes, 24

St. George Cathedral, 26, 82

Strabo, 57, 58, 68

Stratis the Sailor, 40–41

stress, 9

Sue (surgeon), 109

suffering, 12

"Summer Solstice," 45

sustainability, 191–92

symbolism, 130–32

Symposium, 86, 218

Taurus, 76

tavernas, 149–53

Temple of Athena Apaturia, 82–83, *83*

Tennyson, Alfred Lord, 41

Themis, 57–58

Themistokles, 25

theology, of the taverna, 149–53

therapeut, 8

therapists, 9

Thermopylae, 198

Theseus, 9, 24, 40–41, 53, 81–85

Thetis, 87

thunderstorms, 12–13

Tick, Edward

    connecting with Seferis, 38–41

    deep connection with Poros, 6–10

    experience of the chapel, 169–72

    first visit to Poros, 12–13

    identifications of, 8

    meeting in Poseidon's Sanctuary, 51–56

    sea turtles and, 52–56, 214–15

    travels to Poros, 42–46

    wandering the streets, 136–39

Tick, Izzy, 74

Tiryns, 200

Titan missiles, 197

tourism, 2, 11, 155–56, 191

tranquility, 46–47

trauma, 183–91

Trizina Landscape, pl. 14

Troizen (ruin site), 24–25, 194

Trojan War, 41, 55

Trump, Donald, 216

Tsichla, 18, 37

Turkey, 36–37

turtle. *See sea turtles.*

Twelve Olympians, 9

Underworld, 40–41, 63, 64, 197, 199

Vagonia Beach, 34–35

veterans, 183–91, 195–204

Viet Nam, 195

240 INDEX

Virgin of the Life-giving Spring, 10
Visigoths, 69, 91
vision, 133–35
Vlachou, Konstantina, 177–81
voice, 133–35
volcanoes, 176–77

War of Independence, 32
warriors, 183–91
weather, 30
Who Stole the Arms of the Venus de Milo, 40
World War I, 24, 27
World War II, 4, 18, 27, 119, 184

writers and artists
American writers in Poros, 118–23
Chagall and Poros, 124–26
in the houses of art, 126–30
modern artists, 123–24
symbolism on the strait, 130–32
voice and vision, 133–35

Xenokrates, 25
Xenoulis, Giorgos, 27

Zeus, 4, 57, 59, 64–65, 178–79
Zorba the Greek, 41